June 10th 1969

To my sister (and in more
than) law, Cecily —
who has always been there
in the Big moments. With
much love.

The author

THE AMERICAN NEGRO

HIS HISTORY AND LITERATURE

The Social Implications of Early Negro Music In the United States

With over 150 of the Songs
Many of them with their Music

Edited with an Introduction
by Bernard Katz

ARNO PRESS and THE NEW YORK TIMES

NEW YORK 1969

General Editor

WILLIAM LOREN KATZ

CONTENTS

INTRODUCTION

It is now generally agreed that the major force in the shaping of America's music was the contribution of our black fellow citizens. To them we must credit the largest share of the acclaim that this music has won, not only from the youth of the world, but from virtually all serious composers of the present and past century.

Today the black American's primary role in the shaping of the early minstrel songs, ragtime, the Spirituals, the blues, the various phases of Jazz, swing, Dixieland, be-bop, modern, soul music, or rock and roll is no longer the matter of debate it was in the first quarter of this century.

In that era, the noted music critic of the New York *Tribune*, Henry Edward Krehbiel, had to contend with unknowing European pedants who refused to believe the ex-slave capable of any such contribution. And, as recently as the 1920's, Negro scholars James Weldon Johnson and Nathaniel Dett still had to answer those who preferred to believe that the psalm-singing plantation owner or his piano-playing wife and daughter was the true source of the music. Even today some of this mythology persists.

The pages that follow contain pioneering writings on the history of early Afro-American music.[1] Never before have they been gathered together for the easy access of the general reader or the research of the musicologist and the historian. And, a pleasant bonus is the more than one hundred and fifty songs contained in these articles, many with their music.

So thorough are the facts contained in the pioneer texts that follow, that little more is needed to set them properly in their time and in the music's early history.

*　*　*　*　*

One of the earliest descriptions of Negro music is that of the slave-ship captain, Theodore Canot: "During afternoons of serene weather, men, women, girls, and boys are allowed while on deck to unite in

African melodies which they always enhance by extemporaneous *tom-tom* on the bottom of a tub or tin kettle."[2]

Canot confirms the fact that the black man brought both his songs and his musicianship with him from Africa. Soon after the earliest of many slave uprisings, Negroes would be forbidden the use of these tubs and kettles, or anything else resembling a drum that might be used to communicate between plantations. However, they were allowed to keep their songs—even encouraged to sing them. The slave owner, as we shall see, found them useful and profitable.

Edward Long heard an early form of the West Indian music known as Calypso, long before the year 1774 when his *History of Jamaica* was published. This is how he describes it:

> The tunes consist of a solo part'. . . and this is accompanied with a full or general chorus . . . for their subject matter, they generally prefer one of derision, and not infrequently at the expence of the overseer, if he happens to be near and listening: this only serves to add a poignancy to their satire and heightens the fun. In the [sugar] crop season, the mill-feeders entertain themselves very often with these *jeux d'esprit* in the night-time; and this merriment helps to keep them awake.[3]

George Washington Cable was to point out that in early New Orleans too, one found—"the mingled humor and outrage of . . . satirical songs of double meaning. They readily passed unchallenged among the numerous nonsense rhymes—that often rhymed lamely or not at all—which beguiled the hours afield or the moonlight gatherings in the 'quarters', as well as served to fit the wild chants of their dances."[4]

The explorer-naturalist William Bartram heard another variation on these songs on a plantation in Georgia in 1775. Here the slave was improvising flattery of his master, rather than satire, into his work-songs: " . . . the regular heavy strokes of their gleaming axes re-echoed in the deep forests: at the same time, contented and joyful, the sooty sons of Afric forgetting their bondage, in chorus sung the virtues and beneficence of their master in songs of their own composition."[5]

At least a century before Booker T. Washington, American Negroes were already putting into practice one of his famous policies: "When your head is in the lion's mouth—pet him!" or, in this case, sing him a song!

In 1781 Thomas Jefferson wrote in his *Notes on Virginia* that, "In music," the Negroes "are more generally gifted than the whites, with accurate ears for tune and time, and they have been found capable of imagining a small catch." But he thought that "Whether they will be equal to the composition of a more extensive run of melody, or of complicated harmony is yet to be proved."[6]

He did, however, hand down to us a valuable footnote for musical history. "The instrument proper to them," he wrote, "is the Banjar, which they brought hither from Africa, and which is the original of the guitar, its chords being precisely the four lower chords of the guitar.—T. J. "[7]

In 1838, when Fanny Kemble, the noted English actress-abolitionist, married a slave owner and went to live for an embattled year on his Georgia plantation, the songs of the Negro boatmen, the slave congregation, and the field hands were so much a part of the life around her that in her letters this skilled musician most often takes the music for granted. Her usual comments on it are casual—except for rare occasions such as this:

> I told you formerly that I thought I could trace distinctly some popular national melody with which I was familiar in almost all their songs; but I have been quite at a loss to discover any such foundation for many that I have heard lately, and which have appeared to me extraordinarily wild and unaccountable. The way in which the chorus strikes in with the burden, between each phrase of the melody chanted by a single voice, is very curious and effective, especially with the rhythm of the rowlocks for accompaniment. The high voices all in unison, and the admirable time and true accent with which their responses are made, always make me wish that some great musical composer could hear these semi-savage performances. With a very little skillful adaptation and instrumentation, I think one or two barbaric chants and choruses might be evoked from them that would make the fortune of an opera.[8]

With "the very little skillful adaptation" that Fanny Kemble suggested, a horde of white professionals had already started in search of the "fortune" she promised—at least a decade before. A decade later the field was packed to overflowing with people grinding out—not the opera Miss Kemble wanted—but sheet music and orchestrations of this "Ethiopian" music that was needed by the burnt-cork-faced minstrel companies playing in the civilized parts of this bustling new country and in Europe. When Stephen Foster was seventeen or eighteen he sold his first song, "Open thy lattice, Love." Front-parlor soloists, barber-shop quartettes, and singing groups of all kinds were singing these "adapted" Ethiopian Melodies.

Most prominent, of course, were men like Stephen Foster, Edwin P. Christy, David and John Braham, Dan Emmett, who wrote "Dixie," and "Daddy" Thomas Rice—all whites. The black bards, whose music was being "adapted" were, for the most part, unknown. When a Philadelphia Negro barber, Richard Milburn, sold a song he had written, the publisher put his mother's name on the sheet music as author; Alice Hawthorne. The song was "Listen to the Mocking Bird."

Stephen Foster first heard Negro songs in a little Pittsburgh church when he was a child. He never traveled farther south than Kentucky where relatives lived, and his brother suggested the name "Swanee" for the river he was to immortalize. Thomas Rice learned his world-famous Jim Crow dance and its accompanying forty-four-verse song from a black cripple who performed in the alley in back of a Louisville theatre.

Most of the Negro composers who would eventually get a small share of the musical fame and an even smaller portion of the fortune would not be heard from until after the Civil War—in the 70's and 80's.[9] In 1853, when the Swedish novelist Fredrika Bremer came to visit the United States every tourist was expected to see Niagara Falls, New York City, Washington, D. C., and to travel south and hear the genuine "Ethiopian" melodies and see the original Jim Crow dance. Miss Bremer's two-volume record of her visit, *Homes of the New World*, a valuable source for the social historian, includes worthless descriptions of the music she heard. It turned out, when she finally got around to naming the tunes she had been writing about so ecstatically as the "naive" but lovely creations of the southern blacks, that invariably she had been referring to such songs as Stephen Foster's "Oh, Susannah," and his "Old Uncle Ned." The only "Negro" song she might have heard, "Carry Me Back to Old Virginny," wasn't the one written by the Negro James A. Bland.[10] His, the famous version of that song, wasn't written until the 1870's. All the songs that had been dutifully rendered for the lady-novelist from Sweden, were early white minstrel songs, sung by the plantation owner's hand-picked troupe of singers, or a Negro musician who had heard or read the sheet music Miss Bremer could have purchased.[11]

So it was that when J. Miller McKim and his daughter Lucy and the hundreds of other northern teachers and missionaries came to the Sea Islands in 1861-1862, and met the slaves for the first time without the former master's presence, they actually began to hear songs that few had heard before—or had bothered to hear. Even by 1867, when *The Slave Songs of the United States* had been gathered in a book, some of the songs had already been identified as folk versions of old Baptist and Methodist hymns. But the great body of songs, like those Fanny Kemble found so "unaccountable" and so extraordinary, had a strange beauty like the one—

> I know moon-rise, I know star-rise,
> Lay this body down . . .
> *I'll lie in de grave and stretch out my arms*

This final line had led Colonel Higginson to write, "Never, it seems to me, since man first lived and suffered, was his infinite longing for peace uttered more plaintively than in that line."

These white and Negro teachers, missionaries, ministers, and Federal officials, heard the songs and began as best they could, without any special musical skill, to put them on paper. James Weldon Johnson admits that "Except for the work of these pioneer collectors, done mostly as a labor of love, the number of the Spirituals recorded and preserved would have been a small fraction of what it was."[12] It was not alone the neglect of the slave owners that would have led to the disappearance of most of this music; the slave himself would have allowed it to die as part of his grim life as a chattel.

It is important to recognize that the men and women who first recorded these songs were white, and most of them were ministers of one religious denomination or another. Both of these factors were to prove important in determining the kind and number of these songs that were recorded.

Though according to Dr. DuBois, "For the first time the North met the Southern slave face to face and heart to heart with no third witness," it was inevitable that color should still stand as a steel wall between them. Centuries of white oppression could not possibly be erased by even the most wholehearted show of good will. And a white man, no matter how powerful and convincing his credentials, could hardly have expected to breach the barrier.

So the whites heard only the songs the black man wanted him to hear. Because he was tentatively counted as a friend, he heard more of them than the slave master ever had, but it is clear that there were many songs these early pioneers never heard. Colonel Higginson mentions passing one of his black squads coming in on a wet morning after a rainy night out on picket duty. They were singing as their

commander met them: "My presence apparently checked the performance of another verse beginning 'De buchra [white man] [en] list for
money,' apparently in reference to the controversy about the pay-
question then just beginning, and to the more mercenary aims they
attributed to the white soldiers."[13]

This episode casts some doubt on the Colonel's assertion that his
men's songs "all had a religious motive," or his observation that "I
never overheard in camp a profane or vulgar song." A Fanny Kemble
comment supplies additional evidence that whites probably heard only
the songs that they wanted to hear: "One of their songs displeased me
not a little [she tells us], for it embodied the opinion that 'twenty-six
black girls not make mulatto yellow girl'; and as I told them I did not
like it, they have omitted it since."[14]

Thus it is very possible that a great body of songs of secular social
comment, too difficult to disguise for white ears, stayed underground
during the last years of slavery and the violent reconstruction years
that followed. They would surface later in the blues and other forms,
undoubtedly affected by urbanization and other factors of the Negro's
postwar life and transformed into something quite different.

The end result should not have proved surprising, if one studied the
list of those early collectors, for McKim, Barton, Spaulding, and Higginson were all ministers. The vast majority of the songs that were
rescued from oblivion were the songs of the Sabbath—of church worship. The songs of the rest of the week would have to creep out of
hiding during a time when fewer men of the cloth were around.

In Sterling Brown's *The Negro in American Fiction*, appears this
quotation: "I swear their nature is beyond my comprehension. A
strange people!—merry 'mid their misery—laughing through their tears,
like the sun shining through the rain. Yet what simple philosophers
they! They tread life's path as if 'twere strewn with roses devoid of
thorns, and make the most of life with natures of sunshine and
song."[15]

"Most American readers," comments Brown, "would take this to
refer to the Negro, but it was spoken of the Irish, in a play dealing
with one of the most desperate periods of Ireland's tragic history."

This is precisely the way the Negro has been pictured by those
who have pointed to the singing slave as proof of his reasonably
humane treatment under slavery, proof of his childlike, joyful, and
uncomplaining acceptance of that fate. Ex-slave Frederick Douglass
wrote:

It is impossible to conceive of a greater mistake. I have been utterly astonished, since I came to the north, to find persons who could speak of the singing, among slaves, as evidence of their contentment and happiness. . . . Slaves sing most when they are most unhappy. The songs of the slave represent the sorrows of his heart; and he is relieved by them, only as an aching heart is relieved by tears. . . . I have often sung to drown my sorrow, but seldom to express my happiness. Crying for joy, and singing for joy, were alike uncommon to me while in the jaws of slavery.[16]

It is hardly to be argued that the description found by Sterling Brown was no more an accurate picture of the Negro than it was of the Irish, and, if there is any question of that, one need only add a singularly appropriate observation by Frederick Douglass on the deep sorrow he heard in the slave songs: "I have never heard any songs like those anywhere since I left slavery, except when in Ireland. . . . It was during the famine of 1845-46."[17]

But what still must be examined is the important role the master or the slave institution itself played in the slave's singing or in his songs. It is still not generally recognized that the master or his agents often controlled the very choice of songs, the tempo of those used, and even the character of their lyrics.

The hard-headed, down-to-earth, thoroughly unromantic calculation of slaveholders is openly admitted by Georgia Bryan Conrad in her *Reminiscences of a Southern Woman.* She explained why she and her fellow slave owners refused to allow slaves to learn to read or write: "Self-preservation is the first law of nature, and the country was so flooded with abolition literature that the slave-owner felt his only safety lay in keeping the Negroes ignorant."[18]

Frederick Douglass provides an instance of the master's use of slave songs:

Slaves are generally expected to sing as well as to work. A silent slave is not liked by masters or overseers. *"Make a noise*, make a noise," and "bear a hand," are the words usually addressed to the slaves when there is silence amongst them. This may account for the almost constant singing heard in the southern states. There is generally more or less singing among the teamsters, as it was one means of letting the overseer know where they were, and that they were moving on with the work.[19]

This continuous singing obviously was not the slaves' choice. It was a device of the master, similar to hanging a bell on a cow; the owner could thus know exactly where his property was to be found at any given moment. Thus masters not only encouraged continuous singing, they often insisted on it.

Julien Tiersot, Librarian of the Paris Conservatory, in his *La Musique Chez les Peuples Indigènes de l'Amérique du Nord*, explains another value of the music for the master. The songs, he says, "are sung in harvest season to stimulate the gathering of grain. The efficiency of these songs is so well recognized that the owners of plantations pay extra wages to singers capable of leading the chorus of laborers."[20]

This also is confirmed by ex-slave Booker T. Washington: "Oftentimes in slavery, as to-day in certain parts of the South [1905], some man or woman with an exceptional voice was paid to lead the singing, the idea being to increase the amount of labor by such singing."[21]

The American History and Encyclopedia of Music (1908 edition) included this report from an observer: "Work on the plantation was often to the accompaniment of songs whose rhythmic swing acted as an incentive to a steadier and better labor. . . . Charles Peabody tells of a leader in a band of slaves who was besought by his companions not to sing a certain song because it made them work too hard."[22]

And the anonymous writer added that the songs were used for the same purpose on Baltimore ships with black crews sailing for the West Indies. The songs were used, too, during the Civil War, by slaves employed in the construction and building of Confederate fortifications.

Speed-up, as another function of the songs, is so generally recognized that Mary Wylie McCarty, a southern writer, in a recent booklet notes, "The plantation owners encouraged them in their singing while at work, and through some of the Negroes who sang the leads, regulated the tempo so as to get from the slaves the maximum amount of labor."[23] This would also explain why slow tunes were discouraged and faster ones demanded, as reported by several eyewitnesses.

There is much evidence that the slave owner and his overseer attempted to control the very character of the songs, insisting on happy tunes rather than sad ones. The dean of America's music critics, Henry E. Krehbiel of the New York *Tribune*, commented on this "innate lightness of heart and carelessness of disposition, carefully cultivated by the slaveholders for obvious reasons."[24] Fanny Kemble was more explicit:

> I have heard that many masters and overseers on these plantations prohibit melancholy tunes or words and encourage nothing but cheerful music . . . deprecating the effect of sadder strains upon the slaves

whose peculiar musical sensibilities might be expected to make them especially excitable by any songs of a plaintive character, and having any reference to their particular hardships.[25]

The master's careful observation and strict supervision of any and everything that might affect his working force is proved by this comment by one of the plantation South's most stalwart defenders, Ulrich B. Phillips:

> A black preacher might meet rebuke and even run the risk of being lynched if he harped too loudly upon the liberation of the Hebrews from Egyptian bondage; but a moderate supervision would prevent such indiscretions. The Sermon on the Mount would be harmless despite its suggestion of an earthly inheritance for the meek; the Decalogue was utterly sound; and "servants obey your masters," "render unto Caesar the things that are Caesar's," and "well done, thou good and faithful servant" were invaluable texts for homilies.[26]

There was another use for a singing slave; he was not only a source of entertainment for himself and his fellows, but a much used source of entertainment for the master and his friends. Some talented groups were sent out on limited tours for the financial benefit of their owners.

Dr. John Lovell, Jr. demonstrates that the spirituals were not in any way an acceptance of the miseries of this life for the joys of the next one. His study highlights some of the hidden meanings of the slave songs. Contemporary documentation reinforces this view. Ex-slave Booker T. Washington, who aided many a Negro cause in the same kind of secrecy, explains:

> Most of the verses of the plantation songs had some references to freedom. True, they had sung those same verses before, but they had been careful to explain that the "freedom" in these songs referred to the next world, and had no connection with life in this world. Now they gradually threw off the mask, and were not afraid to let it be known that the "freedom" in their songs meant freedom of the body in this world.[27]

And, from Sarah Bradford, the biographer of Harriet Tubman, who with a $40,000 price on her head went into the South and brought parties of slaves to freedom, using as her signals and codes the very songs we have been writing about, comes this report:

Slaves must not be seen talking together, and so it came about that their communication was often made by singing, and the words of their familiar hymns, telling of the heavenly journey, and the land of Canaan, while they did not attract the attention of the masters, conveyed to their brethren and sisters in bondage something more than met the ear.[28]

New York City, 1968   Bernard Katz

NOTES TO INTRODUCTION

1. The designation "Afro-American" is not as recent an innovation as supposed. Henry E. Krehbiel's classic study published in 1914 was called *Afro-American Folksongs*.

2. Brantz Mayer, *Captain Canot; or Twenty Years of an African Slaver* (New York: D. Appleton, 1854), pp. 103-104. Republished, Arno Press-N.Y. Times (N.Y.) 1968.

3. Edward Long, *History of Jamaica*, (London, 1774), II, 423.

4. George Washington Cable, "Creole Slave Songs," *The Century Magazine* (April, 1886), p. 808.

5. William Bartram, *Travels Through North & South Carolina, Georgia, East & West Florida* (Philadelphia: James & Johnson, 1791), p. 312.

6. Jefferson was the Renaissance man of his times, but like most Americans of this early period, he was unfamiliar with anything but European music. The extraordinary harmonies of Negro instrumental and vocal music, together with their melody and rhythm, won them the accolades of the world's renowned composers including Mendelssohn, Dvorak, Milhaud, Debussy, Stravinsky, and Antheil.

7. Thomas Jefferson, *Notes on the State of Virginia* (Philadelphia: Prichard & Hall, 1788), p. 150.

8. Frances Anne Kemble, *Journal of a Residence on a Georgian Plantation, 1838-1839* (New York: Harper & Bros., 1863), p. 218.

9. Among the black composers to emerge in the 1870's and afterwards were: Samuel Coleridge-Taylor, Edmund Dede, Joseph White, and besides James A. Bland, these writers of popular music: Kerry Mills, Scott Joplin, Bob Cole, Will Marion Cook, Gussie L. Davis, W. C. Handy, Rosamond Johnson, William Grant Still, and Edward "Duke" Ellington.

10. James A. Bland wrote over 700 songs, only 38 of which are in the files of the Library of Congress. Others of his well-known songs were "Oh, Dem Golden Slippers," and "In The Evening By The Moonlight." Neither he nor Stephen Foster were southerners: Foster was from Pittsburgh; Bland was born in Flushing, Long Island.

11. Other of the songs Fredrika Bremer mistook for Negro melodies were the white minstrel songs "Rosa Lee," "Dearest May," "Mary Blaine," and a song about the Pedee River that may have been an early version of Stephen Foster's "Swanee River."

12. James Weldon Johnson, *The Book of American Negro Spirituals* (New York: Viking Press, 1926), p. 47.

13. Thomas Wentworth Higginson, "Negro Spirituals," *The Atlantic Monthly* (June, 1867), p. 693.

14. Frances Anne Kemble, *op. cit.*, p. 219.

15. Sterling Brown, *The Negro in American Fiction* (Washington, D.C.: Associates in Negro Folk Education, 1937), p. 1. Republished, Arno Press-N.Y. Times (N.Y.) 1969.

16. Frederick Douglass, *Narrative of the Life of Frederick Douglass, An American Slave* (Boston: Anti-Slavery Office, 1845), p. 15.

17. Frederick Douglass, quoted by Harriet Beecher Stowe, *Men of Our Times* (Hartford, Conn.: Hartford Publishing Co., 1868), p. 395.

18. Georgia Bryan Conrad, "Reminiscences of a Southern Woman," *Southern Workman* (April, 1901), p. 253.

19. Frederick Douglass, quoted by Harriet Beecher Stowe, *op. cit.*, p. 394.

20. Julien Tiersot, *La Musique Chez les Peuples Indigènes de l'Amérique du Nord* ("Notes d'Ethnographie Musicale," 2nd Series [Paris: Librairie Fischbacher, 1910]). The translated paragraph is from Krehbiel.

21. Booker T. Washington, Preface to Samuel Coleridge-Taylor's *Twenty-Four Negro Melodies*, transcribed for the Piano (Boston: Oliver Ditson, 1905), p. viii.

22. *American History and Encyclopedia of Music* (Toledo-New York-Chicago: Irving Squire, 1908), IV, 56.

23. Mary Wylie McCarty, "Negro Spirituals, Shouts and Chanteys," in *Flags of Five Nations* (Sea Islands, Ga.: Cloister Hotel, n.d.), p. 31.

24. Henry E. Krehbiel, *Afro-American Folksongs* (New York: G. Schirmer, 1914), p. 45; (2nd ed.; New York: Frederick Ungar, 1962).

25. Frances Anne Kemble, *op. cit.*, p. 129.

26. Ulrich B. Phillips, *Life and Labor in the Old South* (Boston: Little, Brown, 1929), p. 202.

27. Booker T. Washington, *Up From Slavery* (New York: Doubleday, Page, 1901), pp. 19-20.

28. Sara Bradford, *Harriet, Moses of Her People* (New York: George Lockwood, 1886), p. 27.

PROLOGUE

William Edward Burghardt DuBois

[In his historic *Souls of Black Folk*, first published in 1903
and reprinted many times thereafter, Dr. William Edward
Burghardt DuBois included this remarkable essay on early
Negro music and its role in his own life.]

OF THE SORROW SONGS

> I walk through the churchyard
> To lay this body down;
> I know moon-rise, I know star-rise;
> I walk in the moonlight, I walk in the starlight;
> I'll lie in the grave and stretch out my arms,
> I'll go to judgment in the evening of the day,
> And my soul and thy soul shall meet that day,
> When I lay this body down.
>
> N<small>EGRO</small> S<small>ONG</small>.

THEY that walked in darkness sang songs in
the olden days — Sorrow Songs — for they
were weary at heart. And so before each
thought that I have written in this book I have set
a phrase, a haunting echo of these weird old songs
in which the soul of the black slave spoke to men.
Ever since I was a child these songs have stirred me
strangely. They came out of the South unknown to
me, one by one, and yet at once I knew them as of
me and of mine. Then in after years when I came
to Nashville I saw the great temple builded of these

songs towering over the pale city. To me Jubilee
Hall seemed ever made of the songs themselves, and
its bricks were red with the blood and dust of toil.[1]
Out of them rose for me morning, noon, and night,
bursts of wonderful melody, full of the voices of my
brothers and sisters, full of the voices of the past.

Little of beauty has America given the world save
the rude grandeur God himself stamped on her bosom;
the human spirit in this new world has expressed
itself in vigor and ingenuity rather than in beauty.
And so by fateful chance the Negro folk-song — the
rhythmic cry of the slave — stands to-day not simply
as the sole American music, but as the most beautiful expression of human experience born this side the
seas. It has been neglected, it has been, and is, half
despised, and above all it has been persistently mis-
taken and misunderstood; but notwithstanding, it
still remains as the singular spiritual heritage of
the nation and the greatest gift of the Negro people.

Away back in the thirties the melody of these slave
songs stirred the nation, but the songs were soon
half forgotten. Some, like "Near the lake where
drooped the willow," passed into current airs and
their source was forgotten; others were caricatured
on the "minstrel" stage and their memory died away.
Then in war-time came the singular Port Royal ex-
periment after the capture of Hilton Head, and perhaps for the first time the North met the Southern
slave face to face and heart to heart with no third
witness. The Sea Islands of the Carolinas, where
they met, were filled with a black folk of primitive
type, touched and moulded less by the world about
them than any others outside the Black Belt. Their
appearance was uncouth, their language funny, but
their hearts were human and their singing stirred
men with a mighty power. Thomas Wentworth
Higginson hastened to tell of these songs, and Miss

1. Jubilee Hall in Nashville is a monument to those twelve young
men and women of Fisk University who, in a day when dollars
were worth considerably more than today, toured the United
States and Europe as the Fisk Jubilee Singers and raised more
than $150,000 for their university.

McKim and others urged upon the world their rare beauty. But the world listened only half credulously until the Fisk Jubilee Singers sang the slave songs so deeply into the world's heart that it can never wholly forget them again.

There was once a blacksmith's son born at Cadiz, New York, who in the changes of time taught school in Ohio and helped defend Cincinnati from Kirby Smith. Then he fought at Chancellorsville and Gettysburg and finally served in the Freedman's Bureau at Nashville. Here he formed a Sunday-school class of black children in 1866, and sang with them and taught them to sing. And then they taught him to sing, and when once the glory of the Jubilee songs passed into the soul of George L. White, he knew his life-work was to let those Negroes sing to the world as they had sung to him. So in 1871 the pilgrimage of the Fisk Jubilee Singers began. North to Cincinnati they rode, — four half-clothed black boys and five girl-women, — led by a man with a cause and a purpose. They stopped at Wilberforce, the oldest of Negro schools, where a black bishop blessed them. Then they went, fighting cold and starvation, shut out of hotels, and cheerfully sneered at, ever northward; and ever the magic of their song kept thrilling hearts, until a burst of applause in the Congregational Council at Oberlin revealed them to the world. They came to New York and Henry Ward Beecher dared to welcome them, even though the metropolitan dailies sneered at his "Nigger Minstrels." So their songs conquered till they sang across the land and across the sea, before Queen and Kaiser, in Scotland and Ireland, Holland and Switzerland. Seven years they sang, and brought back a hundred and fifty thousand dollars to found Fisk University.

Since their day they have been imitated — sometimes well, by the singers of Hampton and Atlanta, sometimes ill, by straggling quartettes. Caricature has sought again to spoil the quaint beauty of the music, and has filled the air with many debased melodies which vulgar ears scarce know from the real.

But the true Negro folk-song still lives in the hearts of those who have heard them truly sung and in the hearts of the Negro people.

What are these songs, and what do they mean? I know little of music and can say nothing in technical phrase, but I know something of men, and knowing them, I know that these songs are the articulate message of the slave to the world. They tell us in these eager days that life was joyous to the black slave, careless and happy. I can easily believe this of some, of many. But not all the past South, though it rose from the dead, can gainsay the heart-touching witness of these songs. They are the music of an unhappy people, of the children of disappointment; they tell of death and suffering and unvoiced longing toward a truer world, of misty wanderings and hidden ways.

The songs are indeed the siftings of centuries; the music is far more ancient than the words, and in it we can trace here and there signs of development. My grandfather's grandmother was seized by an evil Dutch trader two centuries ago; and coming to the valleys of the Hudson and Housatonic, black, little, and lithe, she shivered and shrank in the harsh north winds, looked longingly at the hills, and often crooned a heathen melody to the child between her knees, thus:

Do ba - na co - ba, ge - ne me, ge - ne me!

Do ba - na co - ba, ge - ne me, ge - ne me!

Ben d' nu - li, nu - li, nu - li, nu - li, ben d' le.

The child sang it to his children and they to their

children's children, and so two hundred years it has
travelled down to us and we sing it to our children,
knowing as little as our fathers what its words may
mean, but knowing well the meaning of its music.

This was primitive African music; it may be seen
in larger form in the strange chant . . .

> " You may bury me in the East,
> You may bury me in the West,
> But I 'll hear the trumpet sound in that morning,"

— the voice of exile.

Ten master songs, more or less, one may pluck
from this forest of melody — songs of undoubted
Negro origin and wide popular currency, and songs
peculiarly characteristic of the slave.

[In *Souls of the Black Folk* Dr. DuBois has headed
his chapters with the melodies of the songs he now
lists. At this point, he refers to them in a way that
would be confusing out of the context of the rest
of the book. This is his list:

You May Bury Me in the East	Roll, Jordan, Roll
Swing Low, Sweet Chariot	Been A-Listening
My Lord, What a Mourning!	My Way's Cloudy
Wrestlin' Jacob	Steal Away
Nobody Knows the Trouble I've Seen	

He then adds four additional songs. "Bright Spark-
les," an Easter carol, "Dust, Dust and Ashes," a
dirge, "My Mother's Took Her Flight," and the
melody, "I Hope My Mother Will Be There in that
Beautiful World on High." He comments on these
last four as follows:]

These represent a third step in the development of
the slave song, of which "You may bury me in the
East" is the first, and songs like "March on"
. . . and "Steal away" are the second. The first
is African music, the second Afro-American, while the
third is a blending of Negro music with the music
heard in the foster land. The result is still distinctively Negro and the method of blending original,
but the elements are both Negro and Caucasian.

One might go further and find a fourth step in this development, where the songs of white America have been distinctively influenced by the slave songs or have incorporated whole phrases of Negro melody, as "Swanee River" and "Old Black Joe." Side by side, too, with the growth has gone the debasements and imitations — the Negro "minstrel" songs, many of the "gospel" hymns, and some of the contemporary "coon" songs, — a mass of music in which the novice may easily lose himself and never find the real Negro melodies.

In these songs, I have said, the slave spoke to the world. Such a message is naturally veiled and half articulate. Words and music have lost each other and new and cant phrases of a dimly understood theology have displaced the older sentiment. Once in a while we catch a strange word of an unknown tongue, as the "Mighty Myo," which figures as a river of death; more often slight words or mere doggerel are joined to music of singular sweetness. Purely secular songs are few in number, partly because many of them were turned into hymns by a change of words, partly because the frolics were seldom heard by the stranger, and the music less often caught. Of nearly all the songs, however, the music is distinctly sorrowful. The ten master songs I have mentioned tell in word and music of trouble and exile, of strife and hiding; they grope toward some unseen power and sigh for rest in the End.

The words that are left to us are not without interest, and, cleared of evident dross, they conceal much of real poetry and meaning beneath conventional theology and unmeaning rhapsody. Like all primitive folk, the slave stood near to Nature's heart. Life was a "rough and rolling sea" like the brown Atlantic of the Sea Islands; the "Wilderness" was the home of God, and the "lonesome valley" led to the way of life. "Winter'll soon be over," was the picture of life and death to a tropical imagination. The sudden wild thunder-storms of the South awed and impressed the Negroes, — at times the rumbling seemed to them "mournful," at times imperious:

> "My Lord calls me,
> He calls me by the thunder,
> The trumpet sounds it in my soul."

The monotonous toil and exposure is painted in many words. One sees the ploughmen in the hot, moist furrow, singing:

> "Dere's no rain to wet you,
> Dere's no sun to burn you,
> Oh, push along, believer,
> I want to go home."

The bowed and bent old man cries, with thrice-repeated wail:

> "O Lord, keep me from sinking down,"

and he rebukes the devil of doubt who can whisper:

> "Jesus is dead and God's gone away."

Yet the soul-hunger is there, the restlessness of the savage, the wail of the wanderer, and the plaint is put in one little phrase:

My soul wants something that's new, that's new

Over the inner thoughts of the slaves and their relations one with another the shadow of fear ever hung, so that we get but glimpses here and there, and also with them, eloquent omissions and silences. Mother and child are sung, but seldom father; fugitive and weary wanderer call for pity and affection, but there is little of wooing and wedding; the rocks and the mountains are well known, but home is unknown. Strange blending of love and helplessness sings through the refrain:

> "Yonder's my ole mudder,
> Been waggin' at de hill so long;
> 'Bout time she cross over,
> Git home bime-by."

Elsewhere comes the cry of the "motherless" and the "Farewell, farewell, my only child."

Love-songs are scarce and fall into two categories

— the frivolous and light, and the sad. Of deep successful love there is ominous silence, and in one of the oldest of these songs there is a depth of history and meaning:

Poor Ro - sy, poor gal; Poor Ro - sy,

poor gal; Ro - sy break my poor heart,

Heav'n shall - a - be my home.

A black woman said of the song, "It can't be sung without a full heart and a troubled sperrit." The same voice sings here that sings in the German folk-song:

"Jetz Geh i' an's brunele, trink' aber net."

Of death the Negro showed little fear, but talked of it familiarly and even fondly as simply a crossing of the waters, perhaps — who knows? — back to his ancient forests again. Later days transfigured his fatalism, and amid the dust and dirt the toiler sang:

"Dust, dust and ashes, fly over my grave,
But the Lord shall bear my spirit home."

The things evidently borrowed from the surrounding world undergo characteristic change when they enter the mouth of the slave. Especially is this true of Bible phrases. "Weep, O captive daughter of Zion," is quaintly turned into "Zion, weep-a-low," and the wheels of Ezekiel are turned every way in the mystic dreaming of the slave, till he says:

"There's a little wheel a-turnin' in-a-my heart."

As in olden time, the words of these hymns were improvised by some leading minstrel of the religious band. The circumstances of the gathering, however, the rhythm of the songs, and the limitations of allowable thought, confined the poetry for the most part to single or double lines, and they seldom were expanded to quatrains or longer tales, although there are some few examples of sustained efforts, chiefly paraphrases of the Bible. Three short series of verses have always attracted me, — the one that heads this chapter, of one line of which Thomas Wentworth Higginson has fittingly said, "Never, it seems to me, since man first lived and suffered was his infinite longing for peace uttered more plaintively." The second and third are descriptions of the Last Judgment, — the one a late improvisation, with some traces of outside influence:

> "Oh, the stars in the elements are falling,
> And the moon drips away into blood,
> And the ransomed of the Lord are returning unto God,
> Blessed be the name of the Lord."

And the other earlier and homelier picture from the low coast lands:

> "Michael, haul the boat ashore,
> Then you'll hear the horn they blow,
> Then you'll hear the trumpet sound,
> Trumpet sound the world around,
> Trumpet sound for rich and poor,
> Trumpet sound the Jubilee,
> Trumpet sound for you and me."

Through all the sorrow of the Sorrow Songs there breathes a hope — a faith in the ultimate justice of things. The minor cadences of despair change often to triumph and calm confidence. Sometimes it is faith in life, sometimes a faith in death, sometimes assurance of boundless justice in some fair world beyond. But whichever it is, the meaning is always clear: that sometime, somewhere, men will judge men by their souls and not by their skins. Is such a hope justified? Do the Sorrow Songs sing true?

The silently growing assumption of this age is that the probation of races is past, and that the backward races of to-day are of proven inefficiency and not worth the saving. Such an assumption is the arrogance of peoples irreverent toward Time and ignorant of the deeds of men. A thousand years ago such an assumption, easily possible, would have made it difficult for the Teuton to prove his right to life. Two thousand years ago such dogmatism, readily welcome, would have scouted the idea of blond races ever leading civilization. So wofully unorganized is sociological knowledge that the meaning of progress, the meaning of "swift" and "slow" in human doing, and the limits of human perfectability, are veiled, unanswered sphinxes on the shores of science. Why should Æschylus have sung two thousand years before Shakespeare was born? Why has civilization flourished in Europe, and flickered, flamed, and died in Africa? So long as the world stands meekly dumb before such questions, shall this nation proclaim its ignorance and unhallowed prejudices by denying freedom of opportunity to those who brought the Sorrow Songs to the Seats of the Mighty?

Your country? How came it yours? Before the Pilgrims landed we were here. Here we have brought our three gifts and mingled them with yours: a gift of story and song — soft, stirring melody in an ill-harmonized and unmelodious land; the gift of sweat and brawn to beat back the wilderness, conquer the soil, and lay the foundations of this vast economic empire two hundred years earlier than your weak hands could have done it; the third, a gift of the Spirit. Around us the history of the land has centred for thrice a hundred years; out of the nation's heart we have called all that was best to throttle and subdue all that was worst; fire and blood, prayer and sacrifice, have billowed over this people, and they have found peace only in the altars of the God of Right. Nor has our gift of the Spirit been merely passive. Actively we have woven ourselves with the very warp and woof of this nation, — we fought their battles, shared their sorrow, mingled our blood with theirs, and generation after generation have pleaded with a headstrong, careless people to despise not Justice, Mercy, and Truth, lest the nation be smitten with a curse. Our song, our toil, our cheer, and warning have been given to this nation in blood-brotherhood. Are not these gifts worth the giving? Is not this work and striving? Would America have been America without her Negro people?

Even so is the hope that sang in the songs of my fathers well sung. If somewhere in this whirl and chaos of things there dwells Eternal Good, pitiful yet masterful, then anon in His good time America shall rend the Veil and the prisoned shall go free. Free, free as the sunshine trickling down the morning into these high windows of mine, free as yonder fresh young voices welling up to me from the caverns of brick and mortar below — swelling with song, instinct with life, tremulous treble and darkening bass. My children, my little children, are singing to the sunshine, and thus they sing:

-long   the   heav - en - ly   way.

And the traveller girds himself, and sets his face toward the Morning, and goes his way.

THREE PREFACES

These are portions of the Introductions to three of the most significant collections of early Afro-American songs. They supply a concise but useful history and explanation of that musical heritage.[1]

1

[This is an excerpt from the Introduction to the historic, first-published collection, *Slave Songs of the United States*, jointly edited by William Francis Allen, Charles Pickard Ware and Lucy McKim Garrison in 1867.][2]

The musical capacity of the Negro race has been recognized for so many years that it is hard to explain why no systematic effort has hitherto been made to collect and preserve their melodies. More than thirty years ago those plantation songs made their appearance which were so extraordinarily popular for a while; and if "Coal-black Rose," "Zip Coon" and "Ole Virginny nebber tire" have been succeeded by spurious imitations, manufactured to suit the somewhat sentimental taste of our community, the fact that these were called "Negro melodies" was itself a tribute to the musical genius of the race.

The public had well-nigh forgotten these genuine slave songs, and with them the creative power from which they sprung, when a fresh interest was excited through the educational mission to the Port Royal islands, in 1861. The agents of this mission were not long in discover-

---

1. The introduction to Fisk University's collection of Jubilee Songs is omitted since it is largely a history of the group which is already covered in the DuBois and William E. Barton contributions.
2. William Francis Allen, Charles Pickard Ware, and Lucy McKim Garrison, *Slave Songs of the United States* (New York: A. Simpson & Co., 1867).

ing the rich vein of music that existed in these half-barbarous people, and when visitors from the North were on the islands, there was nothing that seemed better worth their while than to see a "shout" or hear the "people" sing their "sperichils." A few of these last, of special merit, soon became established favorites among the whites, and hardly a Sunday passed at the church on St. Helena without "Gabriel's Trumpet," "I hear from Heaven today," or "Jehovah Hallelujah." The last time I myself heard these was at the Fourth of July celebration, at the church, in 1864. All of them were sung, and then the glorious shout, "I can't stay behind, my Lord," was struck up, and sung by the entire multitude with a zest and spirit, a swaying of the bodies and nodding of the heads and lighting of the countenances and rhythmical movement of the hands, which I think no one present will ever forget.

Attention was, I believe, first publicly directed to these songs in a letter from Miss McKim, of Philadelphia, to *Dwight's Journal of Music*, November 8, 1862, from which some extracts will presently be given. At about the same time, Miss McKim arranged and published two of them, "Roll, Jordan" and "Poor Rosy"—probably on all accounts the two best specimens that could be selected. Mr. H. G. Spaulding not long after gave some well-chosen specimens of the music in an article entitled "Under the Palmetto," in the *Continental Monthly* for August, 1863, among them, "O Lord, remember me" and "The Lonesome Valley." Many other persons interested themselves in the collection of words and tunes, and it seems time at last that the partial collections in the possession of others, should not be forgotten and lost, but that these relics of a state of society which has passed away should be preserved while it is still possible. . . .

A gentleman in Delaware writes: "We must look among their non-religious songs for the purest specimens of Negro minstrelsy. It is remarkable that they have themselves transferred the best of these to the uses of their churches—I suppose on Mr. Wesley's principle that 'it is not right the Devil should have all the good tunes.' Their leaders and preachers have not found this change difficult to effect; or at least they have taken so little pains about it that one often detects the profane *cropping out*, and revealing the origin of their most solemn 'hymns,' in spite of the best intentions of the poet and artist. Some of the best *pure Negro* songs I have heard were those that used to be sung by the black stevedores, or perhaps the crews themselves, of the West India vessels, loading and unloading at the wharves in

Philadelphia and Baltimore. I have stood for more than an hour, often, listening to them, as they hoisted and lowered the hogsheads and boxes of their cargoes; one man taking the burden of the song (and the slack of the rope) and the others striking in with the chorus. They would sing in this way more than a dozen different songs in an hour; most of which might indeed be warranted to contain 'nothing religious'—a few of them, 'on the contrary, quite the reverse'—but generally rather innocent and proper in their language, and strangely attractive in their music; and with a volume of voice that reached a square or two away. That plan of labor has now passed away, in Philadelphia at least, and the songs, I suppose, with it. So that these performances are to be heard only among black sailors on their vessels, or 'long-shore men in out-of-the-way places, where opportunities for respectable persons to hear them are rather few.''

*   *   *   *   *

I never fairly heard a secular song among the Port Royal freedmen, and never saw a musical instrument among them. The last violin, owned by a "wordly man," disappeared from Coffin's Point "de year gun shoot at Bay Point." In other parts of the South, "fiddle-sings," "devil-songs," "corn-songs," "jig-tunes," and what not, are common; all the world knows the banjo, and the "Jim Crow" songs of thirty years ago. We have succeeded in obtaining only a very few songs of this character. Our intercourse with the colored people has been chiefly through the work of the Freedmen's Commission, which deals with the serious and earnest side of the Negro character. It is often, indeed, no easy matter to persuade them to sing their old songs, even as a curiosity, such is the sense of dignity that has come with freedom. It is earnestly to be desired that some person, who has the opportunity, should make a collection of these now, before it is too late. . . .

Our title, "Slave Songs," was selected because it best described the contents of the book. A few of those here given were, to be sure, composed since the proclamation of emancipation, but even these were inspired by slavery. "All, indeed, are valuable as an expression of the character and life of the race which is playing such a conspicuous part in our history. The wild, sad strains tell, as the sufferers themselves could, of crushed hopes, keen sorrow, and a dull, daily misery, which covered them as hopelessly as the fogs from the rice swamps. On the other hand, the words breathe a trusting faith in rest for the future—in 'Canaan's air and happy land,' to which their eyes seem constantly turned."

2

[James Weldon Johnson was one of those rare, multi-talented men—a novelist, poet, diplomat, historian, and writer of popular songs. He and his brother, Rosamond, wrote the songs "Under the Bamboo Tree," "Didn't He Ramble," and "Lift Every Voice and Sing," which has been called the Negro national anthem. This introduction to his first *Book of American Negro Spirituals*[1] took its title from his well-known poem that starts it— "O Black and Unknown Bards." Published in 1925 with musical arrangements by his brother Rosamond and Lawrence Brown, it was combined with a second volume in 1940.]

O Black And Unknown Bards[2]

O black and unknown bards of long ago,
How came your lips to touch the sacred fire?
How, in your darkness, did you come to know
The power and beauty of the minstrel's lyre?
Who first from midst his bonds lifted his eyes?
Who first from out the still watch, lone and long,
Feeling the ancient faith of prophets rise
Within his dark-kept soul, burst into song?

Heart of what slave poured out such melody
As "Steal away to Jesus"? On its strains
His spirit must have nightly floated free,
Through still about his hands he felt his chains.
Who heard great "Jordan roll"? Whose starward eye
Saw chariot "swing low"? And who was he
That breathed that comforting, melodic sigh,
"Nobody knows de trouble I see"?

1. From *The Books of American Negro Spirituals*, Book I, edited by James Weldon Johnson. Copyright © 1925 by The Viking Press, Inc., renewed 1953 by Grace Nail Johnson, J. Rosamond Johnson and Lawrence Brown. Reprinted by permission of The Viking Press, Inc.
2. From *Saint Peter Relates An Incident* by James Weldon Johnson. Copyright 1917 by James Weldon Johnson. All rights reserved. Reprinted by permission of The Viking Press, Inc.

What merely living clod, what captive thing,
Could up toward God through all its darkness grope,
And find within its deadened heart to sing
These songs of sorrow, love and faith, and hope?
How did it catch that subtle undertone,
That note in music heard not with the ears?
How sound the elusive reed so seldom blown,
Which stirs the soul or melts the heart to tears?

Not that great German master in his dream
Of harmonies that thundered amongst the stars
At the creation, ever heard a theme
Nobler than "Go down, Moses." Mark its bars
How like a mighty trumpet call they stir
The blood. Such are the notes that men have sung
Going to valorous deeds; such tones there were
That helped make history when time was young.

There is a wide, wide wonder in it all,
That from degraded rest and servile toil
The fiery spirit of the seer should call
These simple children of the sun and soil.
O black slave singers, gone forgot, unfamed,
You—you alone, of all the long, long line
Of those who've sung untaught, unknown, unnamed,
Have stretched out upward, seeking the divine.

You sang not deeds of heroes or of kings;
No chant of bloody war, no exulting paean
Of arms-won triumphs; but your humble strings
You touched in chord with music empyrean.
You sang far better than you knew; the songs
That for your listeners' hungry hearts sufficed
Still live,—but more than this to you belongs:
You sang a race from wood and stone to Christ.

*   *   *   *   *

As the years go by and I understand more about this music and its
origin the miracle of its production strikes me with increasing wonder.

It would have been a notable achievement if the white people who settled this country, having a common language and heritage, seeking liberty in a new land, faced with the task of conquering untamed nature, and stirred with the hope of building an empire, had created a body of folk music comparable to the Negro Spirituals. But from whom did these songs spring—these songs unsurpassed among the folk songs of the world and, in the poignancy of their beauty, unequalled?

*   *   *   *   *

The statement that the Spirituals are imitations made by the Negro of other music that he heard is an absurdity. What music did American Negroes hear to imitate? . . . Some have gone so far as to say that they caught snatches of airs from the French Opera at New Orleans; but the songs of the Negroes who fell most directly under that influence are of a type distinct from the Spirituals. It was in localities far removed from New Orleans that the great body of Spirituals were created and sung. There remains then the music which the American Negroes heard their masters sing; chiefly religious music. Now if ignorant Negroes evolved such music as *Deep River*, *Steal Away to Jesus*, *Somebody's Knockin' at Yo Do'*, *I Couldn't Hear Nobody Pray* and *Father Abraham* by listening to their masters sing gospel hymns, it does not detract from the achievement but magnifies it. . . .

The white people among whom the slaves lived did not originate anything comparable even to the mere titles of the Spirituals. In truth, the power to frame the poetic phrases that make the titles of so many of the Spirituals betokens the power to create the songs. Consider the sheer magic of:

> Swing Low Sweet Chariot
> I've Got to Walk My Lonesome Valley
> Steal Away to Jesus
> Singing With a Sword in My Hand
> Rule Death in His Arms
> Ride on King Jesus
> We Shall Walk Through the Valley in Peace
> The Blood Came Twinklin' Down
> Deep River
> Death's Goin' to Lay His Cold, Icy Hand on Me

and confess that none but an artistically endowed people could have evoked it. . . .

The Spirituals are purely and solely the creation of the American Negro; that is, as much so as any music can be the pure and sole creation of any particular group. And their production, although seemingly miraculous, can be accounted for naturally. The Negro brought with him from Africa his native musical instinct and talent, and that was no small endowment to begin with.

Many things are now being learned about Africa. It is being learned and recognized that the great majority of Africans are in no sense "savages"; that they possess a civilization and a culture, primitive it is true but in many respects quite adequate; that they possess a folk literature that is varied and rich; that they possess an art that is quick and sound. Among those who know about art it is generally recognized that the modern school of painting and sculpture in Europe and America is almost entirely the result of the direct influence of African art, following the discovery that it was art. Not much is yet known about African music, and, perhaps, for the reason that the conception of music by the Africans is not of the same sort as the conception of music by the people of Western Europe and the United States. Generally speaking, the European concept of music is melody and the African concept is rhythm. Melody has, relatively, small place in African music, and harmony still less; but in rhythms African music is beyond comparison with any other music in the world. . . .

Now the Negro in America had his native musical endowment to begin with; and the Spirituals possess the fundamental characteristics of African music. They have a striking rhythmic quality, and show a marked similarity to African songs in form and intervallic structure. But the Spirituals, upon the base of the primitive rhythms, go a step in advance of African music through a higher melodic and an added harmonic development. For the Spirituals are not merely melodies. The melodies of many of them, so sweet or strong or even weird, are wonderful, but hardly more wonderful than the harmonies. One has never experienced the full effect of these songs until he has heard their harmonies in the part singing of a large number of Negro voices. . . . But what led to this advance by the American Negro beyond his primitive music? Why did he not revive and continue the beating out of complex rhythms on tom-toms and drums while he uttered barbaric and martial cries to their accompaniment? It was because at the precise and psychic moment there was blown through or fused into the vestiges of his African music the spirit of Christianity as he knew Christianity.

At the psychic moment there was at hand the precise religion for the condition in which he found himself thrust. Far from his native land and customs, despised by those among whom he lived, experiencing the pang of separation of loved ones on the auction block, knowing the hard task master, feeling the lash, the Negro seized Christianity, the religion of compensations in the life to come for the ills suffered in the present existence, the religion which implied the hope that in the next world there would be a reversal of conditions, of rich man and poor man, of proud and meek, of master and slave. The result was a body of songs voicing all the cardinal virtues of Christianity—patience—forbearance—love—faith—and hope—through a necessarily modified form of primitive African music. The Negro took complete refuge in Christianity, and the Spirituals were literally forged of sorrow in the heat of religious fervor. They exhibited, moreover, a reversion to the simple principles of primitive, communal Christianity.

The thought that the Negro might have refused or failed to adopt Christianity—and there were several good reasons for such an outcome, one being the vast gulf between the Christianity that was preached to him and the Christianity practiced by those who preached it—leads to some curious speculations. One thing is certain, there would have been no Negro Spirituals. His musical instinct would doubtless have manifested itself; but is it conceivable that he could have created a body of songs in any other form so unique in the musical literature of the world and with such a powerful and universal appeal as the Spirituals? Indeed, the question arises, would he have been able to survive slavery in the way which he did? It is not possible to estimate the sustaining influence that the story of the trials and tribulations of the Jews as related in the Old Testament exerted upon the Negro. This story at once caught and fired the imaginations of the Negro bards, and they sang, sang their hungry listeners into a firm faith that as God saved Daniel in the lion's den, so would He save them; as God preserved the Hebrew children in the fiery furnace, so would He preserve them; as God delivered Israel out of bondage in Egypt, so would He deliver them. How much this firm faith had to do with the Negro's physical and spiritual survival of two and a half centuries of slavery cannot be known.

Thus it was by sheer spiritual forces that African chants were metamorphosed into the Spirituals; that upon the fundamental throb of African rhythms were reared those reaches of melody that rise above earth and soar into the pure, ethereal blue. And this is the miracle of the creation of the Spirituals.

3

[For the 1927 edition of the 1874 *Religious Folk-Songs of the Negro as Sung at Hampton Institute*,[1] Hampton's musical director R. Nathaniel Dett wrote the important Foreword of which this is a partial text.]

"Folk-songs," says the late Henry E. Krehbiel, "are the echoes of the heart-beats of the vast folk and in them are preserved feelings, beliefs, and habits of vast antiquity, not only in the words, but also in the music and perhaps more truthfully in the music than in the words. Music cannot lie, for the reason that the things which are at its base, the things without which it could not be, are unconscious, unvolitional human products." Folk-songs, then, quite aside from their music value are of inestimable worth because of the light which they throw upon those individualizing elements in the character of the race that produced them.

*   *   *   *   *

But as such an index of character, Negro music, at the very outset, made a bad start. The singing and dancing in a New Orleans theatre of "Jim Crow," a Negro folk-nonsense-ballad by a Negro cripple who was able to flop himself about the stage in imitation of the motions of a crow, was such an uproarious success that it was imitated throughout the country by "black-face" comedians of both races as a sure-fire hit. Thereby an early tradition of the Negro as essentially a humorous character was established, the effect of which exists to the present day.

Romanticists who have pictured the bondsman as a happy, carefree being have seen in the ecstatic expression of his song an extension of this established idea and so have added their bit in emphasizing the supposedly rollicking nature of his contribution.

An old book of minstrel songs reveals the fact that almost all of them are meant to be Negro in character, but they are hilarious and insincere. The melodies are interrupted only that the singer may "do the buck." The most unfortunate feature is that many are out-and-out parodies of Negro church songs. The words of one run:—

1. R. Nathaniel Dett, Foreword to *Religious Folk-Songs of the Negro as Sung at Hampton Institute* (Hampton, Va.: Hampton Institute Press, 1927).

> Monkey dressed in soldier clothes
> All cross over Jordan
> Went in de woods to drill some crows
> O Jerusalem—

another begins with:—

> Angels meet me at the crossroads
> Don't charge sinner any toll—

and is followed by sixteen measures of an instrumental jig. In still another, there is a graphic account of Gabriel's blowing his horn "early in de mornin' " and all of the sinners are warned to be present to

> Jine in de army fo' dey close de door
> Ob de big white house on de todder shore.

Between the verses of this, there is also an instrumental polka of eight measures.

The fact that one minstrel company alone, Rice's Minstrels, featuring such songs as those above quoted, ran eight consecutive years in New York, that the ditties of Stephen Foster have enjoyed world-wide popularity, that some of the Broadway shows run by Negroes themselves have dance-parodied their own religious music for commercial appeal, reveals something of what has been, and to a large extent still is, the popular idea of the Negro and his music.

But in the delineation of character, if truth rather than mere effect for effect's sake, is the end desired, too much emphasis must not be laid upon any one element which may later be found to be but a mere phase. Human nature, even in primitive peoples, is more or less complex and cannot be revealed by a sort of peep-show exhibition which permits but one part to be seen at a time, anymore than a picture of a countenance can be impressed on the intelligence of an onlooker by the single revelation of one feature at a time, such as an ear or an eye. The stage character of the Irishman and the Jew, which graced (or disgraced) the American stage a decade or so ago never existed in real life; neither did, or does, the Negro character as embodied in the familiar and conventional stage "darkey." But as thousands of people have no other source of information except the theatre or popular fiction (which employs a similar method) these pseudo-types finally come to be accepted as true.

So the average audience almost everywhere expects the Negro to be funny. All things associated with him, and all things which he has made, being supposedly created in a mind but dimly lit with the half-light of a feeble intelligence or stimulated by emotions which were, or are, but the reflections of the emotions of others around him, are presumed consequently to be taken humorously, even as the words of a child who accidentally hits upon a great truth are expected to be taken.

In those primitive Negro churches where original songs are still sung, there is often hand-clapping, patting and rattling of the feet, swaying of the body, and sometimes, but rarely now, snapping of the fingers in accompaniment. The attention of visitors or casual observers is generally attracted by these obvious and dramatic evidences of emotion, and they are amused by them because it is the style to be amused, and because Americans have rather formed the bad habit of laughing at other people or at almost anything which is "different"; but being too far removed from the actual spirit of the song by this very lack of sympathy (in the broader sense of the word) they entirely miss the real essence of what is going on.

Such visitors are like those who, standing on a hill-top, watch a bonfire in the valley below; they enjoy all the visual effects of the conflagration but feel none of its heat.

It was once the privilege of the writer to attend a backwoods "after-service" at which, when the regular service had "let out," a small group of not more than seven or ten (they were all old women if he remembers rightly) grouped themselves together by standing in a ring with a criss-cross clasping of hands. To the strong rhythm of a sort of chant, they violently thrust each other backwards and forwards with an intense fervor. There was no shuffling of feet or rotating of the ring as described by Mr. [James Weldon] Johnson, but the effect was crudely fantastic, savoring of a barbaric incantation. But this I soon forgot, for, looking into the faces of the singers, I was struck by evidences of spiritual elevation, and I realized that in some mysterious way these unlettered people, by a common consent, were mutually enjoying a communion with eternal forces by a method of evocation beyond the reach of the uninitiated.

*   *   *   *   *

That the Negro as a race had, and still has, an outlook on life which is quite his own, and that his songs express moods born of his own peculiar experience and which are quite original with him, may strike many as new. But how, otherwise, shall one explain the strong unwavering note of hope of final recompense, and the assurance of the perfectness of another life to come, unless one is willing to admit that the slave brought with him from Africa a religious inheritance which, far from being shaken in any way, was strengthened by his American

experience? Does it seem natural to suppose that there could be anything in slave life, not only as it existed in our Southern States, but
even in slave life as it has existed anywhere in the world, to inspire
such an idea? It was nothing else, then, than this religious inheritance,
this oriental regard for parable and prophecy, which made easy the
incorporation into the spiritual of so much of Bible story; for in striving to give voice to his experiences the slave found in the Testaments,
in the story of the children of Israel, for instance, much in the way of
a text that was ready made; all of which was quite to his liking though,
of course, unconsciously, *for he could thus sing of one thing and mean
another.* This indirect mode of expression, it is well known, is one of
the most characteristic earmarks by which the art of the East is dis-
tinguished from that of the West; it is characteristic of Negro music,
often hiding, mask-like, its fundamental mood and not a little of its
real meaning.

There are many songs, however, in which the Negro's soul-sorrow
is hidden by no mask. How poignantly it is revealed in "Farewell,
farewell to my only child"; how prayerfully in "O Lord, O My Lord,
keep me from sinking down"; how filled with longing in "Deep River!
My home is over Jordan, Lord, I want to cross over into camp ground";
with what philosophical self-analysis in "Sometimes I feel like a
motherless child" or in "I'm troubled in mind; if Jesus don't help me,
I surely will die."

*   *   *   *   *

But the worth of native Negro genius to America is paramount; for
certainly it is most important that in a country given over to commercial enterprise, there should be at least one wellspring of spiritual
issue.

I

NEGRO SONGS

James Miller McKim

[James Miller McKim was a former Presbyterian minister, one of the youngest founders of the Anti-Slavery Society, and a close associate of William Lloyd Garrison its noted leader. He, his Quaker wife, and their daughter Lucy were leading participants in the Underground Railroad. The following report, published in *Dwight's Journal of Music* (Boston, 9 August 1862), is drawn from a talk he gave before a Philadelphia gathering known as the "Port Royal Freed-men's Association." It is an early example of the serious interest in the slave songs that led to their first published collection in *Slave Songs of the United States*. Interestingly, these first two examples, unlike most that followed, were secular songs.]

Negro Songs.

Mr. J. McKim, of Philadelphia, an agent of the Port Royal Relief Society, who last month visited the Sea Islands of South Carolina, makes the following remarks upon the negroes' songs :

That the present condition of these people is in favorable contrast with that under their masters is evident from their songs, which constitute a striking feature in their manifestations of character. They are a musical people. When they work in concert, as in rowing or grinding at the mill, their hands keep time to music. Their boat songs are the ones most frequently heard. The islands are made and permeated by rivers and creeks, and the boat furnishes the most common mode of locomotion.

When the negroes begin to row, they at the same time begin to sing. All their songs are in the minor key. If one chances to begin on the major, it quickly saddens and passes into the minor. Their songs are all religious, barcaroles and all. I speak without exception. So far as I heard or was told of their singing, it was all religious. None of their songs express mirth or present joy. The only joy expressed. or implied is that of hope. "Rest at last" was their general burthen ; "Heaven is my home ;" "Have a little patience ;" "God will deliver"—these and the like were the refrains of all their ballads.

There was one which on shore we heard more than any other, and which was irresistibly touching. It was a sort of ballad, known as "Poor Rosy, Poor Gal." It is almost impossible to give an idea of the effect of this or any of their songs by a mere recital or description. They are all exceedingly simple, both in sentiment and in music. Each stanza contains but a single thought, set in perhaps two or three bars of music ; and yet as they sing it, in alternate recitatives and choruses, with varying inflections and dramatic effect, this simple and otherwise monotonous melody will, to a musical ear and a heart susceptible of impression, have all the charm of variety. Take, for instance, a few stanzas from the dirge of "Poor Rosy." Fancy the first line sung in the major key, and the two following changed by an easy transition, and with varying inflections, into the minor, and you will have some idea of the effect.

Poor Rosy, poor gal !
Poor—Rosy—poor—gal !
P-o-o-r R-o-s-y, p-o-o-r gal !
　　Heaven shall be my home.

Hard trial on my way !
Hard—trial—on—my—way !
H-a-r-d t-r-l-a-l o-n m-y w-a-y !
　　Heaven shall be my home.

Wonder what de people want of me,
Wonder—what—de—people—want—of—me,
W-o-n-d-e-r w-h-a-t de p-e-o-p-l-e w-a-n-t o-f m-e,
　　Heaven shall be my home.

When I talk I talk with God !
When—I—talk—I—talk—with—God !
W-h-e-n I t-a-l-k I t-a-l-k w-i-t-h G-o-d !
　　Heaven shall be my home.

I asked one of these blacks—one of the most intelligent I had met—where they got these songs. "Dey make em, sah." "How do they make them ?" After a pause, evidently casting about for an explanation, he said, "I'll tell you ; it's dis way. My master call me up and order me a short peck of corn and a hundred lash. My friends see it and is sorry for me. When dey come to de praise meeting dat night dey sing about it. Some very good singers and know how ; and dey work it in, work it in, you know ; till dey get it right ; and dat's de way." A very satisfactory explanation.

I said these songs were all in the minor key. This was a mistake. They have one that has a cheerful, and, as it sounded when I first heard it, a hilarious ring. It is a new one, made, as they said, "since secesh times." It runs thus :

　　No more driver call for me,
　　　　No more driver call ;
　　No more driver call for me,
　　　　Many a thousand die !

　　No more peck of corn for me,
　　　　No more peck of corn ;
　　No more peck of corn for me,
　　　　Many a thousand die !

　　No more hundred lash for me,
　　　　No more hundred lash,
　　No more hundred lash for me,
　　　　Many a thousand die !

and so on, recounting all the incidents of slave life.

When I first heard this song I was going up from Hilton Head to Beaufort in a boat rowed by a half dozen men detailed from the first regiment of South Carolina volunteers. They were in fine voice and spirits, and the echoes came back from the inlets of Ladies' and St. Helena with fine effect. As we passed we encountered a boat load of black people rowing in the opposite direction. They were acquaintances of our oarsmen, and after the first salutation, asked what those clothes meant? Our crew were dressed in the blue blouse and pants and felt hat, which constitutes the uniform of the regiment. They explained—one of them adding, in a tone of laughing triumph,

"We'se Uncle Sam's chil'n now ; we'se Uncle Sam's chil'n ; we're none of your fiel' hans."

The others looked envious and passed on. The fact that these people are thought worthy to be enlisted as soldiers, adds to their self-respect.

I dwell on these songs not as a matter of entertainment but of instruction. They tell the whole story of these people's life and character. There is no need after hearing them, to inquire into the history of the slave's treatment. Recitals of this kind one will hear enough of, whether he desires it or not ; for these people, having now, for the first time in their lives, sympathetic listeners, pour out their hearts in narrations which nothing but flint can resist. I ought to add before leaving this subject, that their songs, like their talk, are couched in a barbarous, Africanized sort of English, and are sometimes quite unintelligible. In the specimens I have here given I have not followed their pronunciation.

[2]

II

NEGRO "SHOUTS" AND SHOUT SONGS

Henry George Spaulding

[Henry George Spaulding, a Unitarian minister and a member of the
U. S. Sanitary Commission during the Civil War, visited Port Royal
in the South Carolina Sea Islands during a Navy stopover in 1863.
In Port Royal, St. Helena, and Beaufort, South Carolina, he witnessed
the scenes he described and heard the songs he transcribed for the
readers of the popular *Continental Monthly*. The following was published in the issue of August 1863 (pp. 196-200), as part of an article
entitled "Under the Palmetto."]

NEGRO "SHOUTS" AND SHOUT SONGS

At the 'praise meetings' on the plantations, one of the elders usually presides, and conducts the exercises with great solemnity. Passages of Scripture are quoted from memory, and the hymns, which constitute the principal feature of the meeting, are deaconed off as at church. Sometimes the superintendent or one of the teachers attends these meetings, and is then expected to conduct the exercises and make an address. After the praise meeting is over, there usually follows the very singular and impressive performance of the 'Shout,' or religious dance of the negroes. Three or four, standing still, clapping their hands and beating time with their feet, commence singing in unison one of the peculiar shout melodies, while the others walk round in a ring, in single file, joining also in the song. Soon those in the ring leave off their singing, the others keeping it up the while with increased vigor, and strike into the shout step, observing most accurate time with the music. This step is something halfway between a shuffle and a dance, as difficult for an uninitiated person to describe as to imitate. At the end of each stanza of the song the dancers stop short with a slight stamp on the last note, and then, putting the other foot forward, proceed through the next verse. They will often dance to the same song for twenty or thirty minutes, once or twice, perhaps, varying the monotony of their movement by walking for a little while and joining in the singing. The physical exertion, which is really very great, as the dance calls into play nearly every muscle of the body, seems never to weary them in the least, and they frequently keep up a shout for hours, resting only for brief intervals between the different songs. Yet, in trying to imitate them, I was completely tired out in a very short time. The children are the best dancers, and are allowed by their parents to have a shout at any time, though, with the adults, the shout always follows a religious meeting, and none but church members are expected to join. It is to one of these shouts of the negro children that Mr. Russell alludes in his Diary when describing a visit which he paid to a plantation near Charleston in April, 1861. He speaks of the children as a set of ' ragged, dirty, and shoeless urchins, who came in shyly, oftentimes running away till they were chased and captured, dressed into line with much difficulty, and, then, shuffling their flat feet, clapping their hands, and drawling out in a monotonous sort of chant something about the ' River Jawdam.'' Such a sketch conveys no idea of the shout as it may be witnessed to-day on any of the plantations among the Sea Islands.

You will find the children clean, and, in general, neatly dressed, coming into the room when asked by the superintendent, rendering their impressive and oftentimes pleasing melodies in a manner seldom surpassed in our schools at the North, while their ' shouting' reveals a suppleness of limb and peculiar grace of motion beyond the power of our dancing masters to impart.

There are many features of the negro shout which amuse us from their strangeness ; some, also, that strike the observer as wholly absurd. Yet, viewed as a religious exercise—and in this light it is always considered by the older negroes—I cannot help regarding it, in spite of many of its characteristics, as both a natural and a rational expression of devotional feeling. ' The negroes never indulge in it when, for any reason, they feel downhearted or sad at their meetings. The shout is a simple outburst and manifestation of religious fervor—a ' rejoicing in the Lord '—making a ' joyful noise unto the God of their salvation.'

The words of the shout songs are a singular medley of things sacred and profane, and are the natural outgrowth of the imperfect and fragmentary knowledge of the Scriptures which the negroes have picked up. The substitution for these crude productions of appropriate hymns, would remove from the shout that which is now the chief objection to it in intelligent minds, and would make of the dance, to which the negroes are so much attached, a useful auxiliary in their religious culture. The tunes to which these songs are sung, are some of them weird and wild —' barbaric madrigals '—while others are sweet and impressive melodies. The most striking of their barbaric airs it would be impossible to write out, but many of their more common melodies are easily caught upon being heard a few times. This music of the negro shout opens a new and rich field of melody—a mine in which there is much rough quartz, but also many veins of sparkling ore.[1]

What, for example, could be more animated, and at the same time more expressive of the thought conveyed in the verse than the following chorus ?— the introduction to which is a sort of recitative or chant :

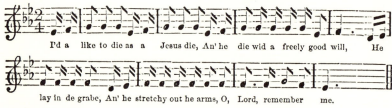

I'd a like to die as a Jesus die, An' he die wid a freely good will, He

lay in de grabe, An' he stretchy out he arms, O, Lord, remember me.

Chorus. *Lively.*

O, Lord, remember me, Do, Lord, remember me ; Re-

member me when de year rolls round, O, Lord, remember me.

The words of the chant are evidently a very childlike expression of the wish to die with the same good will and spirit of forgiveness which were manifested in the Saviour's death.

Of a very different character is the following verse, sung to the same recitative :

'O, Death he is a little man,
He goes from do' to do',
He kill some soul, an he wounded some,
An' he lef' some soul for to pray.'

A most striking contrast between the recitative and chorus, is presented in the following :

Recitative (*Sung to one note like a chant, with a cadence at the end*) :—

'I wonder why Satan do follow me so ?
Satan hab noting 't all for to do, long 'wid me.'

Chorus. *Slow and forcibly.*

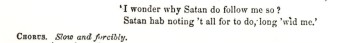

Hold your light, Hold your light, Hold your light on Canaan's shore.

The next song presents a greater variety in melody, as well as in the different verses, which seem to have no connection whatever with each other. The

'Parson Fuller' referred to is the Rev. Dr. Fuller, of Baltimore, who owns a plantation on one of the islands :

Dar's a meetin' here to - night, Dar's a meetin' here to - night, Dar's a

1. All of the early collectors, James Weldon Johnson has observed, were "more or less successful in getting the melodies down correctly, but none of these pioneers even attempted to set down the anarchic harmonies which they heard." None were trained so they merely jotted down the melodies and words. James Weldon Johnson, *The Book of American Negro Spirituals*, p. 47.

meetin' here to - night, I hope to meet you dar. { 1. Parson Fuller sittin' on de
{ 2. Little children learn to
{ 3. Let no angry word or

Tree of Life, An' he heary when Jordan roll.)
fear de Lord, An' let your days be long. } Roll, Jordan, roll, Jordan,
spiteful boast Be heard up - on your tongue.)

Roll, Jor - dan, roll, Roll, Jordan, roll, O roll, Jordan, roll, O my

soul will rise to heab'n above, An' heary when Jordan roll.

The following has evidently been composed since the negroes became free, and expresses very forcibly their feelings toward ' driber, massa, and missus ':

Done wid driber's dribin', Done wid driber's dribin',

Done wid driber's drib - in', Roll, Jordan, roll.

2. Done wid massa's hollerin',
   Done wid massa's hollerin',
   Done wid massa's hollerin',
      Roll, Jordan, roll.

3. Done wid missus' scoldin',
   Done wid missus' scoldin',
   Done wid missus' scoldin',
      Roll, Jordan, roll.

4. Sins so heaby dat I cannot get along,
   Sins so heaby dat I cannot get along,
   Sins so heaby dat I cannot get along,
      Roll, Jordan, roll.

5. Cast my sins to de bottom ob de sea,
   Cast my sins to de bottom ob de sea,
   Cast my sins to de bottom ob de sea,
      Roll, Jordan, roll.

Perhaps the best illustration of the Scriptural patchwork which characterizes many of the shout songs, is seen in the ' Lonesome Valley,' the music of which is very quaint and plaintive :

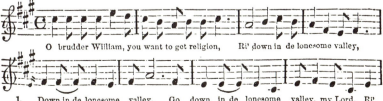

O brudder William, you want to get religion, Ri' down in de lonesome valley,

1. Down in de lonesome valley, Go down in de lonesome valley, my Lord, Ri'
2. You feed on milk and honey, You feed on milk and honey, my Lord, You

down	in de	lonesome	valley,	You	meet my	Jesus	dere.
feed	on	milk and	honey,	And	meet my	Jesus	dere.

The third and fourth stanzas are:

3. When Johnny brought a letter,
   When Johnny brought a letter, my Lord,
   When Johnny brought a letter,
      He meet my Jesus dere. '

4. An' Mary and Marta read 'em,
   An' Mary and Marta read 'em, my Lord,
   An' Mary and Marta read 'em,
      Dey meet my Jesus dere.

The example above given will convey a good idea of the general character of the shout songs. Apart from these religious songs, there is no music among the South Carolina freedmen, except the simple airs which are sung by the boatmen, as they row on the rivers and creeks. A tinge of sadness pervades all their melodies, which bear as little resemblance to the popular Ethiopian melodies of the day as twilight to noonday. The joyous, merry strains which have been associated in the minds of many with the Southern negro, are never heard on the Sea Islands. Indeed, by most of the negroes, such songs as 'Uncle Ned' and 'O Susanna' are considered as highly improper. In the schools, many of the best songs which are sung in our Sunday and public schools have been introduced, and are opening new sources of pleasure to a race so musical by their very nature as are the negroes of the South.

While in Beaufort, I attended a concert given by a band of genuine 'negro minstrels.' The company had taken the name of the 'Charleston Minstrels,' and was composed mainly of refugees from Charleston, who were then servants to various officers in General Saxton's Department. The concert was held in the Episcopal Church, and the proceeds devoted to the benefit of the sick and wounded of the First South Carolina Volunteers. The first view of the performers, as they sat round the stage, a dozen finely formed and good-looking negroes, caused the spectator to fancy himself in the presence of the famous band of Christy, or some other company of white Ethiopian serenaders. Soon, the opera glass revealed the amusing fact, that, although every minstrel was by nature as black as black could be, yet all the performers had given their faces a coating of burnt cork, in order that their resemblance to Yankee minstrels might be in every respect complete. There were excellent voices among the singers, and some of the players handled their instruments with surprising skill; but the presence of an audience composed entirely of white people, and including many of the highest officers in the Department, evidently caused great embarrassment to performers so unaccustomed to the stage. Not a single song which could be called comic was included in the programme; and, with the exception of a few patriotic airs, the songs were of the 'Lily Dale,' half-mournful sort. Between the pieces there was the customary telling of anecdotes and cracking of jokes, some of which were quite amusing, while others excited laughter from the manner in which they were told. As an imitation of our Northern minstrelsy given by a band of uneducated negro musicians, the performance was a wonderful success. Yet the general impression left upon the mind of the hearer was far from pleasing. One could not help feeling that a people, whose very natures are attuned to harmony, are capable of something better than even the most perfect imitation of those who have so grossly caricatured their race.

CONTRABANDS IN THE WAKE OF SHERMAN'S ARMY.

III

SONGS OF THE PORT ROYAL "CONTRABANDS"

Lucy McKim Garrison

[Lucy McKim Garrison was one of the three editors and compilers of
the historic *Slave Songs of the United States*. In this letter she mentions her musical notations of such songs, the first ever published being
the song "Poor Rosy" which appeared in William Lloyd Garrison's
crusading paper *The Liberator*. The daughter of J. Miller McKim, she
was the sister of America's noted architect Charles Nollen McKim,
who designed the now demolished Pennsylvania Railroad depot in
New York, the Morgan Library, and the Arlington Memorial Bridge
and Water Gate. Stanford White was his partner. She later married
Garrison's son Wendell, who with the help of her father founded *The
Nation*. The following letter appeared in *Dwight's Journal of Music*
(Boston, 8 November 1862). She died 11 May 1877, ten years after
her book on the slave songs was published.]

Songs of the Port Royal "Contrabands."

We have received No. 1 of "Songs of the Freedmen of Port Royal, collected and arranged by Miss LUCY McKIM," with the following interesting letter, which speaks for itself. We trust we violate no confidence in printing it. The melody has a simple and touching pathos, a flavor of individuality which makes one desire to know more of these things; and we trust that "Poor Rosy" will be followed by other specimens as genuine.

PHILADELPHIA, Nov. 1st. 1862.

Mr. Dwight,

SIR :—In a recent number of your journal there appeared an article relating to the music of the slaves of Port Royal, taken from an address delivered by my father before the members and friends of the Port Royal Freed-men's Association of this city. The extract included the words of one of their songs, beginning " Poor Rosy, poor gal ! "

My chief object in writing to you, is to say, that having accompanied my father on his tour to Port Royal, and being much struck with the songs of its people, I reduced a number of them to paper ; among them, the ballad referred to. I send you herewith a copy of it, hoping it may interest you. Whether to have the others printed, is as yet, a question with me,

It is difficult to express the entire character of these negro ballads by mere musical notes and signs. The odd turns made in the throat; and tha curious rhythmic effect produced by single voices chiming in at different irregular intervals, seem almost as impossible to place on score, as the singing of birds, or the tones of an Æolian Harp. The airs, however, can be reached, They are too decided not to be easily understood, and their striking originality would catch the ear of any musician. Besides this, they are valuable as an expression of the character and life of the race which is playing such a conspicuous part in our history. The wild, sad strains tell, as the sufferers themselves never could, of crushed hopes, keen sorrow, and a dull daily misery which covered them as hopelessly as the fog from the rice-swamps. On the other hand, the words breathe a trusting faith in rest in the future—in " Canaan's air and happy land," to which their eyes seem constantly turned.

A complaint might be made against these songs on the score of monotony. It is true there is a great deal of repetition of the music, but that is to accommodate the *leader*, who, if he be a good one, is always an improvisator. For instance, on one occasion, the name of each of our party who was present, was dexterously introduced.

As the same songs are sung at every sort of work, of course the *tempo* is not always alike. On the water, the oars dip " Poor Rosy " to an even andante ; a stout boy and girl at the hominy-mill will make the same " Poor Rosy " fly to keep up with the whirling stone ; and in the evening, after the day's work is done, " Heab'n shall-a be my home " peals up slowly and mournfully from the distant quarters. One woman,—a respectable houseservant, who had lost all but one of her twenty-two children, said to me :

" Pshaw ! dont har to dese yer chil'en, misse. Dey just rattles it off,—dey dont know how for sing it. I likes " Poor Rosy " better dan all de songs, but it cant be sung widout *a full heart and a troubled sperrit* ! "

All the songs make good barcaroles. Whittier "builded better than he knew " when he wrote his " Song of the Negro Boatman." It seemed wonderfully applicable as we were being rowed across Hilton Head Harbor among United States gunboats,—the Wabash and the Vermont towering on either side. I thought the crew *must* strike up

" And massa tink it day ob doom,
And we ob jubilee."

Perhaps the *grandest* singing we heard was at the Baptist Church on St. Helena Island, when a congregation of three hundred men and women joined in a hymn—

" Roll, Jordan, roll. Jordan !
Roll, Jordan, roll ! "

It swelled forth like a triumphal anthem. That same hymn was sung by thousands of negroes on the 4th. of July last, when they marched in procession under the Stars and Stripes, cheering them for the first time as the " flag of *our* country," A friend writing from there, says that the chorus was indescribably grand,—" that the whole woods and world seemed joining in that rolling sound."

There is much more in this new and curious music, of which it is a temptation to write, but I must remember that it can speak for itself better than any one for it.

Very respectfully,   LUCY McKIM.

FLAG PRESENTED BY CITIZENS OF NEW YORK
TO THE FIRST S. C. VOLUNTEERS
The Colonel (Higginson) commanding charging Sergeant Prince
Rivers, as color-bearer, never to give it up.

IV

NEGRO SPIRITUALS

Thomas Wentworth Higginson

[By almost any standard Thomas Wentworth Higginson was an extraordinary man. A Unitarian minister, he had been the leader in the
Boston attempt to free Anthony Burns, a fugitive slave, that had ended
in the shooting down of a federal marshal and the sending of an army
of marines into Boston. Higginson and Wendell Phillips had stood
trial and been freed of charges in the shooting. During the Kansas
"Border Ruffian" days Higginson had twice entered the fight to keep
Kansas free. Later he was one of the "Secret Six" who aided John
Brown. He is best known for his command of the first Civil War regiment recruited from former slaves, the First South Carolina Volunteers, and he also fought for women's rights and was the confidant
of the lonely New England poet Emily Dickinson. His was easily the
most thorough study of slave songs. The following article was published in *The Atlantic Monthly*, XIX (June, 1867), pp. 685-694.]

[11]

NEGRO SPIRITUALS.

THE war brought to some of us, besides its direct experiences, many a strange fulfilment of dreams of other days. For instance, the present writer had been a faithful student of the Scottish ballads, and had always envied Sir Walter the delight of tracing them out amid their own heather, and of writing them down piecemeal from the lips of aged crones. It was a strange enjoyment, therefore, to be suddenly brought into the midst of a kindred world of unwritten songs, as simple and indigenous as the Border Minstrelsy, more uniformly plaintive, almost always more quaint, and often as essentially poetic.

This interest was rather increased by the fact that I had for many years heard of this class of songs under the name of "Negro Spirituals," and had even heard some of them sung by friends from South Carolina. I could now gather on their own soil these strange plants, which I had before seen as in museums alone. True, the individual songs rarely coincided; there was a line here, a chorus there, — just enough to fix the class, but this was unmistakable. It was not strange that they differed, for the range seemed almost endless, and South Carolina, Georgia, and Florida seemed to have nothing but the generic character in common, until all were mingled in the united stock of camp-melodies.

Often in the starlit evening I have returned from some lonely ride by the swift river, or on the plover-haunted barrens, and, entering the camp, have silently approached some glimmering fire, round which the dusky figures moved in the rhythmical barbaric dance the negroes call a "shout," chanting, often harshly, but always in the most perfect time, some monotonous refrain. Writing down in the darkness, as I best could, — perhaps with my hand in the safe covert of my pocket, — the words of the song, I have afterwards carried it to my tent, like some captured bird or insect, and then, after examination, put it by. Or, summoning one of the men at some period of leisure, — Corporal Robert Sutton, for instance, whose iron memory held all the details of a song as if it were a ford or a forest, — I have completed the new specimen by supplying the absent parts. The music I could only retain by ear, and though the more common strains were repeated often enough to fix their impression, there were others that occurred only once or twice.

The words will be here given, as nearly as possible, in the original dialect; and if the spelling seems sometimes inconsistent, or the misspelling insufficient, it is because I could get no nearer. I wished to avoid what seems to me the only error of Lowell's "Biglow Papers" in respect to dialect, — the occasional use of an extreme misspelling, which merely confuses the eye, without taking us any closer to the peculiarity of sound.

The favorite song in camp was the following, — sung with no accompaniment but the measured clapping of hands and the clatter of many feet. It was sung perhaps twice as often as any other. This was partly due to the fact that it properly consisted of a chorus alone, with which the verses of other songs might be combined at random.

I. HOLD YOUR LIGHT.

"Hold your light, Brudder Robert, —
　　Hold your light,
　Hold your light on Canaan's shore.

"What make ole Satan for follow me so?
　Satan ain't got notin' for do wid me.
　　Hold your light,
　　Hold your light,
　Hold your light on Canaan's shore."

This would be sung for half an hour at a time, perhaps, each person present being named in turn. It seemed the simplest primitive type of "spiritual." The next in popularity was almost as elementary, and, like this, named successively each one of the circle. It was, however, much more resounding and convivial in its music.

II. BOUND TO GO.

" Jordan River, I 'm bound to go,
  Bound to go, bound to go, —
  Jordan River, I 'm bound to go,
  And bid 'em fare ye well.

" My Brudder Robert, I 'm bound to go,
  Bound to go, &c.

" My Sister Lucy, I 'm bound to go,
  Bound to go," &c.

Sometimes it was "tink 'em" (think them) "fare ye well." The *ye* was so detached, that I thought at first it was " very " or " vary well."

Another picturesque song, which seemed immensely popular, was at first very bewildering to me. I could not make out the first words of the chorus, and called it the "Romandàr," being reminded of some Romaic song which I had formerly heard. That association quite fell in with the Orientalism of the new tent-life.

III. ROOM IN THERE.

" O, my mudder is gone ! my mudder is gone !
My mudder is gone into heaven, my Lord !
  I can't stay behind !
Dere 's room in dar, room in dar,
Room in dar, in de heaven, my Lord !
  I can't stay behind,
Can't stay behind, my dear,
  I can't stay behind !

" O, my fader is gone !" &c.

" O, de angels are gone ! " &c.

" O, I 'se been on de road ! I 'se been on de road !
I 'se been on de road into heaven, my Lord !
  I can't stay behind !
O, room in dar, room in dar,
Room in dar, in de heaven, my Lord !
  I can't stay behind !"

By this time every man within hearing, from oldest to youngest, would be wriggling and shuffling, as if through some magic piper's bewitchment ; for even those who at first affected contemptuous indifference would be drawn into the vortex erelong.

Next to these in popularity ranked a class of songs belonging emphatically to the Church Militant, and available for camp purposes with very little strain upon their symbolism. This, for in-

stance, had a true companion-in-arms heartiness about it, not impaired by the feminine invocation at the end.

IV. HAIL MARY.

' One more valiant soldier here,
  One more valiant soldier here,
  One more valiant soldier here,
    To help me bear de cross.
  O hail, Mary, hail !
  Hail, Mary, hail !
  Hail, Mary, hail !
    To help me bear de cross."

I fancied that the original reading might have been " soul," instead of " soldier," — with some other syllable inserted, to fill out the metre, — and that the " Hail, Mary," might denote a Roman Catholic origin, as I had several men from St. Augustine who held in a dim way to that faith. It was a very ringing song, though not so grandly jubilant as the next, which was really impressive as the singers pealed it out, when marching or rowing or embarking.

V. MY ARMY CROSS OVER.

" My army cross over,
  My army cross over.
  O, Pharaoh's army drownded !
  My army cross over.

" We 'll cross de mighty river,
    My army cross over ;
  We 'll cross de river Jordan,
    My army cross over ;
  We 'll cross de danger water,
    My army cross over ;
  We 'll cross de mighty Myo,
    My army cross over. (*Thrice.*)
  O, Pharaoh's army drownded !
  My army cross over."

I could get no explanation of the " mighty Myo," except that one of the old men thought it meant the river of death. Perhaps it is an African word. In the Cameroon dialect, " Mawa " signifies "to die."

The next also has a military ring about it, and the first line is well matched by the music. The rest is conglomerate, and one or two lines show a more Northern origin. " Done " is a Virginia shibboleth, quite distinct from the " been " which replaces it in South Carolina. Yet one of their best choruses, without any fixed words, was, " De bell done ringing," for which, in proper South Carolina dialect, would have been substituted, " De bell been a-ring." This refrain may have gone South with our army.

VI. RIDE IN, KIND SAVIOUR.

" Ride in, kind Saviour !
 No man can hinder me.
O, Jesus is a mighty man !
 No man, &c.
We 're marching through Virginny fields.
 No man, &c.
O, Satan is a busy man,
 No man, &c.
And he has his sword and shield,
 No man, &c.
O, old Secesh done come and gone !
 No man can hinder me."

Sometimes they substituted " hinder *we*," which was more spicy to the ear, and more in keeping with the usual head-over-heels arrangement of their pronouns.

Almost all their songs were thoroughly religious in their tone, however quaint their expression, and were in a minor key, both as to words and music.[1] The attitude is always the same, and, as a commentary on the life of the race, is infinitely pathetic. Nothing but patience for this life, — nothing but triumph in the next. Sometimes the present predominates, sometimes the future ; but the combination is always implied. In the following, for instance, we hear simply the patience.

VII. THIS WORLD ALMOST DONE.

" Brudder, keep your lamp trimmin' and a-burnin',
Keep your lamp trimmin' and a-burnin',
Keep your lamp trimmin' and a-burnin',
 For dis world most done.
So keep your lamp, &c.
 Dis world most done."

But in the next, the final reward of patience is proclaimed as plaintively.

VIII. I WANT TO GO HOME.

" Dere 's no rain to wet you,
 O, yes, I want to go home.
Dere 's no sun to burn you,
 O, yes, I want to go home ;
O, push along, believers,
 O, yes, &c.
Dere 's no hard trials,
 O, yes, &c.
Dere 's no whips a-crackin',
 O, yes, &c.
My brudder on de wayside,
 O, yes, &c.

O, push along, my brudder,
 O, yes, &c.
Where dere 's no stormy weather,
 O, yes, &c.
Dere 's no tribulation,
 O, yes, &c."

This next was a boat-song, and timed well with the tug of the oar.

IX. THE COMING DAY.

" I want to go to Canaan,
I want to go to Canaan,
I want to go to Canaan,
 To meet 'em at de comin' day.
O, remember, let me go to Canaan, (*Thrice.*)
 To meet 'em, &c.
O brudder, let me go to Canaan, (*Thrice.*)
 To meet 'em, &c.
My brudder, you — oh ! — remember (*Thrice.*)
 To meet 'em at de comin' day."

The following begins with a startling affirmation, yet the last line quite outdoes the first. This, too, was a capital boat-song.

X. ONE MORE RIVER.

O, Jordan bank was a great old bank !
 Dere ain't but one more river to cross.
We have some valiant soldier here,
 Dere ain't, &c.
O, Jordan stream will never run dry,
 Dere ain't, &c.
Dere 's a hill on my leff, and he catch on my right,
 Dere ain't but one more river to cross."

I could get no explanation of this last riddle, except, " Dat mean, if you go on de leff, go to 'struction, and if you go on de right, go to God, for sure."

In others, more of spiritual conflict is implied, as in this next.

XI. O THE DYING LAMB !

" I wants to go where Moses trod,
 O de dying Lamb !
For Moses gone to de promised land,
 O de dying Lamb !
To drink from springs dat never run dry,
 O, &c.
Cry O my Lord !
 O, &c.
Before I 'll stay in hell one day,
 O, &c.
I 'm in hopes to pray my sins away,
 O, &c.
Cry O my Lord !
 O, &c.
Brudder Moses promised for be dar too,
 O, &c.
To drink from streams dat never run dry,
 O de dying Lamb !"

In the next, the conflict is at its height, and the lurid imagery of the

---

1. Krehbiel points out Higginson's error. The songs are in a major mode, not minor. It is
 a common mistake, says Krehbiel, among those without technical training in music.

Apocalypse is brought to bear. This book, with the books of Moses, constituted their Bible ; all that lay between, even the narratives of the life of Jesus, they hardly cared to read or to hear.

XII. DOWN IN THE VALLEY.

"We 'll run and never tire,
We 'll run and never tire,
We 'll run and never tire,
Jesus set poor sinners free.
Way down in de valley,
Who will rise and go with me ?
You 've heern talk of Jesus,
Who set poor sinners free.

"De lightnin' and de flashin',
De lightnin' and de flashin',
De lightnin' and de flashin',
Jesus set poor sinners free.
I can't stand de fire. (*Thrice.*)
Jesus set poor sinners free,
De green trees a-flamin'. (*Thrice.*)
Jesus set poor sinners free,
Way down in de valley,
Who will rise and go with me ?
You 've heern talk of Jesus
Who set poor sinners free."

" De valley " and "de lonesome valley " were familiar words in their religious experience. To descend into that region implied the same process with the " anxious-seat " of the camp-meeting. When a young girl was supposed to enter it, she bound a handkerchief by a peculiar knot over her head, and made it a point of honor not to change a single garment till the day of her baptism, so that she was sure of being in physical readiness for the cleansing rite, whatever her spiritual mood might be. More than once, in noticing a damsel thus mystically kerchiefed, I have asked some dusky attendant its meaning, and have received the unfailing answer, — framed with their usual indifference to the genders of pronouns, — " He in de lonesome valley, sa."

The next gives the same dramatic conflict, while its detached and impersonal refrain gives it strikingly the character of the Scotch and Scandinavian ballads.

XIII. CRY HOLY.

"Cry holy, holy !
Look at de people dat is born of God.
And I run down de valley, and I run down to pray,
Says, look at de people dat is born of God.

When I get dar, Cappen Satan was dar,
Says, look at, &c.
Says, young man, young man, dere 's no use for pray,
Says, look at, &c.
For Jesus is dead, and God gone away,
Says, look at, &c.
And I made him out a liar and I went my way,
Says, look at, &c.
Sing holy, holy !

"O, Mary was a woman, and he had a one Son,
Says, look at, &c.
And de Jews and de Romans had him hung,
Says, look at, &c.
Cry holy, holy !

"And I tell you, sinner, you had better had pray,
Says, look at, &c.
For hell is a dark and dismal place,
Says, look at, &c.
And I tell you, sinner, and I would n't go dar !
Says, look at, &c.
Cry holy, holy !"

Here is an infinitely quaint description of the length of the heavenly road : —

XIV. O'ER THE CROSSING.

" Yonder 's my old mudder,
Been a-waggin' at de hill so long.
It 's about time she 'll cross over ;
Get home bimeby.
Keep prayin', I do believe
We 're a long time waggin' o'er de crossin'.
Keep prayin', I do believe
We 'll get home to heaven bimeby.

" Hear dat mournful thunder
Roll from door to door,
Calling home God's children ;
Get home bimeby.
Little chil'en, I do believe
We 're a long time, &c.
Little chil'en, I do believe
We 'll get home, &c.

" See dat forked lightnin'
Flash from tree to tree,
Callin' home God's chil'en ;
Get home bimeby.
True believer, I do believe
We 're a long time, &c.
O brudders, I do believe,
We 'll get home to heaven bimeby."

One of the most singular pictures of future joys, and with a fine flavor of hospitality about it, was this : —

XV. WALK 'EM EASY.

" O, walk 'em easy round de heaven,
Walk 'em easy round de heaven,
Walk 'em easy round de heaven,
Dat all de people may join de band.
Walk 'em easy round de heaven. (*Thrice.*)
O, shout glory till 'em join dat band !"

The chorus was usually the greater

part of the song, and often came in paradoxically, thus : —

XVI. O YES, LORD.

" O, must I be like de foolish mans ?
        O yes, Lord !
Will build de house on de sandy hill.
        O yes, Lord !
I 'll build my house on Zion hill,
        O yes, Lord !
No wind nor rain can blow me down
        O yes, Lord ! "

The next is very graceful and lyrical, and with more variety of rhythm than usual : —

XVII. BOW LOW, MARY.

" Bow low, Mary, bow low, Martha,
        For Jesus come and lock de door,
        And carry de keys away.
Sail, sail, over yonder,
        And view de promised land.
        For Jesus come, &c.
Weep, O Mary, bow low, Martha,
        For Jesus come, &c.
Sail, sail, my true believer ;
Sail, sail, over yonder ;
Mary, bow low, Martha, bow low,
        For Jesus come and lock de door
        And carry de keys away."

But of all the "spirituals" that which surprised me the most, I think, — perhaps because it was that in which external nature furnished the images most directly, — was this. With all my experience of their ideal ways of speech, I was startled when first I came on such a flower of poetry in that dark soil.

XVIII. I KNOW MOON-RISE.

"I know moon-rise, I know star-rise,
        Lay dis body down.
I walk in de moonlight, I walk in de starlight,
        To lay dis body down.
I 'll walk in de graveyard, I 'll walk through de
                graveyard,
        To lay dis body down.
I 'll lie in de grave and stretch out my arms ;
        Lay dis body down.
I go to de judgment in de evenin' of de day,
        When I lay dis body down ;
And my soul and your soul will meet in de day
        When I lay dis body down."

" I 'll lie in de grave and stretch out my arms." Never, it seems to me, since man first lived and suffered, was his infinite longing for peace uttered more plaintively than in that line.

The next is one of the wildest and most striking of the whole series : there is a mystical effect and a passionate

striving throughout the whole. The Scriptural struggle between Jacob and the angel, which is only dimly expressed in the words, seems all uttered in the music. I think it impressed my imagination more powerfully than any other of these songs.

XIX. WRESTLING JACOB.

" O wrestlin' Jacob, Jacob, day 's a-breakin' ;
        I will not let thee go !
O wrestlin' Jacob, Jacob, day 's a-breakin' ;
        He will not let me go !
O, I hold my brudder wid a tremblin' hand ;
        I would not let him go !
I hold my sister wid a tremblin' hand ;
        I would not let her go !

" O, Jacob do hang from a tremblin' limb,
        He would not let him go !
O, Jacob do hang from a tremblin' limb ;
        De Lord will bless my soul.
O wrestlin' Jacob, Jacob," &c.

Of "occasional hymns," properly so called, I noticed but one, a funeral hymn for an infant, which is sung plaintively over and over, without variety of words.

XX. THE BABY GONE HOME.

" De little baby gone home,
De little baby gone home,
De little baby gone along,
        For to climb up Jacob's ladder.
And I wish I 'd been dar,
I wish I 'd been dar,
I wish I 'd been dar, my Lord,
        For to climb up Jacob's ladder."

Still simpler is this, which is yet quite sweet and touching.

XXI. JESUS WITH US.

" He have been wid us, Jesus,
        He still wid us, Jesus,
He will be wid us, Jesus,
        Be wid us to the end."

The next seemed to be a favorite about Christmas time, when meditations on "de rollin' year" were frequent among them.

XXII. LORD, REMEMBER ME !

" O do, Lord, remember me !
        O do, Lord, remember me !
O, do remember me, until de year roll round !
        Do, Lord, remember me !

" If you want to die like Jesus died,
        Lay in de grave,
You would fold your arms and close your eyes
        And die wid a free good will.

" For Death is a simple ting,
  And he go from door to door,
  And he knock down some, and he cripple up some,
  And he leave some here to pray.

" O do, Lord, remember me !
  O do, Lord, remember me !
  My old fader 's gone till de year roll round ;
  Do, Lord, remember me !"

The next was sung in such an operatic and rollicking way that it was quite hard to fancy it a religious performance, which, however, it was. I heard it but once.

XXIII. EARLY IN THE MORNING.

" I meet little Rosa early in de mornin',
  O Jerusalem ! early in de mornin' ;
  And I ax her, How you do, my darter?
  O Jerusalem ! early in de mornin'.

" I meet my mudder early in de mornin',
  O Jerusalem ! &c.
  And I ax her, How you do, my mudder?
  O Jerusalem ! &c.

" I meet Budder Robert early in de mornin',
  O Jerusalem ! &c.
  And I ax him, How you do, my sonny?
  O Jerusalem ! &c.

" I meet Tittawisa early in de mornin',
  O Jerusalem ! &c.
  And I ax her, How you do, my darter?
  O Jerusalem ! " &c.

" Tittawisa " means " Sister Louisa." In songs of this class the name of every person present successively appears.

Their best marching song, and one which was invaluable to lift their feet along, as they expressed it, was the following. There was a kind of spring and *lilt* to it, quite indescribable by words.

XXIV. GO IN THE WILDERNESS.

" Jesus call you. Go in de wilderness,
  Go in de wilderness, go in de wilderness,
  Jesus call you. Go in de wilderness
  To wait upon de Lord.
  Go wait upon de Lord,
  Go wait upon de Lord,
  Go wait upon de Lord, my God,
  He take away de sins of de world.

" Jesus a-waitin'. Go in de wilderness,
  Go, &c.
  All dem chil'en go in de wilderness
  To wait upon de Lord."

The next was one of those which I had heard in boyish days, brought North from Charleston. But the chorus alone was identical ; the words were mainly different, and those here given are quaint enough.

XXV. BLOW YOUR TRUMPET, GABRIEL.

" O, blow your trumpet, Gabriel,
  Blow your trumpet louder ;
  And I want dat trumpet to blow me home
  To my new Jerusalem.

" De prettiest ting dat ever I done
  Was to serve de Lord when I was young.
  So blow your trumpet, Gabriel, &c.

" O, Satan is a liar, and he conjure too,
  And if you don't mind, he 'll conjure you.
  So blow your trumpet, Gabriel, &c.

" O, I was lost in de wilderness,
  King Jesus hand me de candle down.
  So blow your trumpet, Gabriel," &c.

The following contains one of those odd transformations of proper names with which their Scriptural citations were often enriched. It rivals their text, " Paul may plant, and may polish wid water," which I have elsewhere quoted, and in which the sainted Apollos would hardly have recognized himself.

XXVI. IN THE MORNING.

" In de mornin',
  In de mornin',
  Chil'en ? Yes, my Lord !
  Don't you hear de trumpet sound ?
  If I had a-died when I was young,
  I never would had de race for run.
  Don't you hear de trumpet sound ?

" O Sam and Peter was fishin' in de sea,
  And dey drop de net and follow my Lord.
  Don't you hear de trumpet sound ?

" Dere 's a silver spade for to dig my grave
  And a golden chain for to let me down.
  Don't you hear de trumpet sound ?
  In de mornin',
  In de mornin',
  Chil'en ? Yes, my Lord !
  Don't you hear de trumpet sound ?"

These golden and silver fancies remind one of the King of Spain's daughter in " Mother Goose," and the golden apple, and the silver pear, which are doubtless themselves but the vestiges of some simple early composition like this. The next has a humbler and more domestic style of fancy.

XXVII. FARE YE WELL.

" My true believers, fare ye well,
  Fare ye well, fare ye well,
  Fare ye well, by de grace of God,
  For I 'm going home.

Massa Jesus give me a little broom
For to sweep my heart clean,
And I will try, by de grace of God,
To win my way home."

Among the songs not available for marching, but requiring the concentrated enthusiasm of the camp, was "The Ship of Zion," of which they had three wholly distinct versions, all quite exuberant and tumultuous.

XXVIII. THE SHIP OF ZION.

"Come along, come along,
  And let us go home,
  O, glory, hallelujah !
  Dis de ole ship o' Zion,
    Halleloo ! Halleloo !
  Dis de ole ship o' Zion,
    Hallelujah !

"She has landed many a tousand,
  She can land as many more.
  O, glory, hallelujah ! &c.

"Do you tink she will be able
  For to take us all home ?
  O, glory, hallelujah ! &c.

"You can tell 'em I 'm a comin',
    Halleloo ! Halleloo !
  You can tell 'em I 'm a comin',
    Hallelujah !
  Come along, come along," &c.

XXIX. THE SHIP OF ZION. (*Second version.*)

"Dis de good ole ship o' Zion,
Dis de good ole ship o' Zion,
Dis de good ole ship o' Zion,
  And she 's makin' for de Promise Land.
She hab angels for de sailors, (*Thrice.*)
  And she 's, &c.
And how you know dey 's angels ? (*Thrice.*)
  And she 's, &c.
Good Lord, shall I be de one ? (*Thrice.*)
  And she 's, &c.

"Dat ship is out a-sailin', sailin', sailin',
  And she 's, &c.
She 's a-sailin' mighty steady, steady, steady,
  And she 's, &c.
She 'll neither reel nor totter, totter, totter,
  And she 's, &c.
She 's a-sailin' away cold Jordan, Jordan, Jordan,
  And she 's, &c.
King Jesus is de captain, captain, captain,
  And she 's makin' for de Promise Land."

XXX. THE SHIP OF ZION. (*Third version.*)

"De Gospel ship is sailin',
  Hosann — sann.
O, Jesus is de captain,
  Hosann — sann.
De angels are de sailors,
  Hosann — sann.

O, is your bundle ready ?
  Hosann — sann.
O, have you got your ticket ?
  Hosann — sann."

This abbreviated chorus is given with unspeakable unction.

The three just given are modifications of an old camp-meeting melody ; and the same may be true of the three following, although I cannot find them in the Methodist hymn-books. Each, however, has its characteristic modifications, which make it well worth giving. In the second verse of this next, for instance, "Saviour" evidently has become "soldier."

XXXI. SWEET MUSIC.

"Sweet music in heaven,
  Just beginning for to roll.
Don't you love God ?
  Glory, hallelujah !

"Yes, late I heard my soldier say,
  Come, heavy soul, I am de way.
Don't you love God ?
  Glory, hallelujah !

"I 'll go and tell to sinners round
  What a kind Saviour I have found.
Don't you love God ?
  Glory, hallelujah !

"My grief my burden long has been,
  Because I was not cease from sin.
Don't you love God ?
  Glory, hallelujah ! "

XXXII. GOOD NEWS.

"O, good news ! O, good news !
De angels brought de tidings down,
  Just comin' from de trone.

"As grief from out my soul shall fly,
  Just comin' from de trone ;
I 'll shout salvation when I die,
Good news, O, good news !
  Just comin' from de trone.

"Lord, I want to go to heaven when I die,
Good news, O, good news ! &c.

"De white folks call us a noisy crew,
Good news, O, good news !
But dis I know, we are happy too,
  Just comin' from de trone."

XXXIII. THE HEAVENLY ROAD.

"You may talk of my name as much as you please,
  And carry my name abroad,
But I really do believe I 'm a child of God
  As I walk in de heavenly road.
O, won't you go wid me ? (*Thrice.*)
  For to keep our garments clean.

"O, Satan is a mighty busy ole man,
  And roll rocks in my way ;

But Jesus is my bosom friend,
And roll 'em out of de way.
O, won't you go wid me? (*Thrice.*)
For to keep our garments clean.

" Come, my brudder, if you never did pray,
I hope you may pray to-night :
For I really believe I 'm a child of God
As I walk in de heavenly road.
O, won't you," &c.

Some of the songs had played an historic part during the war. For singing the next, for instance, the negroes had been put in jail in Georgetown, S. C., at the outbreak of the Rebellion. " We 'll soon be free," was too dangerous an assertion ; and though the chant was an old one, it was no doubt sung with redoubled emphasis during the new events. " De Lord will call us home," was evidently thought to be a symbolical verse ; for, as a little drummer-boy explained to me, showing all his white teeth as he sat in the moonlight by the door of my tent, " Dey tink *de Lord* mean for say *de Yankees.*"

XXXIV. WE 'LL SOON BE FREE.

" We 'll soon be free,
We 'll soon be free,
We 'll soon be free,
 When de Lord will call us home.
My brudder, how long,
My brudder, how long,
My brudder, how long,
 'Fore we done sufferin' here ?
It won't be long (*Thrice.*)
 'Fore de Lord will call us home.
We 'll walk de miry road (*Thrice.*)
 Where pleasure never dies.
We 'll walk de golden street (*Thrice.*)
 Where pleasure never dies.
My brudder, how long (*Thrice.*)
 'Fore we done sufferin' here ?
We 'll soon be free (*Thrice.*)
 When Jesus sets me free.
We 'll fight for liberty (*Thrice.*)
 When de Lord will call us home."

The suspicion in this case was unfounded, but they had another song to which the Rebellion had actually given rise. This was composed by nobody knew whom, — though it was the most recent, doubtless, of all these " spirituals," — and had been sung in secret to avoid detection. It is certainly plaintive enough. The peck of corn and pint of salt were slavery's rations.

XXXV. MANY THOUSAND GO.

" No more peck o' corn for me,
 No more, no more, —

No more peck o' corn for me,
 Many tousand go.

" No more driver's lash for me, (*Twice.*)
 No more, &c.

" No more pint o' salt for me, (*Twice.*)
 No more, &c.

" No more hundred lash for me, (*Twice.*)
 No more, &c.

" No more mistress' call for me,
 No more, no more, —
No more mistress' call for me,
 Many tousand go."

Even of this last composition, however, we have only the approximate date, and know nothing of the mode of composition. Allan Ramsay says of the Scotch songs, that, no matter who made them, they were soon attributed to the minister of the parish whence they sprang. And I always wondered, about these, whether they had always a conscious and definite origin in some leading mind, or whether they grew by gradual accretion, in an almost unconscious way. On this point I could get no information, though I asked many questions, until at last, one day when I was being rowed across from Beaufort to Ladies' Island, I found myself, with delight, on the actual trail of a song. One of the oarsmen, a brisk young fellow, not a soldier, on being asked for his theory of the matter, dropped out a coy confession. " Some good sperituals," he said, " are start jess out o' curiosity. I been a-raise a sing, myself, once."

My dream was fulfilled, and I had traced out, not the poem alone, but the poet. I implored him to proceed.

" Once we boys," he said, " went for tote some rice, and de nigger-driver, he keep a-callin' on us ; and I say, ' O, de ole nigger-driver ! ' Den anudder said, ' Fust ting my mammy tole me was, notin' so bad as nigger-driver.' Den I made a sing, just puttin' a word, and den anudder word."

Then he began singing, and the men, after listening a moment, joined in the chorus as if it were an old acquaintance, though they evidently had never heard it before. I saw how easily a new " sing " took root among them.

XXXVI. THE DRIVER.

" O, de ole nigger-driver !
    O, gwine away !
Fust ting my mammy tell me,
    O, gwine away !
Tell me 'bout de nigger-driver,
    O, gwine away !
Nigger-driver second devil,
    O, gwine away !
Best ting for do he driver,
    O, gwine away !
Knock he down and spoil he labor,
    O, gwine away ! "

It will be observed that, although this song is quite secular in its character, its author yet called it a "spiritual." I heard but two songs among them, at any time, to which they would not, perhaps, have given this generic name. One of these consisted simply in the endless repetition — after the manner of certain college songs — of the mysterious line,

" Rain fall and wet Becky Martin."

But who Becky Martin was, and why she should or should not be wet, and whether the dryness was a reward or a penalty, none could say. I got the impression that, in either case, the event was posthumous, and that there was some tradition of grass not growing over the grave of a sinner; but even this was vague, and all else vaguer.

The other song I heard but once, on a morning when a squad of men came in from picket duty, and chanted it in the most rousing way. It had been a stormy and comfortless night, and the picket station was very exposed. It still rained in the morning when I strolled to the edge of the camp, looking out for the men, and wondering how they had stood it. Presently they came striding along the road, at a great pace, with their shining rubber blankets worn as cloaks around them, the rain streaming from these and from their equally shining faces, which were almost all upon the broad grin, as they pealed out this remarkable ditty : —

HANGMAN JOHNNY.

" O, dey call me Hangman Johnny !
    O, ho ! O, ho !
But I never hang nobody,
    O, hang, boys, hang ! "

" O, dey call me Hangman Johnny !
    O, ho ! O, ho !
But we 'll all hang togedder,
    O, hang, boys, hang ! "

My presence apparently checked the performance of another verse, beginning, " De buckra 'list for money," apparently in reference to the controversy about the pay-question, then just beginning, and to the more mercenary aims they attributed to the white soldiers. But " Hangman Johnny " remained always a myth as inscrutable as " Becky Martin."

As they learned all their songs by ear, they often strayed into wholly new versions, which sometimes became popular, and entirely banished the others. This was amusingly the case, for instance, with one phrase in the popular camp-song of " Marching Along," which was entirely new to them until our quartermaster taught it to them, at my request. The words, " Gird on the armor," were to them a stumbling-block, and no wonder, until some ingenious ear substituted, " Guide on de army," which was at once accepted, and became universal.

"We 'll guide on de army, and be marching along,"

is now the established version on the Sea Islands.

These quaint religious songs were to the men more than a source of relaxation ; they were a stimulus to courage and a tie to heaven. I never overheard in camp a profane or vulgar song. With the trifling exceptions given, all had a religious motive, while the most secular melody could not have been more exciting. A few youths from Savannah, who were comparatively men of the world, had learned some of the " Ethiopian Minstrel " ditties, imported from the North. These took no hold upon the mass ; and, on the other hand, they sang reluctantly, even on Sunday, the long and short metres of the hymn-books, always gladly yielding to the more potent excitement of their own "spirituals." By these they could sing themselves, as had their fathers before them, out of the contemplation of their own low estate, into the sublime scenery of the Apocalypse. I remember that this minor-keyed pathos used to seem to me almost too sad to dwell upon, while slavery seemed destined to last for generations; but now that their patience has had its perfect work, history cannot afford to lose this portion of its record. There is no parallel instance of an oppressed race thus sustained by the religious sentiment alone. These songs are but the vocal expression of the simplicity of their faith and the sublimity of their long resignation.

V

SONGS OF THE SLAVE

John Mason Brown

[John Mason Brown was the grandfather of the well-known drama critic, essayist, and raconteur of our own day, and of the same name. A Yale graduate, he chose to live for a time (like his Harvard contemporary Francis Parkman) among the western Indian tribes. At the outbreak of the Civil War, Brown split with pro-Confederate members of his Kentucky family, joined the Union Army, and rose to the rank of Colonel. Afterward he became a prominent attorney and author of many articles, mostly on the law. The article that follows was published in *Lippincott's Magazine*, II (December, 1868), pp. 617-623.]

SONGS OF THE SLAVE

THE characteristics of the negro race in the United States are rapidly changing. The abolition of slavery, and the new privileges and responsibilities growing out of his changed condition, are speedily making of the freedman a being totally different from the slave of former years. Care and want and self-dependence are new ideas to the bulk of the negro population, but they are now ever present and demand recognition. As a consequence, the negro is daily becoming more reflective, more cautious and more shrewd. He grows taciturn as compared with his former habits, and keenly alive to the practical relations between labor and compensation. As might be expected, a new set of qualities are developing, which lay dormant in former years—useless to the slave, but indispensable to the freedman; and peculiarities, very marked under the old régime, are fast disappearing. A tendency to graver views of life and sobriety of thought is very observable.

In nothing has this mental change been more unmistakably shown than in the rapid disuse of a class of songs long popular with negro slaves, and in many instances exquisitely illustrative of their habits of thought. The round of sacred and secular song that for many years was so familiar to every ear throughout the Southern States, is now fading from use and remembrance. It is giving place to a totally different system of words and melody. It could not be perpetuated without perpetuating slavery as it existed, and with the fall of slavery its days were numbered.

A very erroneous idea has long prevailed which accepts "negro minstrelsy" as a mirror of the musical taste and feeling of the negro race in the United States. Nothing could be farther from truth. Beyond the external resemblance, due to burnt cork, there is in negro minstrelsy scarcely a feature of person, music, dialect or action that recalls, with any dramatic accuracy, the genuine negro slave of former years. True it is that Christy, Bryant and Newcomb have achieved great success as Ethiopian comedians, and are accepted as interpreters of the negro ; but it is none the less true that their delineations are mere conventionalisms, and their Ethiopian music even farther from the truth than their very amusing but very inaccurate impersonations. No genuine negro song, composed by a negro slave, ever betrayed a straining after *vowel endings*. Such words as " Swanee," " Tennessee," " Ohio " (the final *o* lengthened *ad libitum*), are by no means as frequently used by the negro as minstrels would have us suppose. Triple time, too, it may be remarked, is such a rarity in negro music that but one instance now occurs to us, and *it* may be plausibly traced to an old Scotch air.

But it is not to the subject of negro minstrelsy that the present sketch will be devoted. It is proposed to offer a few specimens of genuine negro-slave song and music. If they be found neither touching in sentiment, graceful in expression nor well balanced in rhythm, they may, at least, possess interest as peculiarities of a system now no more for ever in this country.

Many eloquent writers have described the religious services of negro slaves and the thrilling effect of their hymns, sung to quaint and unusual tunes by congregations of impassioned and impressible worshipers. The effect can hardly be overstated. Their hymns, " lined out " by the preacher, are full of unpremeditated and irresistible dramatic power. We have seen negroes alternately agonized with fear and transported with a bliss almost frantic as they sang a revival hymn called " The Book of Seven Seals," replete with the imagery of the Apocalypse, picturing the golden streets of the New Jerusalem and the horrible pit of destruction. Such a chorus, sung with the energy of a people of simple and literal faith and strong and inflammable emotions, has often quickened the pulse and set aglow the heart of those whose social position or philosophy made them ashamed to acknowledge the effect.

The religious songs of the negro slave were composed and communicated without the aid of writing, and were unmistakably marked in their construction. As a general rule, but few hymns were borrowed from the collections used by white congregations. Of those that were adopted by the negroes, the favorites were always such as abounded in bold imagery or striking expressions, appealing to ardent hope or vivid fear. Hence the unction with which those well-known hymns, " Am I a Soldier of the Cross ?" and " Hark, from the Tombs," were sung in negro churches.

But the religious songs composed by negro preachers or " exhorters " for the use of their congregations abounded to excess in metaphor of the most striking character. The saints were styled the " Army of the Lord," led by King Jesus, the " Captain " and " Conqueror." They were exhorted to listen to the summons of silver trumpets, marshaling the faithful to victory, and were described as sweeping down all the obstructions of evil, and marching forward, with measured tread, up the hill on which stands the city reserved for their habitation. The banners, trumpets, drums and other paraphernalia of an army were used without stint, and often with most graphic effect. Wherever a figure was attempted, it was fearlessly carried to its limit. There was current, not many years since, a hymn in which the Christian was likened to a traveler on a railway train. The conductor was the Lord Jesus, the brakemen were eminent servants of the Church, and stoppages were made at Gospel depôts to take up waiting converts or replenish the engine with the water of life or the fuel of holy zeal. The allegory was developed with as much accuracy and verisimilitude as though the author of the hymn had carefully studied the *Pilgrim's Progress;* yet it was imagined and composed by Oscar Buckner, an illiterate and ignorant negro slave.

It is doubtful if the authorship of that famous hymn, "The Old Ship of Zion," so popular among negroes everywhere, can be traced. It must have originated (judging from internal evidence) among the Maryland or Virginia negroes of the seaboard. As its name would indicate, the imagery of the hymn is exclusively nautical. A stanza or two will give an idea of many peculiarities of negro-slave religious song. This hymn is the original of very numerous imitations :

THE OLD SHIP OF ZION.

2. Oh, what are the timbers for buildin' of the ship?
    Oh glory, halleloo!
  She is made o' gospel timbers, halleloo!
  She is made o' gospel timbers, halleloo!

3. Oh, what is the compass you've got aboard the ship?
    Oh glory, halleloo!
  The Bible is our compass, halleloo!
  Oh, the Bible is our compass, halleloo!

As regards this hymn, it may be observed that the refrain of "glory, halleloo!" is not a singularity. It is found in many, perhaps most, negro songs of devotion. It serves to mark the time and keep the congregation well together in their singing, and also gives the leader time to recall the next verse. "The Old Ship of Zion" was a hymn of thirty or forty stanzas, each descriptive of some equipment, in a style similar to those already quoted.

A very popular hymn, still much sung, and evidently based upon the air of "The Old Ship of Zion," commences thus:

PRAY ON! PRAY ON!

Another quite popular but far inferior hymn runs thus:

OH WAKE THE NATIONS!

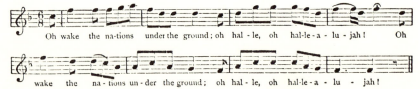

Did time and space allow, examples might be multiplied of a remarkably distinctive character of religious music; but there are other species of negro song which it is proposed to notice.

For many years the steamboats on Western and Southern rivers were, almost without exception, manned by crews of negro slaves. Even after white labor began to encroach upon the occupation of the "deck-hand" and "roustabout," the vocation of "fireman" was peculiarly the negro's. He basked in an atmosphere insupportable to whites, and delighted in the alternation of very hard labor and absolute idleness. It was not uncommon for large steamers to carry a crew of forty or fifty negro hands, and it was inevitable that these should soon have their songs and peculiar customs. Nine-tenths of the "river songs" (to give them a name) have the same refrain, and nearly all were constructed on single lines, separated by a barbarous and unmeaning chorus. The leader would mount the capstan as the steamer left or entered port, and affect to sing the *solo* part from a scrap of newspaper, "the full strength of the company" joining in the chorus. The effect was ludicrous, for no imagination was expended on the composition. Such songs were sung only for the howl that was their chief feature. A glance at the following will abundantly satisfy the reader with this department of negro music:

STEAMBOAT SONG.

Occasionally some stirring incident of steamboat achievement, as the great race between the "Shotwell" and the "Eclipse," would wake the Ethiopian muse and inspire special pæans. But as a general rule the steamboat songs were tiresomely similar to the one just given. In the department of farm or plantation songs there is much of singular music and poetry (?) to be found. Some of them are peculiar to the harvest-field, some belong exclusively to corn-shuckings (not huskings), and some are consecrated to fireside games. Long ago, when the mowing-machine and reaper were as yet unthought of, it was not uncommon to see, in a Kentucky harvest-field, fifteen or twenty "cradlers" swinging their brawny arms in unison as they cut the ripened grain, and moving with the regulated cadence of the leader's song. The scene repeated the poet's picture of ancient oarsmen and the chanter seated high above the rowers, keeping time with staff and voice, blending into one impulse the banks of the trireme.

For such a song strong emphasis of rhythm was, of course, more important than words. Each mower kept his stroke and measured his stride by musical intervals. A very favorite song for these harvesting occasions commenced thus:

RISE UP IN DUE TIME

To dignify such a specimen as the last with the name of a song may seem absurd, but in the practical life of the farmer its value was well known. A cheerful and musical leader in the harvest-field was fully appreciated and eagerly sought.

But the brisk melodies of the harvest-field and meadow were abandoned as the declining sun called the hands home to feed the "stock" and prepare for rest. Then the melancholy that tinges every negro's soul would begin to assert itself in dreamy, sad and plaintive airs, and in words that described the most sorrowful pictures of slave life— the parting of loved ones, the separation of mother and child or husband and wife, or the death of those whom the heart cherishes. As he drove his lum-

bering ox-cart homeward, sitting listlessly upon the heavy "tongue" behind the patient brutes, the creaking wheels and rough-hewn yokes exhibiting perhaps his own rude handiwork, the negro slave rarely failed to sing his song of longing. What if its words were rude and its music ill-constructed? Great poets like Schiller have essayed the same theme, and mighty musicians like Beethoven have striven to give it musical form. What their splendid genius failed adequately to express, the humble slave could scarce accomplish; yet they but wrought in the same direction as the poor negro, whose eyes unwittingly swam in tears, and whose heart, he scarce knew why, dissolved in tenderness, as he sang in a plaintive minor key some such song as this:

OH, SU-ZANN !

Oh, Su - zann, Fare you well! And ain't you mighty sorry . . . To think I married you

REFRAIN.

just last night, And gwine away in the morning? Oh, Su-zan-na, fare you well !

Within his cabin, and cheered by good company and a bright firelight, the negro slave resumed his gayety, and sang and danced and laughed as though life were but a long holiday. His day's work done and his appetite appeased, he cast off all care and abandoned himself to mirth and song. Stale anecdotes were told and the old laugh renewed. Venerable songs were sung

and time-honored jigs were fiddled. The origin and meaning of most of this class of songs have long been forgotten, and the jingle of rhyme and tune alone preserved.

We defy any one, however grave, to hear such a song as the following, sung in stentorian chorus by negroes, male and female, big and little, without laughing outright:

THE FIFER'S SON.

Oh there was three young men a-fighting in the wars, And they all got killed but the fif - er's son; They

all got killed but the fif - er's son; And he proved him - self a sol - dier. Oh

take this cane - staff in your hand, And choose that one that you wish to be;

Choose that one that you wish to be, And prove your - self a sol - - dier.

Or who could hear, without a responsive tapping of the foot and unbending of the wrinkled brow,

> "I won't have none of your weavily wheat,
> I won't have none of your barley"?

Who that has listened to the music of "Harry Cain," or "Send for the Barber," or "We'll knock around the Kitchen till the Cook comes in," will forget the merry cadence? And when the old patriarch of a plantation stood forth, before an admiring audience, to dance the famous "Turkey-buzzard Jig," was it not a scene ever to be remembered by the fortunate white who witnessed its performance?

Such events were peculiar to slavery, and disappeared with its extinction. The elements that produced them—compulsory labor and thoughtless relaxation—exist no longer. As the negro's hands are now his own property, so must his brain be used for other purposes than heretofore.

To close this sketch, already too long, a solitary instance of descriptive song may be given.

Many years ago there originated a negro ballad, founded on the incidents of a famous horse-race, on which large sums were staked. Its popularity among the negroes throughout the slaveholding States was very great, and it was their nearest approach to an epic. It was generally sung in chanting style, with marked emphasis and the prolongation of the concluding syllable of each line. The tenor of the narrative indicates that the "Gal-li-ant Gray Mar'" was. imported from Virginia to Kentucky to beat the "Noble Skewball," and the bard is evidently a partisan of the latter. The commencement of the narrative is in approved invocatory style:

> "Oh, ladies and gentlemen, come one and come all;
> Did you ever hear tell of the Noble Skewball?"

and the author plunges at once *in medias res*, and presents to his auditors, regardless of rhyme, a view of the crowded race-course:

THE NOBLE SKEWBALL.

When the day was ap-p'int-ed for Skewball to run, The horses was ready, the peo-ple did come—

Some from old Vir-gin-ny, and from Tennes-see; Some from Al-a-ba-ma, and from eve-ry-where.

The general reader will not probably feel interested in the preparation for the great race and the descriptions given of the horses, riders and owners, and the thread of the ballad may be given in short space.. The owner of the "Noble Skewball" thus instructs his jockey:

> "Stick close to your saddle, and don't be alarmed,
> For you shall not be jostled by the Noble Skewball!"

and appeals confidently to the umpire—

> "Squire Marvin, Squire Marvin, just judge my horse well,
> For all that I want is to see justice done."

At the signal—

> "When the horses was saddled and the word was give, Go !
> Skewball shot like a arrow just out o' a bow;"

and during the early part of the race the listener is assured,

> "If you had a-been there at the first running round,
> You'd a-swore by your life that they never totch ground."

The excitement of the spectators, and the lavish betting of the friends of the "Noble Skewball" and the "Gal-li-ant Gray Mar'," are minutely described, and the listener hurried by a current of incident to the grand climax—the triumph of the "Noble Skewball" and the payment of the stakes. The poetic fire is cooled down gradually through a dozen or more concluding couplets, the last of which proposes

> "A health to Miss Bradley, that gal-li-ant Gray Mar',
> Likewise to the health of the Noble Skewball!"

To convey a correct idea of negro pronunciation by ordinary rules of orthography is almost impossible. Combinations that would satisfy the ear would be grotesquely absurd to the eye. The habits of the negro in his pronunciation of English words are not such as minstrelsy would indicate. Just as the French and German characters in our comedies have passed into a conventional form of mispronunciation which the bulk of playgoers firmly believe to be lifelike and true, so have minstrels given permanency to very great mistakes in reproducing negro pronunciation. The use of "hab" for "have," of "lub" for "love," or "massa" for "mäas," is by no means universal, nor nearly so.

In the preceding samples of slave songs no great care has been taken to convey an accurate idea of the pronunciation. We have rather aimed to put in permanent form a few random selections from a class of songs rapidly perishing, and soon to be entirely disused.

It only remains to be said that all slave songs seem best suited to barytone voices, and that no musical effect so delights the negro's ear as a well-executed swell on an emphatic word. It is in the chorus that the voices of negroes are heard to best advantage, and, though keenly appreciative of melody, it is very rare to hear among them any attempt at harmony. The remark may apply to serfs and very ignorant peasantry everywhere, but it is certainly almost without exception that the negro slaves in the United States never attempted even a rude bass in their singing, and that their most effective hymns were sung in unison.

VI

THE DANCE IN PLACE CONGO

and

CREOLE SLAVE SONGS

George Washington Cable

[George Washington Cable, a native of New Orleans who fought in the Confederate Army, was forced to leave the South because his writings expressed his distaste for southern postwar mistreatment of the Negro. Cable, Henry E. Krehbiel, and the irascible, one-eyed poet and writer, Lafcadio Hearn, at one time collected Creole songs in a project that broke up over the mutual distrust of Cable and Hearn. Some of Cable's Creole songs had already appeared in *Slave Songs of the United States*, nineteen years before the publication of the following articles in *The Century Magazine* (XXXI, February 1886, pp. 517-532, and April 1886, pp. 807-828).]

A MANDINGO.

I.

CONGO SQUARE.

WHOEVER has been to New Orleans with eyes not totally abandoned to buying and selling will, of course, remember St. Louis Cathedral, looking south-eastward — riverward — across quaint Jackson Square, the old Place d'Armes. And if he has any feeling for flowers, he has not forgotten the little garden behind the cathedral, so antique and unexpected, named for the beloved old priest Père Antoine.

The old Rue Royale lies across the sleeping garden's foot. On the street's farther side another street lets away at right angles, north-westward, straight, and imperceptibly downward from the cathedral and garden toward the rear of the city. It is lined mostly with humble ground-floor-and-garret houses of stuccoed brick, their wooden doorsteps on the brick sidewalks. This is Orleans street, so named when the city was founded.

Its rugged round-stone pavement is at times nearly as sunny and silent as the landward side of a coral reef. Thus for about half a mile; and then Rampart street, where the palisade wall of the town used to run in Spanish days, crosses it, and a public square just beyond draws a grateful canopy of oak and sycamore boughs. That is the place. One may shut his buff umbrella there, wipe the beading sweat from the brow, and fan himself with his at. Many's the bull-fight has taken place on that spot Sunday afternoons of the old time. That is Congo Square.

The trees are modern. So are the buildings about the four sides, for all their aged looks. So are all the grounds' adornments. Trémé market, off, beyond, toward the swamp, is not so very old, and the scowling, ill-smelling prison on the right, so Spanish-looking and dilapidated, is not a third the age it seems; not fifty-five. In that climate every year of a building's age counts for ten. Before any of these M. Cayetano's circus and menagerie were here. Cayetane the negroes called him. He was the Barnum of that region and day.

Miché Cayetane, qui sortie de l'Havane,
Avec so chouals et somacaques."

ciety and the haunt of true lovers; not only in the military, but also in the most unwarlike sense the place of arms, and of hearts and hands, and of words tender as well as words noble.

The Place Congo, at the opposite end of the street, was at the opposite end of everything. One was on the highest ground; the other on the lowest. The one was the rendezvous of the rich man, the master, the military

"THE RENDEZVOUS OF THE RICH MAN."

officer — of all that went to make up the ruling class; the other of the butcher and baker, the raftsman, the sailor, the quadroon, the painted girl, and the negro slave. No meaner name could be given the spot. The negro was the most despised of human creatures and the Congo the plebeian among negroes. The white man's plaza had the army and navy on its right and left, the court-house, the council-hall and the church at its back, and the world before it. The black man's was outside the rear gate, the poisonous wilderness on three sides and the proud man's contumely on its front.

That is, "who came from Havana with his horses and baboons."

Up at the other end of Orleans street, hid only by the old padre's garden and the cathedral, glistens the ancient Place d'Armes. In the early days it stood for all that was best; the place for political rallying, the retail quarter of all fine goods and wares, and at sunset and by moonlight the promenade of good so-

Before the city overgrew its flimsy palisade

walls, and closing in about this old stamping-ground gave it set bounds, it was known as Congo Plains. There was wide room for much field sport, and the Indian villagers of the town's outskirts and the lower class of white Creoles made it the ground of their wild ball game of *raquette*. Sunday afternoons were the time for it. Hence, beside these diversions there was, notably, another.

The hour was the slave's term of momentary liberty, and his simple, savage, musical and superstitious nature dedicated it to amatory song and dance tinctured with his rude notions of supernatural influences.

II.

GRAND ORCHESTRA.

THE booming of African drums and blast of huge wooden horns called to the gathering. It was these notes of invitation, reaching beyond those of other outlandish instruments, that caught the Ethiopian ear, put alacrity into the dark foot, and brought their owners, male and female, trooping from all quarters. The drums were very long, hollowed, often from a single piece of wood, open at one end and having a sheep or goat skin stretched across the other. One was large, the other much smaller. The tight skin heads were not held up to be struck; the drums were laid along on the turf and the drummers bestrode them, and beat them on the head madly with fingers, fists, and feet,— with slow vehemence on the great drum, and fiercely and rapidly on the small one. Sometimes an extra performer sat on the ground behind the larger drum, at its open end, and "beat upon the wooden sides of it with two sticks." The smaller drum was often made from a joint or two of very large bamboo, in the West Indies where such

could be got, and this is said to be the origin of its name; for it was called the *Bamboula*.

In stolen hours of night or the basking-hour of noon the black man contrived to fashion these rude instruments and others. The drummers, I say, bestrode the drums; the other musicians sat about them in an arc, cross-legged on the ground. One important instrument was a gourd partly filled with pebbles or grains of corn, flourished violently at the end of a stout staff with one hand and beaten upon the palm of the other. Other performers rang triangles, and others twanged from jew's-harps an astonishing amount of sound. Another instrument was the jawbone of some ox, horse, or mule, and a key rattled rhythmically along its weather-beaten teeth. At times the drums were reënforced by one or more empty barrels or casks beaten on the head with the shank-bones of cattle.

A queer thing that went with these when the affair was pretentious — full dress, as it were — at least it was so in the West Indies, whence Congo Plains drew all inspirations — was the Marimba brett, a union of reed and string principles. A single strand of wire ran lengthwise of a bit of wooden board, sometimes a shallow box of thin wood, some eight inches long by four or five in width, across which, under the wire, were several joints of reed about a quarter of an inch in diameter and of graduated lengths. The performer, sitting cross-legged, held the board in both hands and plucked the ends of the reeds with his thumb-nails. The result was called — music.

But the grand instrument at last, the first violin, as one might say, was the banjo. It had but four strings, not six: beware of the dictionary. It is not the "favorite musical instrument of the negroes of the Southern States of America." Uncle Remus says truly that

BLOWING THE QUILLS.

A FIELD-HAND.

that is the fiddle; but for the true African dance, a dance not so much of legs and feet as of the upper half of the body, a sensual, devilish thing tolerated only by Latin-American masters, there was wanted the dark inspiration of African drums and the banjo's thrump and strum.

And then there was that long-drawn human cry of tremendous volume, richness, and resound, to which no instrument within their reach could make the faintest approach:

> "Eh! pou' la belle Layotte ma mourri 'nocent,
> Oui 'nocent ma mourri!"

all the instruments silent while it rises and swells with mighty energy and dies away distantly, "Yea-a-a-a-a-a!"—then the crash of savage drums, horns, and rattles—

> "For the fair Layotte I must crazy die!
> Yes, crazy I must die!"

To all this there was sometimes added a Pan's-pipe of but three reeds, made from single

Eh-h-h! pou' la belle La - yotte ma mour - ri 'no - cent, Oui, 'no - cent ma mour - ri!
Yea! For the fair La - yotte I must cra - zy die, Yes, cra - zy I must die.

A CONGO WOMAN.

joints of the common brake cane, and called by English-speaking negroes "the quills." One may even at this day hear the black lad, sauntering home at sunset behind a few cows that he has found near the edge of the cane-brake whence he has also cut his three quills, blowing and hooting, over and over,—

But to show how far the art of playing the "quills" could be carried, if we are not going too much aside, see this "quill tune" (page 44), given me by Mr. Krehbiel, musical critic of the "New York Tribune," and got by him from a gentleman who heard it in Alabama.

Such was the full band. All the values of

contrast that discord can furnish must have been present, with whatever there is of ecstasy in maddening repetition, for of this the African can never have too much.

And yet there was entertaining variety. Where? In the dance! There was constant, exhilarating novelty — endless invention — in the turning, bowing, arm-swinging, posturing and leaping of the dancers. Moreover, the music of Congo Plains was not tamed to mere monotone. Monotone became subordinate to many striking qualities. The strain was wild. Its contact with French taste gave it often great tenderness of sentiment. It grew in fervor, and rose and sank, and rose again, with the play of emotion in the singers and dancers.

III.

THE GATHERING.

IT was a weird one. The negro of colonial Louisiana was a most grotesque figure. He was nearly naked. Often his neck and arms, thighs, shanks, and splay feet were shrunken, tough, sinewy like a monkey's. Sometimes it was scant diet and cruel labor that had made them so. Even the requirement of law was only that he should have not less than a barrel of corn — nothing else,— a month, nor get more than thirty lashes to the twenty-four hours. The whole world was crueler those times than now; we must not judge them by our own.

Often the slave's attire was only a cotton shirt, or a pair of pantaloons hanging in indecent tatters to his naked waist. The bondwoman was well clad who had on as much as a coarse chemise and petticoat. To add a *tignon*—a Madras handkerchief twisted into a turban—was high gentility, and the number of kerchiefs beyond that one was the measure of absolute wealth. Some were rich in *tignons ;* especially those who served within the house, and pleased the mistress, or even the master—there were Hagars in those days. However, Congo Plains did not gather the house-servants so much as the "field-hands."

These came in troops. See them; wilder than gypsies; wilder than the Moors and Arabs whose strong blood and features one sees at a glance in so many of them; gangs — as they were called — gangs and gangs of them, from this and that and yonder direction; tall, well-knit Senegalese from Cape Verde, black as ebony, with intelligent, kindly eyes and long, straight, shapely noses; Mandingoes, from the Gambia River, lighter of color,

of cruder form, and a cunning that shows in the countenance; whose enslavement seems specially a shame, their nation the "merchants of Africa," dwelling in towns, industrious, thrifty, skilled in commerce and husbandry, and expert in the working of metals, even to silver and gold; and Foulahs, playfully miscalled "*Poulards*," — fat chickens,— of goodly stature, and with a perceptible rose tint in the cheeks; and Sosos, famous warriors, dexterous with the African targe; and in contrast to these, with small ears, thick eyebrows, bright eyes, flat, upturned noses, shining skin, wide mouths and white teeth, the negroes of Guinea, true and unmixed, from the Gold Coast, the Slave Coast, and the Cape of Palms — not from the Grain Coast; the English had that trade. See them come! Popoes, Cotocolies, Fidas, Socoes, Agwas, short, copper-colored Mines — what havoc the slavers did make! — and from interior Africa others equally proud and warlike : fierce Nagoes and Fonds; tawny Awassas; Iboes, so light-colored that one could not tell them from mulattoes but for their national tattooing; and the half-civilized and quick-witted but ferocious Arada, the original Voudou worshiper. And how many more! For here come, also, men and women from all that great Congo coast,— Angola, Malimbe, Ambrice, etc.,— small, good-natured, sprightly "boys," and gay, garrulous "gals," thick-lipped but not tattooed; chattering, chaffering, singing, and guffawing as they come: these are they for whom the dance and the place are named, the most numerous sort of negro in the colonies, the Congoes and Franc-Congoes, and though serpent worshipers, yet the gentlest and kindliest natures that came from Africa. Such was the company. Among these *bossals* — that is, native Africans — there was, of course, an ever-growing number of negroes who proudly called themselves Creole negroes, that is, born in America;[*] and at the present time there is only here and there an old native African to be met with, vain of his singularity and trembling on his staff.

IV.

THE BAMBOULA.

THE gathering throng closed in around, leaving unoccupied the circle indicated by the crescent of musicians. The short, harsh turf was the dancing-floor. The crowd stood. Fancy the picture. The pack of dark, tattered

---

[*] This broader use of the term is very common. The Creole "dialect" is the broken English *of the Creoles*, while the Creole *patois* is the corrupt French, not of the Creoles, but rather of the former slave race in the country of the Creoles. So of Creole negroes and Creole dances and songs.

figures touched off every here and there with the bright colors of a Madras *tignon*. The squatting, cross-legged musicians. The low-roofed, embowered town off in front, with here and there a spire lifting a finger of feeble remonstrance ; the flat, grassy plain stretching around and behind, dotted with black stumps ; in the distance the pale-green willow undergrowth, behind it the *cyprière* — the cypress swamp — and in the pale, seven-times-heated sky the sun, only a little declined to south and westward, pouring down its beams.

With what particular musical movements the occasion began does not now appear. May be with very slow and measured ones ; they had such that were strange and typical. I have heard the negroes sing one — though it was not of the dance-ground but of the cane-field — that showed the emphatic barbarism of five bars to the line, and was confined to four notes of the open horn.*

But I can only say that with some such slow and quiet strain the dance may have been preluded. It suits the Ethiopian fancy for a beginning to be dull and repetitious ; the bottom of the ladder must be on the ground.

The singers almost at the first note are many. At the end of the first line every voice is lifted up. The strain is given the second time with growing spirit. Yonder glistening black Hercules, who plants one foot forward, lifts his head and bare, shining chest, and rolls out the song from a mouth and throat like a cavern, is a *candio*, a chief, or was before he was overthrown in battle and dragged away, his village burning behind him, from the mountains of High Soudan. That is an African amulet that hangs about his neck — a *greegree*. He is of the Bambaras, as you may know by his solemn visage and the long tattoo streaks running down from the temples to the neck, broadest in the middle, like knife-gashes. See his play of restrained enthusiasm catch from one bystander to another. They swing and bow to right and left, in slow time to the piercing treble of the Congo women. Some are responsive ; others are competitive. Hear that bare foot slap the ground ! one sudden stroke only, as it were the foot of a stag. The musicians warm up at the sound. A smiting of breasts with open hands begins very softly and becomes vigor-

ous. The women's voices rise to a tremulous intensity. Among the chorus of Franc-Congo singing-girls is one of extra good voice, who thrusts in, now and again, an improvisation. This girl here, so tall and straight, is a Yaloff. You see it in her almost Hindoo features, and hear it in the plaintive melody of her voice. Now the chorus is more piercing than ever. The women clap their hands in time, or standing with arms akimbo receive with faint courtesies and head-liftings the low bows of the men, who deliver them swinging this way and that.

See ! Yonder brisk and sinewy fellow has taken one short, nervy step into the ring, chanting with rising energy. Now he takes another, and stands and sings and looks here and there, rising upon his broad toes and sinking and rising again, with what wonderful lightness ! How tall and lithe he is. Notice his brawn shining through his rags. He too, is a *candio*, and by the three long rays of tattooing on each side of his face, a Kiamba. The music has got into his feet. He moves off to the farther edge of the circle, still singing, takes the prompt hand of an unsmiling Congo girl, leads her into the ring, and leaving the chant to the throng, stands her before him for the dance.

Will they dance to that measure ? Wait ! A sudden frenzy seizes the musicians. The measure quickens, the swaying, attitudinizing crowd starts into extra activity, the female voices grow sharp and staccato, and suddenly the dance is the furious Bamboula. (See page 44.)

Now for the frantic leaps ! Now for frenzy ! Another pair are in the ring ! The man wears a belt of little bells, or, as a substitute, little tin vials of shot, " bram-bram sonnette ! " And still another couple enter the circle. What wild — what terrible delight ! The ecstasy rises to madness ; one — two — three of the dancers fall — *bloucoutoum ! boum !* — with foam on their lips and are dragged out by arms and legs from under the tumultuous feet of crowding new-comers. The musicians know no fatigue ; still the dance rages on :

" Quand patate la cuite na va mangé li ! "

And all to that one nonsense line meaning only,

" When that 'tater's cooked don't you eat it up ! "

An - no - qué,   An - no - bia,   Bia - ta - ia,   Que - re - qué,   Nal - lé - oua.

Au - mon - dé,   Au - tap - o - té,   Au - pé - to - té,   Au - qué - ré - qué,   Bo.

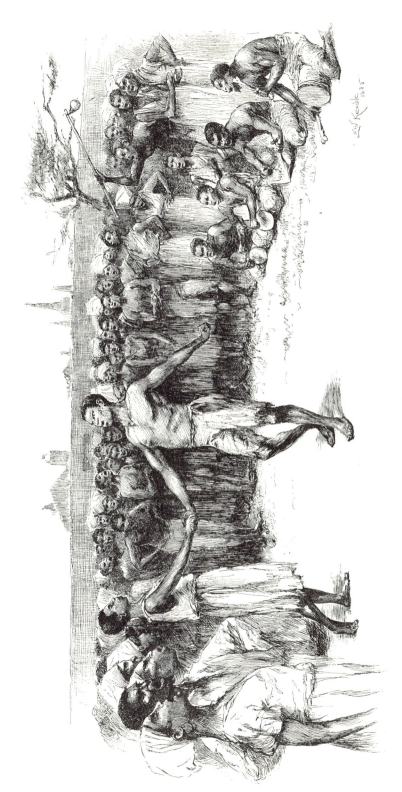

THE BAMBOULA.

It was a frightful triumph of body over mind, even in those early days when the slave was still a genuine pagan; but as his moral education gave him some hint of its enormity, and it became a forbidden fruit monopolized by those of reprobate will, it grew everywhere more and more gross. No wonder the police stopped it in Congo Square. Only the music deserved to survive, and does survive — coin snatched out of the mire. The one just given, Gottschalk first drew from oblivion. I have never heard another to know it as a bamboula; but Mr. Charles P. Ware, in "Slave Songs of the United States," has printed one got from Louisiana, whose characteristics resemble the bamboula reclaimed by Gottschalk in so many points that here is the best place for it:* As much as to say, in English, "Look at that darky," — we have to lose the saucy double meaning between *mulet* (mule) and *mulâtre* (mulatto) —

> "Look at that darky there, Mr. Banjo,
>   Doesn't he put on airs!
> Hat cocked on one side, Mr. Banjo,
> Walking-stick in hand, Mr. Banjo,
> Boots that go 'crank, crank,' Mr. Banjo, —
> *Look* at that darky there, Mr. Banjo,
>   *Doesn't* he put on airs!"

THE LOVE SONG.

It is odd that such fantastical comicality of words should have been mated to such fierce and frantic dancing, but so it was. The reeking faces of the dancers, moreover, always solemnly grave. So we must picture it now if we still fancy ourselves spectators on Congo Plains. The bamboula still roars and rattles, twangs, contorts, and tumbles in terrible earnest, while we stand and talk. So, on and on. Will they dance nothing else? Ah! — the music changes. The rhythm stretches out heathenish and ragged. The quick contagion is caught by a few in the crowd, who take it up with spirited smitings of the bare sole upon the ground, and of open hands upon the thighs. From a spot near the musicians a single male voice, heavy and sonorous, rises in improvisation, — the Mandingoes brought that art from Africa, — and in a moment many others have joined in refrain, male voices in rolling, bellowing resonance, female responding in high, piercing unison. Partners are stepping into the ring. How strangely the French language is corrupted on the thick negro tongue,

ARR. BY H. E. KREHBIEL.

VOICE.

Vo - yez ce mu - let la, Mi - ché Bain - jo, comme il est in - so - lent. Cha - peau sur co -

PIANO—*Sempre staccato.*

té, Mi-ché Bain-jo, La canne a la main, Miché Bain-jo, Bottes qui fé crin, crin, Miché Bain-jo.

as with waving arms they suit gesture to word and chant (the translation is free, but so is the singing and posturing) :

and chanting and swinging and writhing has risen with it, and the song is changed. (See RÉMON, page 45.)

En bas hé, en bas hé, Par en bas yé pé-lé-lé moin, yé pé-lé-lé, Counjaille
'Way yon-der, 'way yon-der, 'Way down there they're call-ing me, they are calling, but Coonjye,

a dé-baut-ché. Par en haut yé pé-lé-lé moin, yé pé-lé-lé pou' Mom-selle Su-zette,
has bewitched me. 'Way up there they're call-ing me, They are calling for Mom-selle Su-zette,

Par en bas yé pé-lé-le moin, yé pé-lé-lé, Coun-jaille a dé-baut-ché.
'Way down there they're call-ing me, they are call-ing, (but) Coonjye has be-witched me.

V.

THE COUNJAILLE.

SUDDENLY the song changes. The rhythm sweeps away long and smooth like a river escaped from its rapids, and in new spirit, with louder drum-beat and more jocund rattle, the voices roll up into the sky and the dancers are at it. Aye, ya, yi!*

I could give four verses, but let one suffice; it is from a manuscript copy of the words, probably a hundred years old, that fell into my hands through the courtesy of a Creole lady some two years ago. It is one of the best known of all the old Counjaille songs. The four verses would not complete it. The Counjaille was never complete, and found its end, for the time being, only in the caprice of the improvisator, whose rich, stentorian voice sounded alone between the refrains.

But while we discourse other couples have stepped into the grassy arena, the instrumental din has risen to a fresh height of inspiration, the posing and thigh-beating and breast-patting

But the dance is not changed, and love is still the theme. Sweat streams from the black brows, down the shining black necks and throats, upon the men's bared chests, and into dark, unstayed bosoms. Time wears, shadows lengthen; but the movement is brisker than ever, and the big feet and bent shanks are as light as thistles on the air. Let one flag, another has his place, and a new song gives new vehemence, new inventions in steps, turns, and attitudes.

More stanzas could be added in the original *patois*, but here is a translation into African English as spoken by the Creole negro:

CHORUS. I done been 'roun' to evvy spot)
Don't foun' nair match fo' sweet }*Bis.*
Layotte.)

SOLO. I done hunt all dis settle*ment*
All de way 'roun' fum Pierre Soniat';
Never see yalla gal w'at kin
'Gin to lay 'longside sweet Layotte.
I done been, etc.

SOLO. I yeh dey talk 'bout 'Loïse gal—
Loïse, w'at b'long to Pierre Soniat';
I see her, but she can't biggin
Stan' up 'longside my sweet Layotte.
I done been, etc.

Inne, dé, trois, Caroline, Qui ci ça yé comme ça ma chère ? Mo l'aimé toé,
Inne, dé, trois, Caroline, Quo fère t'apé crié ma chère ?

to conné ça, Si-yé to zi-é et vien bo moin ; Mo l'aimé toé, to con-né ça, Si-yé to zié et vien bo moin.

A MARCHANDE DES CALAS.

SOLO. I been meet up wid John Bayou,
       Say to him, "John Bayou, my son,
       Yalla gal nevva meet yo' view
       Got a face lak dat chahmin' one!"
                          I done been, etc.

The fair Layotte appears not only in other versions of this *counjaille* but in other songs. (See MA MOURRI, page 46.)

Or in English:

Well I know, young men, I must die,
       Yes, crazy, I must die.
Well I know, young men, I must crazy die,
       Yes, crazy, I must die. Eh-h-h-h!
For the fair Layotte, I must crazy die,— Yes, etc.
Well I know, young men, I must die,— Yes, etc.
Well I know, young men, I must crazy die,
       I must die for the fair Layotte.

VI.

THE CALINDA.

THERE were other dances. Only a few years ago I was honored with an invitation, which I had to decline, to see danced the Babouille, the Cata (or Chacta), the Counjaille, and the Calinda. Then there were the Voudou, and the Congo, to describe which would not be pleasant. The latter, called Congo also in Cayenne, Chica in San Domingo, and in the Windward Islands confused under one name with the Calinda, was a kind of Fandango, they say, in which the Madras kerchief held by its tip-ends played a graceful part.

The true Calinda was bad enough. In Louisiana, at least, its song was always a grossly personal satirical ballad, and it was the favorite dance all the way from there to Trinidad. To dance it publicly is not allowed this side the West Indies. All this Congo Square business was suppressed at one time; 1843, says tradition. The Calinda was a dance of multitude, a sort of vehement cotillion. The contortions of the encircling crowd were strange and terrible, the din was hideous. One Calinda is still familiar to all Creole ears; it has long been a vehicle for the white Creole's satire; for generations the man of municipal politics was fortunate who escaped entirely a lampooning set to its air.

In my childhood I used, at one time, to hear,

every morning, a certain black *marchande des calas* — peddler-woman selling rice croquettes — chanting the song as she moved from street to street at the sunrise hour with her broad, shallow, laden basket balanced on her head.

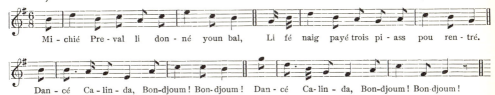

Mi - chié Pre - val li don - né youn bal, Li fé naig payé trois pi - ass pou ren - tré.

Dan - cé Ca - lin - da, Bon-djoum! Bon-djoum! Dan - cé Ca - lin - da, Bon-djoum! Bon-djoum!

In other words, a certain Judge Preval gave a ball — not an outdoor Congo dance — and made such Cuffees as could pay three dollars a ticket. It doesn't rhyme, but it was probably true. " Dance, dance the Calindá! Boujoum! Boujoum!"

The number of stanzas has never been counted; here are a few of them.

" Dans l'equirie la 'y' avé grand gala;
Mo cré choual la yé t b'en étonné.

Miché Preval, li té capitaine bal;
So cocher Louis, té maite cérémonie.

Y avé des négresses belle passé maitresses,
Qui volé bel-bel dans l'ormoire momselle.
   *   *   *   *   *

Ala maite la geôle li trouvé si drôle,
Li dit, "moin aussi, mo fé bal ici."

Ouatchman la yé yé tombé la dans;
Yé fé gran' déga dans léquirie la." etc.

" It was in a stable that they had this gala night," says the song; "the horses there were greatly astonished. Preval was captain; his coachman, Louis, was master of ceremonies. There were negresses made prettier than their mistresses by adornments stolen from the ladies' wardrobes *(armoires)*. But the jailer found it all so funny that he proposed to himself to take an unexpected part; the watchmen came down "——

No official exaltation bought immunity from the jeer of the Calinda. Preval was a magistrate. Stephen Mazureau, in his attorney-general's office, the song likened to a bull-frog in a bucket of water. A page might be covered by the roll of victims. The masters winked at these gross but harmless liberties and, as often as any others, added stanzas of their own invention.

The Calinda ended these dissipations of the summer Sabbath afternoons. They could not run far into the night, for all the fascinations of all the dances could not excuse the slave's tarrying in public places after a certain other *bou-djoum!* (that was not of the Calinda, but of the regular nine-o'clock evening gun) had rolled down Orleans street from the Place d'Armes; and the black man or woman who wanted to keep a whole skin on the back had to keep out of the Calaboose. Times have changed, and there is nothing to be regretted in the change that has come over Congo Square. Still a glamour hangs over its dark past. There is the pathos of slavery, the poetry of the weak oppressed by the strong, and of limbs that danced after toil, and of barbaric love-making. The rags and semi-nakedness, the bamboula drum, the dance, and almost the banjo, are gone; but the *bizarre* melodies and dark lovers' apostrophes live on; and among them the old Counjaille song of Aurore Pradère.

AURORE PRADÈRE.

CHO. ‖ Aurore Pradère, pretty maid, ‖ *(ter)*
She's just what I want and her I'll have.
SOLO. Some folks say she's too pretty, quite;
Some folks they say she's not polite;
All this they say — Psha-a-ah!
   More fool am I!
For she's what I want and her I'll have.

CHO. ‖ Aurore Pradère, pretty maid, ‖ *(ter)*
She's just what I want and her I'll have.
SOLO. Some say she's going to the bad;
Some say that her mamma went mad;
All this they say — Psha-a-ah!
   More fool am I!
For she's what I want and her I'll have.

THE CALABOOSE.

Mr. Ware and his associate compilers have neither of these stanzas, but one very pretty one; the third in the music as printed here, and which we translate as follows:

SOLO.   A muslin gown she doesn't choose,
          She doesn't ask for broidered hose,
          She doesn't want prunella shoes,
          O she's what I want and her I'll have.

CHO.   Aurore Pradère, etc.

This article and another on a kindred theme were originally projected as the joint work of Mr. H. E. Krehbiel, musical editor of the "New York Tribune," author of "The History of Choral Music in New York City," etc.; and the present writer. But under the many prior claims of the journalist's profession, Mr. Krehbiel withdrew from the work, though not until he had furnished a number of instrumental accompaniments, as well as the "Quill Song" credited to him, and much valuable coöperation.

As may in part be seen by the names attached to the musical scores, the writer is indebted to a number of friends: Mr. Krehbiel; Miss Mary L. Bartlett, of Hartford, Conn.; Madame Louis Lejeune, of New Orleans; Dr. Blodgett, of Smith College, Northampton, Mass.; Mr. C. G. Ware, of Brookline, in the same State; Madame Clara Gottschalk Petersen, of Philadelphia; and in his earlier steps — for the work of collection has been slow — to that skillful French translator and natural adept in research, Mr. Lafcadio Hearn, of New Orleans; the late Isaac N. Philips, Mr. Louis Powers, Miss Clara Cooper Hallaran, the late Professor Alexander Dimitry, all of the same city; Madame Sidonie de la Houssaye, of Franklin, La.; and, through the editors of THE CENTURY, to Mr. W. Macrum, of Pittsburg.—G. W. C.

QUILL TUNE.

NOTED BY H. E. KREHBIEL.

Quill notes on the staff; voice notes below.

THE BAMBOULA.

ARR. BY MISS M. L. BARTLETT.

Quand pa-tate la cuite na va man-gé li, Na va man-gé, Na va man-gé.

Quand pa-tate la cuite na va man-gé, Na va man-gé li.

RÉMON, RÉMON.

Arr. by John A. Broekhoven.

Mo parlé Ré-mon, Rémon, Li parlé Si-mon, Si- mon, Li par-lé Ti - tine, Ti - tine li tombé dans chagrin. O

femme Romolus, O-o! Belle femme Romolus, O-o! O femme Romolus, O-o! Belle femme, qui ça volez mo fé.

BELLE LAYOTTE.

Arr. by John A. Broekhoven.

Mo de-ja rou-lé tout la côte, Pancore 'oir pa - reil belle La - yotte, Mo de-ja rou-lé

tout la côte, Pancore 'oir pa - reil belle Layotte. Mo rou-lé tout la co-lo-nie, Di-pi cé Mi-ché

Pierre So - niat, Pancore 'oir in grif-fonne comme ça, Com-pa-rabe a mo belle La - yotte.

MA MOURRI.

ARR. BY H. E. KREHBIEL.

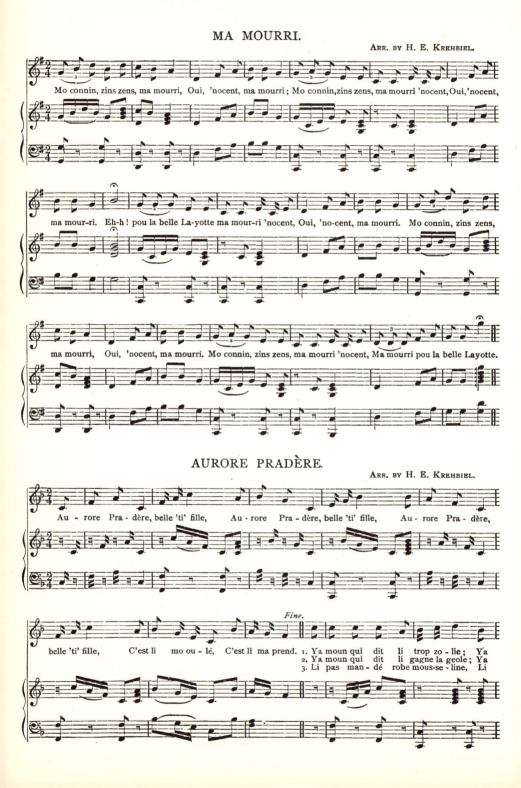

Mo connin, zins zens, ma mourri, Oui, 'nocent, ma mourri; Mo connin, zins zens, ma mourri 'nocent, Oui, 'nocent,

ma mour-ri. Eh-h! pou la belle La-yotte ma mour-ri 'nocent, Oui, 'no-cent, ma mourri. Mo connin, zins zens,

ma mourri, Oui, 'nocent, ma mourri. Mo connin, zins zens, ma mourri 'nocent, Ma mourri pou la belle Layotte.

AURORE PRADÈRE.

ARR. BY H. E. KREHBIEL.

Au - rore Pra - dère, belle 'ti' fille,   Au - rore Pra - dère, belle 'ti' fille,   Au - rore Pra - dère,

Fine.

belle 'ti' fille,   C'est li   mo ou - lé, C'est li ma prend. 1. Ya moun qui   dit   li trop zo - lie; Ya
2. Ya moun qui   dit   li gagne la geole; Ya
3. Li pas man - dé robe mous-se - line, Li

moun qui dit li pas po-lie; Tout ça ye dit Sia! Mo bin fou bin, C'est li mo ou-lé, c'est li ma prend.
moun qui dit so m'man te folle; etc.
pas man-dé des bas brodée; Li pas man-dé sou-liers prinelle, C'est li, etc.

George W. Cable.

CREOLE SLAVE SONGS.

I.

THE QUADROONS.

THE patois in which these songs are found is common, with broad local variations, wherever the black man and the French language are met in the mainland or island regions that border the Gulf and the Caribbean Sea. It approaches probably nearer to good French in Louisiana than anywhere in the Antilles. Yet it is not merely bad or broken French; it is the natural result from the effort of a savage people to take up the language of an old and highly refined civilization, and is much more than a jargon. The humble condition and great numbers of the slave-caste promoted this evolution of an African-Creole dialect. The facile character of the French master-caste, made more so by the languorous climate of the Gulf, easily tolerated and often condescended to use the new tongue. It chimed well with the fierce notions of caste to have one language for the master and another for the slave, and at the same time it was convenient that the servile speech should belong to and draw its existence chiefly from the master's. Its growth entirely by ear where there were so many more African ears than French tongues, and when those tongues had so many Gallic archaisms which they were glad to give away and get rid of, resulted in a broad grotesqueness all its own.

We had better not go aside to study it here. Books have been written on the subject. They may be thin, but they stand for years of labor. A Creole lady writes me almost as I write this, "It takes a whole life to speak such a language in form." Mr. Thomas of Trinidad has given a complete grammar of it as spoken there. M. Marbot has versified some fifty of La Fontaine's fables in the tongue. Père

Gaux has made a catechism in, and M. Turiault a complete grammatical work on, the Martinique variety. Dr. Armand Mercier, a Louisiana Creole, and Professor James A. Harrison, an Anglo-Louisianian, have written valuable papers on the dialect as spoken in the Mississippi delta. Mr. John Bigelow has done the same for the tongue as heard in Hayti. It is an amusing study. Certain tribes of Africa had no knowledge of the v and z sounds. The sprightly Franc-Congos, for all their chatter, could hardly master even this African-Creole dialect so as to make their wants intelligible. The Louisiana negro's *r*'s were ever being lost or mislaid. He changed *dormir* to *dromi'*. His master's children called the little fiddler-crab *Tourlourou*; he simplified the articulations to *Troolooloo*. Wherever the *r* added to a syllable's quantity, he either shifted it or dropped it overboard. *Po'té ça?* *Non!* not if he could avoid it. It was the same with many other sounds. For example, final *le*; a thing so needless — he couldn't be burdened with it; *li pas capab'!* He found himself profitably understood when he called his master *aimab' et nob'*, and thought it not well to be *trop sensib'* about a trifling *l* or two. The French *u* was vinegar to his teeth. He substituted *i* or *ei* before a consonant and *oo* before a vowel, or dropped it altogether; for *une*, he said *eine;* for *puis, p'is ; absolument* he made *assoliment;* *tu* was nearly always *to;* a *mulâtresse* was a *milatraisse*. In the West Indies he changed *s* into *ch* or *tch*, making *songer chongé*, and *suite tchooite;* while in Louisiana he reversed the process and turned *ch* into *ç* — *c'erc'é* for *cherchez* or *chercher*.

He misconstrued the liaisons of correct French, and omitted limiting adjectives where he conveniently could, or retained only their final sound carried over and prefixed to the noun: *nhomme — zanimaux — zherbes' — zaf-*

faires. He made odd substitutions of one word for another. For the verb to go he oftener than otherwise used a word that better signified his slavish pretense of alacrity, the verb to run: *mo courri,—mo* always, never *je,—mo courri, to courri, li courri ;* always seizing whatever form of a verb was handiest and holding to it without change; *no courri, vo courri, yé courri.* Sometimes the plural was *no zôtt —* we others *— courri, vo zôtt courri, yé zôtt courri ; no zôtt courri dans bois —* we are going to the woods. His auxiliary verb in imperfect and pluperfect tenses was not to have, but to be in the past participial form *été,* but shortened to one syllable. I have gone, thou hadst gone: *mo 'té courri, to 'té courri.* There is an affluence of bitter meaning

hidden under these apparently nonsensical lines.* It mocks the helpless lot of three types of human life in old Louisiana whose fate was truly deplorable. *Milatraisse* was, in Creole song, the generic term for all that class, famous wherever New Orleans was famous in those days when all foot-passengers by night picked their way through the mud by the rays of a hand-lantern — the freed or free-born quadroon or mulatto woman. *Cocodrie* (Spanish, *cocodrilla,* the crocodile or alligator) was the nickname for the unmixed black man; while *trouloulou* was applied to the free male quadroon, who could find admittance to the quadroon balls only in the capacity, in those days distinctly menial, of musician — fiddler. Now sing it!

THE FIDDLER.

"Yellow girl goes to the ball;
Nigger lights her to the hall.
            Fiddler man!
Now, what is that to you?
Say, what is that to you,
            Fiddler man?"

It was much to him; but it might as well have been little. What could he do? As they say, "*Ravette zamein tini raison divant poule*" ("Cockroach can never justify himself to the hungry chicken"). He could only let his black half-brother celebrate on Congo Plains the mingled humor and outrage of it in satirical songs of double meaning. They readily passed unchallenged among the numerous nonsense rhymes — that often rhymed lamely or not at all — which beguiled the hours afield or the moonlight gatherings in the "quarters," as well as served to fit the wild chants of some of their dances. Here is one whose characteristics tempt us to suppose it a calinda, and whose humor consists only in a childish play on words. (Quand Mo 'Te, page 64.)

There is another nonsense song that may or may not have been a dance. Its movement has the true wriggle. The dances were many; there were some popular in the West Indies that seem to have remained comparatively unknown in Louisiana: the *belair, bèlè,* or *béla ;* the *cosaque ;* the *biguine.* The *guiouba* was probably the famed *juba* of Georgia and the Carolinas. (Neg' pas Capa' Marché, page 64.)

Mi - la - traisse cour - ri dans bal, Co - co - drie po' - té fa - nal, Trou-lou-lou! C'est pas zaf - faire à tou, C'est pas zaf - faire à tou, Trou-lou-lou!

CALALOU.

II.

THE LOVE-SONG.

AMONG the songs which seem to have been sung for their own sake, and not for the dance, are certain sentimental ones of slow movement, tinged with that faint and gentle melancholy that every one of Southern experience has noticed in the glance of the African slave's eye; a sentiment ready to be turned, at any instant that may demand the change, into a droll, self-abasing humor. They have thus a special charm that has kept for them a place even in the regard of the Creole of to-day. How many ten thousands of black or tawny nurse "mammies," with heads wrapped in stiffly starched Madras kerchief turbans, and holding *'tit mait'e* or *'tit maitresse* to their bosoms, have made the infants' lullabies these gently sad strains of disappointed love or regretted youth, will never be known. Now and then the song would find its way through some master's growing child of musical ear, into the drawing-room; and it is from a Creole drawing-room in the Rue Esplanade that we draw the following, so familiar to all Creole ears and rendered with many variations of text and measure. (Ah Suzette, page 6 4 .)

One may very safely suppose this song to have sprung from the poetic invention of some free black far away in the Gulf. A Louisiana slave would hardly have thought it possible to earn money for himself in the sugar-cane fields. The mention of mountains points back to St. Domingo.

It is strange to note in all this African-Creole lyric product how rarely its producers seem

A NURSE MAMMIE.

to have recognized the myriad charms of nature. The landscape, the seasons, the sun, moon, stars, the clouds, the storm, the peace that follows, the forest's solemn depths, the vast prairie, birds, insects, the breeze, the flowers — they are passed in silence. Was it because of the soul-destroying weight of bondage? Did the slave feel so painfully that the beauties of the natural earth were not for him? Was it because the overseer's eye was on him that his was not lifted upon them? It may have been — in part. But another truth goes with these. His songs were not often contemplative. They voiced not outward nature, but the inner emotions and passions of a nearly naked serpent-worshiper, and these looked not to the surrounding scene for sympathy; the surrounding scene belonged to his master. But love was his, and toil, and anger, and superstition, and malady. Sleep was his balm, food his reënforcement, the dance his pleasure, rum his longed-for nepenthe, and

death the road back to Africa. These were his themes, and furnished the few scant figures of his verse.

The moment we meet the offspring of his contemplative thought, as we do in his apothegms and riddles, we find a change, and any or every object in sight, great or trivial, comely or homely, is wrought into the web of his traditional wit and wisdom. " Vo mié, savon, passé godron," he says, to teach a lesson of gentle forbearance ("Soap is worth more than tar"). And then, to point the opposite truth,— " Pas marré so chien avé saucisse " ("Don't chain your dog with links of sausage"). " Qui zamein 'tendé souris fé so nid dan zoré ç'at?" ("Who ever heard of mouse making nest in cat's ear?") And so, too, when love was his theme, apart from the madness of the dance — when his note fell to soft cooings the verse became pastoral. So it was in the song last quoted. And so, too, in this very African bit, whose air I have not:

"Si to té tit zozo,
Et mo-même, mo té fizi,
Mo sré tchoué toé — boum!
Ah! tchère bizou
D'acazou,
Mo laimein ou
Comme cochon laimein la bou!"

Shall we translate literally?

"If you were a little bird
And myself, I were a gun,
I would shoot you — boum!
Ah! dear jewel
Of mahogany,
I love you
As the hog loves mud."

One of the best of these Creole love-songs — one that the famed Gottschalk, himself a New Orleans Creole of pure blood, made use of — is the tender lament of one who sees the girl of his heart's choice the victim of chagrin in beholding a female rival wearing those vestments of extra quality that could only be the favors which both women had coveted from the hand of some one in the proud master-caste whence alone such favors could come. "Calalou," says the song, "has an embroidered petticoat, and Lolotte, or Zizi," as it is often sung, "has a — heartache." Calalou, here, I take to be a derisive nickname. Originally it is the term for a West Indian dish, a noted ragout. It must be intended to apply here to the quadroon women who swarmed into New Orleans in 1809 as refugees from Cuba, Guadeloupe, and other islands where the war against Napoleon exposed them to Spanish and British aggression. It was with this great influx of persons neither savage nor enlightened, neither white nor black, neither slave nor truly free, that the famous quadroon caste arose and flourished. If Calalou, in the verse, was one of these quadroon fair ones, the song is its own explanation. (See Pov' piti Momzel Zizi, page 65.)

"Poor little Miss Zizi!" is what it means — "She has pain, pain in her little heart." "À li" is simply the Creole possessive form; "corps à moin" would signify simply myself. Calalou is wearing a Madras turban; she has on an embroidered petticoat; [they tell their story and] Zizi has achings in her heart. And the second stanza moralizes: "When you wear the chain of love" — maybe we can make it rhyme:

"When love's chains upon thee lie
Bid all happiness good-bye."

Poor little Zizi! say we also. Triumphant Calalou! We see that even her sort of freedom had its tawdry victories at the expense of the slave. A poor freedom it was, indeed: To have f. m. c. or f. w. c. tacked in small letters upon one's name perforce and by law, that all might know that the bearer was not a real freeman or freewoman, but only a free man (or woman) of color,—a title that could not be indicated by capital initials; to be the unlawful mates of luxurious bachelors, and take their pay in muslins, embroideries, prunella, and good living, taking with them the loathing of honest women and the salacious derision of the blackamoor; to be the sister, mother, father, or brother of Calalou; to fall heir to property by sufferance, not by law; to be taxed for public education and not allowed to give that education to one's own children; to be shut out of all occupations that the master class could reconcile with the vague title of gentleman; to live in the knowledge that the law pronounced "death or imprisonment at hard labor for life" against whoever should be guilty of "writing, printing, publishing, or distributing anything having a tendency to create discontent among the free colored population": that it threatened death against whosoever should utter such things in private conversation; and that it decreed expulsion from the State to Calalou and all her kin of any age or condition if only they had come in across its bounds since 1807. In the enjoyment of such ghastly freedom as this the flesh-pots of Egypt sometimes made the mouth water and provoked the tongue to sing its regrets for a past that seemed better than the present. (See Bon D'jé, page 66.)

Word for word we should have to render it,— "In times when I was young I never pondered — indulged in reverie, took on care," an archaic French word, *zongler*, still in use among the Acadians also in Louisiana; "mo zamein zonglé, bon D'jé" — "good Lord!" "Açtair" is "à cette heure" — "at this hour," that is, "now — these days." "These days I am getting old — I am pondering, good Lord!" etc. Some time in the future, it may be, some Creole will give us translations of these things, worthy to be called so. Meantime suffer this:

"In the days of my youth not a dream had I, good
    Lord!
These times I am growing old, full of dreams am I,
    good Lord!
I have dreams of those good times gone by! (*ter*)

When I was a slave, one boss had I, good Lord!
These times when I'm needing rest all hands serve I,
    good Lord!
I have dreams," etc.

III.

THE LAY AND THE DIRGE.

THERE were other strains of misery, the cry or the vagabond laugh and song of the friendless orphan for whom no asylum door would open, but who found harbor and food in the fields and wildwood and the forbidden places of the wicked town. When that Creole whom we hope for does come with his good translations, correcting the hundred and one errors that may be in these pages, we must ask him if he knows the air to this :

" Pitis sans popa, pitis sans moman,
Qui ça 'ou' zaut' fé pou' gagnein l'a'zanc,[1]
  No courri l'aut' bord pou' cercé patt ç'at'[2]
  No tournein bayou pou' péç'é patassa;[3]
  Et v'là comm ça no té fé nou' l'a'zan.

" Pitis sans popa, pitis sans moman,
Qui ça 'ou' zaut' fé, etc.
  No courri dans bois fouillé latanié[4],
  No vend' so racin' pou' fou'bi' planç'é ;
  Et v'là comm' ça, etc.

" Pitis sans popa, etc.
  Pou' fé di thé n'a fouillé sassaf'as,
  Pou' fé di l'enc' no po'té grain' sougras;[5]
  Et v'là, etc.

" Pitis sans popa, etc.
  No courri dans bois ramassé cancos ;
  Avé' nou' la caze no trappé zozos;[7]
  Et v'là, etc.

" Pitis sans popa, etc.
  No courri à soir c'ez Mom'selle Maroto,
  Dans la rie St. Ann ou no té zoué loto ;
  Et v'là," etc.

" Little ones without father, little ones without mother,
What do you to keep soul and body together ?
  The river we cross for wild berries to search ;
  We follow the bayou a-fishing for perch ;
  And that's how we keep soul and body together.

" Little ones without, etc.
  Palmetto we dig from the swamp's bristling stores
And sell its stout roots for scrubbing the floors ;
  And that's how, etc.

" Little ones, etc.
  The sassafras root we dig up ; it makes tea ;
  For ink the ripe pokeberry clusters bring we ;
  And that's how, etc.

" Little ones, etc.
  We go to the woods *cancos* berries to fetch,
  And in our trap cages the nonpareils[8] catch ;
  And that's how, etc.

" Little ones, etc.
  At evening we visit Mom'selle Maroto,
  In St. Ann's street, to gamble awhile at keno ;
  And that's how we keep soul and body together."

Here was companionship with nature — the companionship of the vagabond. We need not

doubt that these little orphan vagrants could have sung for us the song, from which in an earlier article we have already quoted a line or two, of Cayetano's circus, probably the most welcome intruder that ever shared with the man Friday and his song-dancing fellows and sweethearts the green, tough sod of Congo Square.

" C'est Miché Cayétane,
  Qui sorti la Havane
Avec so chouals[9] et so macacs.[10]
Li gagnein ein nhomme qui dancé dans sac ;
Li gagnein qui dancé si yé la main ;
Li gagnein zaut', à choual, qui boir' di vin ;
Li gagnein oussi ein zein, zoli mom'selle,
Qui monté choual sans bride et sans selle !
Pou' di' tou' ça mo pas capab' ;
Mé mo souvien ein qui 'valé sab' !
Yé n'en oussi tou' sort' bétail.
Yé pas montré pou la négrail' ;
Gniapas là dotchians dos-brilé,[11]
Pou' fé tapaze et pou' hirlé ;
Cé gros madame et gros miché,
Qui ménein là tous pitits yé,
  'Oir Miché Cayétane,
  Qui 'rivé la Havane
Avec so chouals et so macacs."

Should the Louisiana Creole negro undertake to render his song to us in English, it would not be exactly the African-English of any other State in the Union. Much less would it resemble the gross dialects of the English-torturing negroes of Jamaica, or Barbadoes, or the Sea Islands of Carolina. If we may venture —

" Dass Cap'm Cayetano,
  W'at comin' fum Havano,*
Wid 'is monkey' an' 'is nag' !
An' one man w'at dance in bag,
An' mans dance on dey han' — cut shine'
An' gallop hoss sem time drink wine !
An' b'u'ful young missy dah beside,
Ridin' 'dout air sadd' aw brid'e ;[12]
To tell h-all dat — he cann' be tole.
Man teck a sword an' swall' 'im whole !
Beas'es ?[13] ev'y sawt o' figgah !
Dat show ain't fo' no common niggah !
Dey don' got deh no po' white cuss'—
Sunbu'nt back ! — to holla an' fuss.
Dass ladies fine, and gennymuns gran',
Fetchin' dey chilluns dah — all han' !
  Fo' see Cayetano,
  W'at come fum Havano
Wid 'is monkey' an' 'is nag' ! "

---

1 L'argent — money.
2 " We go to the other side " [of the river] " to get cats' paws," a delicious little blue swamp berry.
3 The perch. The little sunfish or " pumpkin seed," miscalled through the southwest.
4 Dwarf palmetto, whose root is used by the Creoles as a scrubbing-brush.
5 Pokeberries. 6 Cancos, Indian name for a wild purple berry.
7 Oiseaux, birds.
8 The nonpareil, pape, or painted bunting, is the favorite victim of the youthful bird-trappers.
9 Chevals — chevaux.

10 Macaques.
11 " Gniapas là dotchians dos-brilé."
" Il n'y a pas là des *dotchians* avec les dos brulés."
The *dotchian dos-brilé* is the white trash with sunburnt back, the result of working in the fields. It is an expression of supreme contempt for the *pitits blancs* — low whites — to contrast them with the *gros madames et gros michies.*
12 Riding without e'er a saddle or bridle.
13 Beasts — wild animals.
* To turn final *a* into *o* for the purpose of rhyme is the special delight of the singing negro. I used to hear as part of a moonlight game,—

Come, young man, what chews tobacco,   I had a wife in South Cal-li-no ; Her name was ole Aunt Di-noh.

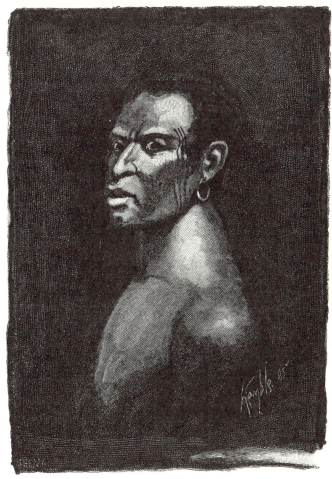

A CANDJO.

A remarkable peculiarity of these African Creole songs of every sort is that almost without exception they appear to have originated in the masculine mind, and to be the expression of the masculine heart. Untrained as birds, their males made the songs. We come now, however, to the only exception I have any knowledge of, a song expressive of feminine sentiment, the capitulation of some belle Layotte to the tender enticement of a Creole-born chief or *candjo*. The pleading tone of the singer's defense against those who laugh at her pretty chagrin is—it seems to me —touching. (See Criole Candjo, page 66.)

But we began this chapter in order to speak of songs that bear more distinctly than anything yet quoted the features of the true lay or historical narrative song, commemorating pointedly and in detail some important episode in the history of the community.

It is interesting to contrast the solemnity with which these events are treated when their heroes were black, and the broad buffoonery of the song when the affair it celebrates was one that mainly concerned the masters. Hear, for example, through all the savage simplicity of the following rhymeless lines, the melancholy note that rises and falls but never intermits. The song is said to be very old, dating from the last century. It is still sung, but the Creole gentleman who procured it for me from a former slave was not able to transcribe or remember the air.

LUBIN.

Tremblant-terr'[1] vini 'branlé moulin;
Tonnerr' chiel[2] tombé bourlé[3] moulin;
　Tou' moun[4] dans moulin là péri.
Temoins vini qui vend'[5] Libin.
Yé dit Libin metté di fé.
Yé hissé saffaud[6] pou' so la tête.[7]

[1] Tremblement de terre.— earthquake.　[2] Ciel.　[3] Brulée.　[4] Tout le monde.　[5] Vendaient — sold, betrayed.
　[6] Echafaud.　[7] So la tête : Creole possessive form for *his head*.

"MISTRESS FLEW INTO A PASSION."

Saïda! m'allé mourri, Saïda!
Mo zamis di comm' ça: "Libin,
Faut to donn' Zilié to bitin[1]."
Cofaire[2] mo sré donnein Zilié?
Pou' moin Zilié zamein lavé;[3]
Zilié zamein 'passé[4] pou moin.
     Saïda! m'allé mourri, Saïda!

An earthquake came and shook the mill;
The heavens' thunders fell and burned it;
Every soul in the mill perished.
Witnesses came who betrayed Lubin.
They said he set the mill on fire.
They raised a scaffold to take off his head.
     Saïda! I am going to die!
My friends speak in this way: "Lubin,
You ought to give Julia your plunder."
Why should I give it to Julia?
For me Julia never washed clothes;
Julia never ironed for me.
     Saïda! I am going to die!

Or notice again the stately tone of lamentation over the fate of a famous negro insurrectionist, as sung by old Madeleine of St. Bernard parish to the same Creole friend already mentioned, who kindly wrote down the lines on the spot for this collection. They are fragmentary, extorted by littles from the shattered memory of the ancient crone. Their allusion to the Cabildo places their origin in the days when that old colonial council administered Spanish rule over the province.

OUARRÂ ST. MALO.

Aïe! zein zens, vini fé ouarrâ
Pou' pôv' St. Malo dans l'embas!
Yé ç'assé li avec yé chien,
Yé tiré li ein coup d'fizi,
         .   .   .
Yé halé li la cyprier,
So bras yé 'tassé[5] par derrier,
Yé 'tassé so la main divant;
Yé 'marré[6] li apé queue choual,
Yé trainein li zouqu'à la ville.
Divant michés là dans Cabil'e
Yé quisé[7] li li fé complot
Pou' coupé cou à tout ye blancs.
Yé 'mandé li qui so compères;
Pôv' St. Malo pas di' a-rien!
Zize[8] là li lir' so la sentence,
Et pis[9] li fé dressé potence.
Yé halé choual — ç'arette parti —
Pôv' St. Malo resté pendi!
Eine hèr soleil deza levée
Quand yé pend li si la levée.
Yé laissé so corps balancé
Pou' carancro gagnein manzé.

THE DIRGE OF ST. MALO.

Alas! young men, come, make lament
For poor St. Malo in distress!
They chased, they hunted him with dogs,
They fired at him with a gun,
         .   .   .
They hauled him from the cypress swamp.
His arms they tied behind his back,
They tied his hands in front of him;

---

[1] Butin: literally plunder, but used, as the word plunder is by the negro, for personal property.   [2] Pourquoi faire.   [3] Washed (clothes).   [4] Ironed.   [5] Attachée.   [6] Amarré, an archaism, common to negroes and Acadians: moored, for fastened.   [7] Accusée.   [8] Juge.   [9] Puis.

THE VOODOO DANCE.

[55]

They tied him to a horse's tail,
They dragged him up into the town.
Before those grand Cabildo men
They charged that he had made a plot
To cut the throats of all the whites.
They asked him who his comrades were;
Poor St. Malo said not a word!
The judge his sentence read to him,
And then they raised the gallows-tree.
They drew the horse — the cart moved off—
And left St. Malo hanging there.
The sun was up an hour high
When on the Levee he was hung;
They left his body swinging there,
For carrion crows to feed upon.

It would be curious, did the limits of these pages allow, to turn from such an outcry of wild mourning as this, and contrast with it the clownish flippancy with which the great events are sung, upon whose issue from time to time the fate of the whole land — society, government, the fireside, the lives of thousands — hung in agonies of suspense. At the same time it could not escape notice how completely in each case, while how differently in the two, the African has smitten his image into every line: in the one sort, the white, uprolled eyes and low wail of the savage captive, who dares not lift the cry of mourning high enough for the jealous ear of the master; in the other, the antic form, the grimacing face, the brazen laugh, and self-abasing confessions of the buffoon, almost within the whisk of the public jailer's lash. I have before me two songs of dates almost fifty years apart. The one celebrates the invasion of Louisiana by the British under Admiral Cochrane and General Pakenham in 1814; the other, the capture and occupation of New Orleans by Commodore Farragut and General Butler in 1862.

It was on the morning of the twenty-third of December, 1814, that the British columns, landing from a fleet of barges and hurrying along the narrow bank of a small canal in a swamp forest, gained a position in the open plain on the banks of the Mississippi only six miles below New Orleans, and with no defenses to oppose them between their vantage-ground and the city. The surprise was so complete that, though they issued from the woods an hour before noon, it was nearly three hours before the news reached the town. But at nightfall General Jackson fell upon them and fought in the dark the engagement which the song commemorates, the indecisive battle of Chalmette.

The singer ends thus:

" Fizi z'Anglé yé fé bim ! bim !
Carabin Kaintock yé fé zim ! zim !
Mo di' moin, sauvé to la peau !
Mo zété corps au bord do l'eau ;
Quand mo rivé li té fé clair.

Madam' li prend' ein coup d'colère ;
Li fé donn' moin ein quat' piquié
Passequé mo pas sivi mouchié ;
Mais moin, mo vo mié quat' piquié
Passé ein coup d'fizi z'Anglé ! "

" The English muskets went bim ! bim !
Kentucky rifles went zim ! zim !
I said to myself, save your skin !
I scampered along the water's edge ;
When I got back it was day-break.
Mistress flew into a passion ;
She had me whipped at the ' four stakes,'
Because I didn't stay with master ;
But the ' four stakes ' for me is better than
A musket shot from an Englishman."

The story of Farragut's victory and Butler's advent in April, 1862, is sung with the still lighter heart of one in whose day the "quatre piquets " was no longer a feature of the calaboose. Its refrain is :

" An-hé !
Qui ça qui rivé r
C'est Ferraguitt et p'i Botlair,
Qui rivé."

The story is long and silly, much in the humor of

" Hark ! hark !
The dogs do bark."

We will lay it on the table.

IV.

THE VOODOOS.

THE dance and song entered into the negro worship. That worship was as dark and horrid as bestialized savagery could make the adoration of serpents. So revolting was it, and so morally hideous, that even in the West Indian French possessions a hundred years ago, with the slave-trade in full blast and the West Indian planter and slave what they were, the orgies of the Voodoos were forbidden. Yet both there and in Louisiana they were practiced.

The Aradas, St. Méry tells us, introduced them. They brought them from their homes beyond the Slave Coast, one of the most dreadfully benighted regions of all Africa. He makes the word Vaudaux. In Louisiana it is written Voudou and Voodoo, and is often changed on the negro's lips to Hoodoo. It is the name of an imaginary being of vast supernatural powers residing in the form of a harmless snake. This spiritual influence or potentate is the recognized antagonist and opposite of Obi, the great African manitou or deity, or him whom the Congoes vaguely generalize as Zombi. In Louisiana, as I have been told by that learned Creole scholar the late Alexander Dimitry, Voodoo bore as a title of

greater solemnity the additional name of Maignan, and that
even in the Calinda dance,
which he had witnessed innumerable times, was sometimes heard, at the height of
its frenzy, the invocation—

"Aïe! Aïe!
Voodoo Magnan!"

The worship of Voodoo is
paid to a snake kept in a box.
The worshipers are not merely
a sect, but in some rude, savage way also an order. A man
and woman chosen from their
own number to be the oracles
of the serpent deity are called
the king and queen. The
queen is the more important
of the two, and even in the
present dilapidated state of the
worship in Louisiana, where
the king's office has almost or
quite disappeared, the queen
is still a person of great note.
She reigns as long as she
continues to live. She comes
to power not by inheritance,
but by election or its barbarous
equivalent. Chosen for such
qualities as would give her a
natural supremacy, personal
attractions among the rest, and
ruling over superstitious fears
and desires of every fierce and
ignoble sort, she wields no trivial influence. I once saw, in
her extreme old age, the famed
Marie Laveau. Her dwelling
was in the quadroon quarter
of New Orleans, but a step or
two from Congo Square, a
small adobe cabin just off the
sidewalk, scarcely higher than
its close board fence, whose
batten gate yielded to the
touch and revealed the crazy
doors and windows spread
wide to the warm air, and one
or two tawny faces within, whose expression
was divided between a pretense of contemptuous inattention and a frowning resentment of
the intrusion. In the center of a small room
whose ancient cypress floor was worn with
scrubbing and sprinkled with crumbs of soft
brick—a Creole affectation of superior clean-
liness—sat, quaking with feebleness in an ill-
looking old rocking-chair, her body bowed,
and her wild, gray witch's tresses hanging
about her shriveled, yellow neck, the queen

A VOODOO.

of the Voodoos. Three generations of her
children were within the faint beckon of her
helpless, waggling wrist and fingers. They
said she was over a hundred years old, and
there was nothing to cast doubt upon the
statement. She had shrunken away from her
skin; it was like a turtle's. Yet withal one
could hardly help but see that the face, now
so withered, had once been handsome and
commanding. There was still a faint shadow
of departed beauty on the forehead, the spark

of an old fire in the sunken, glistening eyes, and a vestige of imperiousness in the fine, slightly aquiline nose, and even about her silent, woe-begone mouth. Her grandson stood by, an uninteresting quadroon between forty and fifty years old, looking strong, empty-minded, and trivial enough; but his mother, her daughter, was also present, a woman of some seventy years, and a most striking and majestic figure. In features, stature, and bearing she was regal. One had but to look on her, impute her brilliancies — too untamable and severe to be called charms or graces — to her mother, and remember what New Orleans was long years ago, to understand how the name of Marie Laveau should have driven itself inextricably into the traditions of the town and the times. Had this visit been postponed a few months it would have been too late. Marie Laveau is dead; Malvina Latour is queen. As she appeared presiding over a Voodoo ceremony on the night of the 23d of June, 1884, she is described as a bright mulattress of about forty-eight, of "extremely handsome figure," dignified bearing, and a face indicative of a comparatively high order of intelligence. She wore a neat blue, white-dotted calico gown, and a " brilliant *tignon* (turban) gracefully tied."

It is pleasant to say that this worship, in Louisiana, at least, and in comparison with what it once was, has grown to be a rather trivial affair. The practice of its midnight forest rites seemed to sink into inanition along with Marie Laveau. It long ago diminished in frequency to once a year, the chosen night always being the Eve of St. John. For several years past even these annual celebrations have been suspended ; but in the summer of 1884 they were — let it be hoped, only for the once — resumed.

When the queen decides that such a celebration shall take place, she appoints a night for the gathering, and some remote, secluded spot in the forest for the rendezvous. Thither all the worshipers are summoned. St. Méry, careless of the power of the scene, draws in practical, unimaginative lines the picture of such a gathering in St. Domingo, in the times when the "*véritable Vaudaux*" had lost but little of the primitive African character. The worshipers are met, decked with kerchiefs more or less numerous, red being everywhere the predominating color. The king, abundantly adorned with them, wears one of pure red about his forehead as a diadem. A blue ornamental cord completes his insignia. The queen, in simple dress and wearing a red cord and a heavily decorated belt, is beside him near a rude altar. The silence of midnight is overhead, the gigantic forms and shadows and still, dank airs of the tropical

forest close in around, and on the altar, in a small box ornamented with little tinkling bells, lies, unseen, the living serpent. The worshipers have begun their devotions to it by presenting themselves before it in a body, and uttering professions of their fidelity and belief in its power. They cease, and now the royal pair, in tones of parental authority and protection, are extolling the great privilege of being a devotee, and inviting the faithful to consult the oracle. The crowd makes room, and a single petitioner draws near. He is the senior member of the order. His prayer is made. The king becomes deeply agitated by the presence within him of the spirit invoked. Suddenly he takes the box from the altar and sets it on the ground. The queen steps upon it and with convulsive movements utters the answers of the deity beneath her feet. Another and another suppliant, approaching in the order of seniority, present, singly, their petitions, and humbly or exultingly, according to the nature of the responses, which hangs on the fierce caprice of the priestess, accept these utterances and make way for the next, with his prayer of fear or covetousness, love, jealousy, petty spite or deadly malice. At length the last petitioner is answered. Now a circle is formed, the caged snake is restored to the altar, and the humble and multifarious oblations of the worshipers are received, to be devoted not only to the trivial expenses of this worship, but also to the relief of members of the order whose distresses call for such aid. Again, the royal ones are speaking, issuing orders for execution in the future, orders that have not always in view, mildly says St. Méry, good order and public tranquillity. Presently the ceremonies become more forbidding. They are taking a horrid oath, smearing their lips with the blood of some slaughtered animal, and swearing to suffer death rather than disclose any secret of the order, and to inflict death on any who may commit such treason. Now a new applicant for membership steps into their circle, there are a few trivial formalities, and the Voodoo dance begins. The postulant dances frantically in the middle of the ring, only pausing from time to time to receive heavy alcoholic draughts in great haste and return more wildly to his leapings and writhings until he falls in convulsions. He is lifted, restored, and presently conducted to the altar, takes his oath, and by a ceremonial stroke from one of the sovereigns is admitted a full participant in the privileges and obligations of the devilish freemasonry. But the dance goes on about the snake. The contortions of the upper part of the body, especially of the neck and shoulders, are such as threaten to dislocate them. The queen shakes the box

MARIE LAVEAU.

and tinkles its bells, the rum-bottle gurgles, the chant alternates between king and chorus —

"Eh! eh! Bomba, honc! honc! *
    Canga bafio tay,
    Canga moon day lay,
    Canga do keelah,
    Canga li ——"

There are swoonings and ravings, nervous tremblings beyond control, incessant writhings and turnings, tearing of garments, even biting of the flesh — every imaginable invention of the devil.

St. Méry tells us of another dance invented in the West Indies by a negro, analogous to

* "Hen! hen!" in St. Méry's spelling of it for French pronunciation. As he further describes the sound in a foot-note, it must have been a horrid grunt.

the Voodoo dance, but more rapid, and in which dancers had been known to fall dead. This was the "Dance of Don Pedro." The best efforts of police had, in his day, only partially suppressed it. Did it ever reach Louisiana? Let us, at a venture, say no.

To what extent the Voodoo worship still obtains here would be difficult to say with certainty. The affair of June, 1884, as described by Messrs. Augustin and Whitney, eye-witnesses, was an orgy already grown horrid enough when they turned their backs upon it. It took place at a wild and lonely spot where the dismal cypress swamp behind New Orleans meets the waters of Lake Pontchartrain in a wilderness of cypress stumps and rushes. It would be hard to find in nature a more painfully desolate region. Here in a fisherman's cabin sat the Voodoo worshipers cross-legged on the floor about an Indian basket of herbs and some beans, some bits of bone, some oddly wrought bunches of feathers, and some saucers of small cakes. The queen presided, sitting on the only chair in the room. There was no king, no snake — at least none visible to the onlookers. Two drummers beat with their thumbs on gourds covered with sheepskin, and a white-wooled old man scraped that hideous combination of banjo and violin, whose head is covered with rattlesnake skin, and of which the Chinese are the makers and masters. There was singing— "*M'allé couri dans déser*" ("I am going into the wilderness"), a chant and refrain not worth the room they would take — and there was frenzy and a circling march, wild shouts, delirious gesticulations and posturings, drinking, and amongst other frightful nonsense the old trick of making fire blaze from the mouth by spraying alcohol from it upon the flame of a candle.

But whatever may be the quantity of the Voodoo *worship* left in Louisiana, its superstitions are many and are everywhere. Its charms are resorted to by the malicious, the jealous, the revengeful, or the avaricious, or held in terror, not by the timorous only, but by the strong, the courageous, the desperate. To find under his mattress an acorn hollowed out, stuffed with the hair of some dead person, pierced with four holes on four sides, and two

small chicken feathers drawn through them so as to cross inside the acorn; or to discover on his door-sill at daybreak a little box containing a dough or waxen heart stuck full of pins; or to hear that his avowed foe or rival has been pouring cheap champagne in the four corners of Congo Square at midnight when there was no moon, will strike more abject fear into the heart of many a stalwart negro or melancholy quadroon than to face a leveled revolver. And it is not only the colored man that holds to these practices and fears. Many a white Creole gives them full credence. What wonder, when African Creoles were the nurses of so nearly all of them! Many shrewd men and women, generally colored persons, drive a trade in these charms and in oracular directions for their use or evasion; many a Creole — white as well as other tints — female, too, as well as male— will pay a Voodoo "*monteure*" to "make a work," *i. e.*, to weave a spell, for the prospering of some scheme or wish too ignoble to be prayed for at any shrine inside the church. These milder incantations are performed within the witch's or wizard's own house, and are made up, for the most part, of a little pound cake, some lighted candle ends, a little syrup of sugar-cane, pins, knitting-needles, and a trifle of anisette. But fear naught; an Obi charm will enable you to smile defiance against all such mischief; or if you will but consent to be a magician, it is they, the Voodoos, one and all, who will hold you in absolute terror. Or, easier, a frizzly chicken! If you have on your premises a frizzly chicken, you can lie down and laugh — it is a checkmate!

A planter once found a Voodoo charm, or *ouanga* (wongah); this time it was a bit of cotton cloth folded about three cow-peas and some breast feathers of a barn-yard fowl, and covered with a tight wrapping of thread. When he proposed to take it to New Orleans his slaves were full of consternation. "Marse Ed, ef ye go on d'boat wid dat-ah, de boat'll sink wi' yer. Fore d'Lord, it will!" For some reason it did not. Here is a genuine Voodoo song, given me by Lafcadio Hearn, though what the words mean none could be more ignorant of than the present writer. They are rendered phonetically in French.

Hé - ron man - dé, Hé - ron man - dé, Ti - gui li pa - pa, Hé - ron man - dé, Ti - gui li pa - pa, Hé - ron man - dé, Hé - ron man - dé, Hé - ron man - dé, Do sé dan go - do.

PLANTER AND VOODOO CHARM.

And another phrase: "Ah tingouai yé, Ah tingouai yé, Ah ouai ya, Ah ouai ya, Ah tingouai yé, Do sé dan go-do, Ah tingouai yé," etc.

V.

SONGS OF WOODS AND WATERS.

A LAST page to the songs of the chase and of the boat. The circumstances that produced them have disappeared. There was a time, not so long ago, when traveling in Louisiana was done almost wholly by means of the paddle, the oar, or the "sweep." Every plantation had its river or bayou front, and every planter his boat and skilled crew of black oarsmen. The throb of their song measured the sweep of the oars, and as their bare or turbaned heads and shining bodies, naked to the waist, bowed forward and straightened back in ceaseless alternation, their strong voices chanted the praise of the silent, broad-hatted master who sat in the stern. Now and then a line was interjected in manly boast to their own brawn, and often the praise of the master softened off into tender laudations of the charms of some black or tawny Zilié, 'Zabette, or Zalli. From the treasures of the old chest already mentioned comes to my hand, from the last century most likely, on a ragged yellow sheet of paper, written with a green ink, one of these old songs. It would

THE BLACK HUNTER.

take up much room; I have made a close translation of its stanzas:

ROWERS' SONG.

Sing, lads; our master bids us sing.
For master cry out loud and strong.
The water with the long oar strike.
Sing, lads, and let us haste along.

'Tis for our master we will sing.
We'll sing for our young mistresses.
And sweethearts we must not forget —
Zoé, Mérente, Zabelle, Louise.

Sing, fellows, for our own true loves.
My lottery prize! Zoé, my belle!
She's like a wild young doe, she knows
The way to jump and dance so well!

Black diamonds are her bright, black eyes,
Her teeth and lilies are alike.
Sing, fellows, for my true love, and
The water with the long oar strike.

See! see! the town! Hurrah! hurrah!
Master returns in pleasant mood.
He's going to treat his boys all 'round.
Hurrah! hurrah for master good!

From the same treasury comes a hunting song. Each stanza begins and ends with the loud refrain: "*Bomboula ! bomboula !*" Some one who has studied African tongues may be able to say whether this word is one with Bamboula, the name of the dance and of the drum that dominates it. *Oula* seems to be an infinitive termination of many Congo verbs, and *boula*, De Lanzières says, means to beat. However, the dark hunters of a hundred years ago knew, and between their outcries of the loud, rumbling word sang, in this song, their mutual exhortation to rise, take guns, fill powder-horns, load up, call dogs, make haste and be off to the woods to find game for master's table and their own grosser *cuisine;* for the one, deer, squirrels, rabbits, birds; for the other, *chat oués* (raccoons), that make "*si bon gombo*" (such good gumbo!). "Don't fail to kill them, boys,— and the tiger-cats that eat men; and if we meet a bear, we'll vanquish him! Bomboula! bomboula!" The lines have a fine African ring in them, but — one mustn't print everything.

Another song, of wood and water both, though only the water is mentioned, I have direct from former Creole negro slaves. It is a runaway's song of defiance addressed to the high sheriff Fleuriau (Charles Jean Baptiste Fleuriau, Alguazil mayor), a Creole of the Cabildo a hundred and fifteen years ago. At least one can think so, for the name is not to be found elsewhere.

of operations, and seeking his adventures not so far from the hen-coop and pig-pen as rigid principles would have dictated. Now that he is free, he is willing to reveal these little pleasantries—as one of the bygones—to the eager historian. Much nocturnal prowling was done on the waters of the deep, forest-darkened bayous, in *pirogues* (dug-outs). For secret signals to accomplices on shore they resorted to singing. What is so innocent as music! The words were in some African tongue. We have one of these songs from the negroes themselves, with their own translation and their own assurance that the translation is correct. The words have a very Congo-ish sound. The Congo tongue knows no *r;* but the fact is familiar that in America the negro interchanges the sounds of *r* and *l* as readily as does the Chinaman. We will use both an English and a French spelling. (De Zab, page 67.)

The whole chant consists of but six words besides a single conjunction. It means, its singers avowed, "Out from under the trees our boat moves into the open water—bring us large game and small game!" *Dé zab* sounds like *des arbs*, and they called it French,

O Zé - né - ral Flo - ri - do! C'est vrai yé pas ca - pab' pran moin! O
O Gen - e - ral Flo - ri - do! In - deed fo' true dey can't catch me! O

Zé - ne - ral La Flo - ri - o! C'est vrai yé pas ca - pab' pran moin!
Gen - e - ral La Fleu - ri - au! In - deed fo' true dey can't catch me!

2. Yen a ein counan si la mer } *Bis.*
   C'est vrai, etc.

2. Dey got* one schooner out at sea } *Bis.*
   Indeed fo' true, etc.

Sometimes the black man found it more convenient not to run away himself, but to make other articles of property seem to escape from custody. He ventured to forage on his own account, retaining his cabin as a base

but the rest they claimed as good "Affykin." We cannot say. We are sappers and miners in this quest, not philologists. When they come on behind, if they ever think it worth their while to do so, the interpretation of this strange song may be not more difficult than that of the famous inscription discovered by Mr. Pickwick. But, as well as the present writer can know, all that have been given here are genuine antiques.

* "**Dey got**" is a vulgarism of Louisiana Creoles, white and colored, for "There is." It is a transfer into English of the French idiom *Il y a.*

QUAND MO 'TE.

ARR. BY MISS M. L. BARTLETT.

Quand mo 'te dans grand chi-min   Mo con-tré nion vié pa-pa.
Mo 'man-dé quel heure li yé,   Li dit moin mi-di pas-sé.
Mo 'man-dé mou-choi' ta-bac,   Li don moin mou-[OMIT............] choi Ma-dras.

Prise to-bac jam-bette à cou-teau,   Taf-fia doux pas-sé si-rop.   sé si-rop.

NEG' PAS CAPA' MARCHE.

ARR. BY MISS M. L. BARTLETT.

Allegro

1. Neg pas ca-pa' mar-ché sans ma, ïs dans poche, c'est pou vo-lé poule.
2. Millate pas ca-pa' mar-ché sans la corde dans poche, c'est pou volé choual.
3. Blanc pas ca-pa' mar-ché sans la'zen dans poche, c'est pou vo-lé filles.

After last verse.

AH! SUZETTE.

ARR. BY MADAME L. LEJEUNE.

Ah! Su-zette,   Su-zette to vé pas chère.   Ah! Su-zette, chère a-mie,

Fine.

to pas lai-mein moin.   1. M'al-lé haut mon-tagne za-mie,   M'al-lé cou-pé
2. Mo cour-ri dans bois, za-mie,   Pou' tou-é zo-

POV' PITI MOMZEL ZIZI.

ARR. BY MME. L. LEJEUNE.

✻ *Ending of Refrain after the Closing Stanza.*

-bo li gag-nin bo-bo, bo-bo,.... bo-bo,.... Li gagnin bo-bo,... dans kèr à li.

BON D'JE.

H. E. KREHBIEL.

1. Dans tan mo té zène Mo zamein zonglé, bon Djé! A ç'tair m'a-pé vi-ni vié, M'a-pé zonglé, bon
2. Dans tan mo té nesclave Mo servis mo maite, bon Djé! A ç'tair mo be-soin re-pos, Mo sers ton moune, bon

Djé! M'apé zon-glé bon tan qui pas-sé, M'apé zonglé bon tan qui pas-sé, M'a-pé zon-glé bon tan qui pas-sé.
Djé! M'apé zon-glé, etc.

CRIOLE CANDJO.

H. E. KREHBIEL.

Andante.

1. In zou' in zène Cri-ole Can-djo, Belle pas-sé blanc dan-dan là
2. Mo cou-ri dans youn bois voi-sin; Mais Cri-ole là prend même ci

Una Corda.

yo, Li té tout tans a-pé dire, "Vi-ni, za-mi, pou' nous rire."
min, Et tous tans li m'a-pé dire, "Vi-ni, etc.

Non, mi-ché, m'pas ou-lé ri - re, moin. Non, mi-ché, m'pas ou-lé ri - re.

rit.

Non, mi-ché, m'pas ou-lé ri - re, moin, Non, mi-ché, m'pas ou-lé ri - re.

rit.

3. Mais li té tant cicané moi,
   Pou' li té quitté moin youn fois
   Mo té 'blizé pou li dire,
   Oui, miché, mo oulé rire.
       Oui miché, etc.

4. Zaut tous qu'ap'es rire moin là bas,
   Si zaut té conné Candjo là,
   Qui belle façon li pou' rire,
   Djé pini moin! zaut s'ré dire,
       "Oui, miché," etc.

One day one young Creole candio,
Mo' fineh dan sho nuf white beau,
   Kip all de time meckin' free —
"Swithawt, meck merrie wid me."
"Naw, sah, I dawn't want meck merrie, me.
Naw, sah, I dawn't want meck merrie."

I go teck walk in wood close by;
But Creole tek' sem road, and try
   All time, all time, to meck free —
"Swithawt, meck merrie wid me."
"Naw, sah, I dawn't want meck merrie, me.
Naw, sah, I dawn't want meck merrie."

But him slide roun' an' roun' dis chile,
Tell, jis' fo' sheck 'im off lill while,
   Me, I was bleedze fo' say, "Shoo!
   If I'll meck merrie wid you?
O, yass, I ziss leave meck merrie, me;
Yass, seh, I ziss leave meck merrie."

You-alls w'at laugh at me so well,
I wish you'd knowed dat Creole swell,
   Wid all 'is swit, smilin' trick'.
   'Pon my soul! you'd done say, quick,
"O, yass, I ziss leave meck merrie, me;
Yass, seh, I ziss leave meck merrie."

DÉ ZAB.

ARR. BY MISS M. L. BARTLETT.

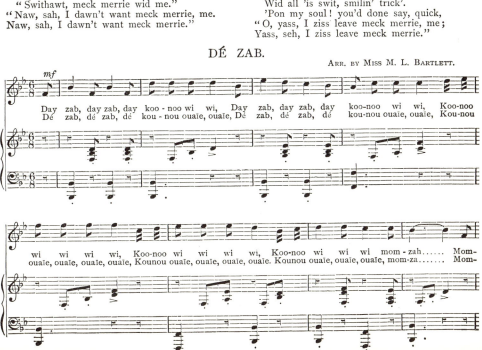

mf

Day zab, day zab, day koo-noo wi wi, Day zab, day zab, day koo-noo wi wi, Koo-noo
Dé zab, dé zab, dé kou-nou ouaïe, ouaïe, Dé zab, dé zab, dé kou-nou ouaïe, ouaïe, Kou-nou

wi wi wi wi, Koo-noo wi wi wi wi, Koo-noo wi wi wi mom-zah...... Mom-
ouaïe, ouaïe, ouaïe, ouaïe, Kounou ouaïe, ouaïe, ouaïe, ouaïe. Kounou ouaïe, ouaïe, ouaïe, mom-za....... Mom-

zah, mom - zah, mom - zah, mom - zah, Ro - zah, ro - zah, ro - zah a-a mom - zah.
za, mom - za, mom - za, mom - za, Ro - za, ro - za, ro - za et mom - za.

George W. Cable.

VII

NEGRO CAMP-MEETING MELODIES

Henry Cleveland Wood

[By 1892 some of the lost "quaintness" in rural Negro worship was being mourned by white observers, many of them with abolitionist backgrounds. The author of the following report in *New England Magazine* (March 1892, pp. 61-64) has to return in memory to the picturesque torchlight outdoor camp-meeting of his youth. In a day when no thought was given to the sensitivities of possible black readers, a handful of songs are embedded in a thicket of minstrel-show mispronunciations and fractured grammar characteristic of the times. In a period when Currier and Ives prints, periodical illustrations, popular music, the "coon" song, and nursery rhymes were subjecting black Americans to derision, the religious folksong collector was no less callous toward the black folk than the rest of white America.]

NEGRO CAMP–MEETING MELODIES.

By Henry Cleveland Wood.

IN my grandfather's land, near a creek which runs through the town of Harrodsburg, Ky., there stood for many years a sycamore tree under which, history relates, the first religious services were held by early settlers on soil then a portion of the extensive wilderness district belonging to Virginia. The genuine camp-meeting was said to have originated in southern Kentucky, and the small gathering of intrepid pioneers under the arching white limbs of a tall sycamore was probably the nucleus of a band of worshippers which has since spread to large proportions. As the wild lands were settled by increasing immigration, the camp-meeting became a recognized feature of the new country on the one hand, from the want of suitable places of worship, and on the other, from the magnificent forest-trees and beautiful woodlands which offered such alluring shade and ample accommodation to the seekers after righteousness.

Dating from the war, the liberated race has taken most kindly to the camp-meeting, perhaps as much on account of the novelty it affords as the freedom of worship and large attendance it permits; for during slavery the race was prohibited from holding large assemblies even of a religious nature.

The negro is nothing if not religious. It matters not how young, or how old, or how good, or how sinful he may be in his normal state, he never fails to extract from religion that fervid enjoyment that characterizes his type. He never wearies of attending church; it comprises not only his religious, but his social life. He cares little for pastime or entertainment, in general. He manages to extract both from his devotional exercises, and is satisfied.

A friend of mine who lives near a church where the congregation is colored, avers that a protracted meeting has been in active progress there for the past twenty years; and the long series of meetings, of one kind and another, which have been held in the building almost constantly, year after year, would almost warrant the assertion.

To see the negro at the height of his religious frenzy, however, and in the full enjoyment of its influence, one should attend camp-meeting, where the dusky worshipper yields up himself fully to the spell of the fervor which enwraps him with its intensity, and sways him with its peculiar forces.

This was especially the case a few years ago. Progress and imitative influence have been at work, and have touched the scene, robbing it of much that was characteristic. The last negro camp-meeting I attended was held under a commodious canvas, while a fashionable choir did the singing and rendered popular hymns of the day to an organ accompaniment. Alas! I sorely missed the picturesque groupings under the forest-trees and the grand volume of powerful voices chanting the weird songs of this dusky people.

There were few scenes more impressive than the old-fashioned camp-meeting, held at night-time beneath the overhanging branches of the trees, through which the moonlight came in subdued rays, while brightly-burning torches amid the deeper gloom made sharp studies in lights and shades. Add to this the rich, sonorous voices of the worshippers, rising and falling in rhythmical cadences, lending to the silence of the night their rare melody, and the scene is one that cannot readily be forgotten.

The words of these tuneful songs are frequently improvised, and are full of repetitions, as is usually the case with compositions by the negroes; and to reproduce them apart from their proper surroundings is to rob them of much of their wild beauty and the strange impressiveness which they possess in so marked a degree, when voiced by the lusty lungs of the camp-meeting worshipper.

The sermons are usually lurid, and carry convictions to the hearts of the hearers, as numerous groans and mournful exclamations testify during its delivery. "Oh ! my soul," "Yes, Lord ! " "Jes' lis'en at 'im ! " "Talkin' ter me ! " "Now yer preachin' ! " "Bress Jesus ! " "Now yer hittin' me hard ! " are some of the expressions heard, on this hand and on that, as the speaker waxes varyingly exhortative and menacing. The climax is reached by a repentant sinner shouting out the joy of a new-found religion ; and amid the moaning and praying and weeping, the excited, swaying congregation takes up some jubilant refrain, until the echoes, far and near, are awakened to tumultous life.

The sermons themselves become almost a chant, delivered in a high-pitched key, and with a sing-song monotony and a catch of the breath between sentences, or a running of one sentence into another, all of which produces an effect that one must hear to fully comprehend. The speakers are often very illiterate, and many amusing mistakes are made in the use of words. The negro orator usually has a great liking for long and high-sounding words, and handles them recklessly at times. I recall hearing one prayer offered up for all "agnominious" sinners, while another speaker grew thankful for the number present of God's "childring," and dropped a tear for those who were "casted away from out his glorifious presence," while yet another spoke of the days that had been "hypothecated an' gone."

While gathering some of the most characteristic songs, I was informed by a dusky singer that I had been "miscorrected" in regard to the words of one of them, and that to have him, for a small consideration, line it out to me while I wrote it down, would be the "supernatural" way to get at the matter.

The old-time melodies are fast disappearing and a new order of things is beginning to supplant them ; therefore, I have striven to preserve a few fragments, at least, of song, in an effort toward perpetuating some of the quaint melodies before the drilled choir and accomplished organist have fully established their innovations on this distinctive feature of the negro camp-meeting.

Chief among those hymns that stir one with their fervor is the one, "Camp-meetin' in de wilderness."

CAMP-MEETIN' IN DE WILDERNESS.

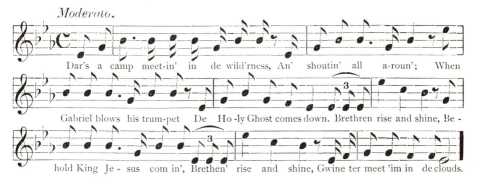

"Some says that nothin' ails me,
  Some gives me up fer lost,
  An' ebery refuge fails me,
  An' all my hopes is crossed.

CHORUS:

"Nex' door ter death they foun' me
  An' snatched me frum de grave,
  I tells ter all aroun' me
  His wondrous power ter save."

CHORUS:

ing mistakes are made in the use of words. The negro orator usually has a great liking for long and high-sounding words, and handles them recklessly at

Several other verses are sung, which, are often improvised to suit the melody. Another fine song is that entitled "I'm jes' from de founting."

I'M JES' FRUM DE FOUNTING.*

Oh! sis-ter   do you love Je-sus? Yes in my soul I love him too— Oh! I'm

jes' from de founting, Oh! I'm jes' from de founting, Oh! I'm jes' from de founting, Dat never runs dry.

How grandly the voices rise and fall as this truly fine old hymn is sung by an enthusiastic congregation, swaying their dusky bodies in rhythmic motion.

AIN'T DAT LOVELY?

Vivace.

Ain't dat love-ly? Ain't dat lovely? Ain't dat love-ly? See dem chillen all dress'd in white.

1st singer:
"I went down in de valley fer ter pray,
  An' I got so happy dat I stayed all day.
            CHORUS:
Ain't dat lovely? Ain't dat lovely? Ain't dat lovely?
See dem childring all dressed in white.
  "I want ter go ter heaben ter hab a good time,
  Eatin' of de bread an' drinkin' of de wine.
            CHORUS:
  "High up in heaben I'll take my seat,
  An' cast my cross at Jesus' feet."
            CHORUS:

Another, somewhat similar, runs:

"Eberybody's talkin' bout de good ole way,
  An' you'd better be prepared fer de jedgmint-
        day.' '

CHORUS:
Yes, go tell de news, Yes, go tell de news,
Yes, go tell de news, Tell de news till you die.

DAVID PLAY ON YOUR HARP.

  "Mary had one only son,
  De Romans an' de Jews dey had him hung,

  Dey hung him twixt de yearth an' sky,
  Fer sinners ter see how brave he did die.
            CHORUS:
  Little David, play on yer harp, hallelujah!
  Little David, play on yer harp, hallelujah!
"Stop, oh sinner, stop, don't run,
  Let me tell yer what de A'mighty's done,
  He tuck his son, had him crucified,
  An' stuck a spear right in his side."
            CHORUS:

KEEP YO' HOUSE CLEAN.

Andante.

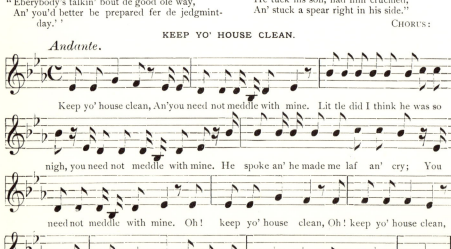

Keep yo' house clean, An' you need not meddle with mine. Lit tle did I think he was so

nigh, you need not meddle with mine. He spoke an' he made me laf an' cry; You

need not meddle with mine. Oh! keep yo' house clean, Oh! keep yo' house clean,

Oh! keep your house clean, An' you need not med-dle with mine.

* Fountain.

One song runs thus:

" Oh dying lamb, oh dying lamb, oh dying lamb,
Eberybody's welcome ter de dying lamb.

" Here a mother wants religion, yes, yes, religion,
Oh glory hallelujah, ter de dying lamb."

Here is a fragment that recalls the John Brown song:

" My body's bound fer ter moulder in de clay,
While my soul goes marchin', erelong,
Hard trials an' tribulations,
Oh, sinner, can't yer jine me,
While my soul goes a marchin' erelong."

A popular song is, " In de valley ":

These are two verses of a pleasing melody:

" Ole Satan's camped aroun' my house,
An's a stumblin' block in my way,
But Jesus is my bosom friend,
He moved it all away.   CHORUS:

Praise Jesus, hallelujah!
Love an' serve de Lord!   (Repeat.)

" De sun run down in a purple stream,
An' de moon hit bled ter death,
An' my soul awoke frum hits wicked dream,
When hit felt my Saviour's breath."

CHORUS:

IN DE VALLEY.

A CAMP-MEETING MELODY.

At the passage " an' its um-m-m," etc., each singer clasps his jaw and cheek in his hand and rocks backwards and forwards, mourning dismally as if suffering with an aggravated case of toothache. The effect is highly grotesque, as one may imagine.

WHO'S DAT A CALLIN'?

I'm boun' ter go ter heaven when I die
Who's dat a callin'?

I don't fear old Nick ner his wicked eye,
Who's dat callin' so low?

Here is a portion of a hymn which reminds one of a Chinese novel that runs into the hundred volumes, it is so lengthy ; indeed, I have never been able to learn just the number of verses which compose it :

" De Lord don't speak like a nat'ral man
He speaks so de heart can understan',
Rocks an' mountings fall on me,
Jesus he walked on de big salt sea.

REFRAIN :

Done tuck my Lord away, away, away, etc.

" An' Nora went ter work an' felt mighty vain,
When hit thundered an' lightened an' begin ter rain,
An' hit rained an' rained 'til de waves did rise
Till dey like ter clim ter de hebenly skies.

" De waters riz an' riz ter de sill o' de door,
An' de dancers moved ter de upper floor,
De water kep' a risin' an' riz all about
Till dey rushed ter de winders an' all peeped out.

" Dey seen ole man Nora come a floatin' by,
An' cried out dey wuz a goin' ter drown an die,
But Nora he felt hisse'f secure,
For he knowed de good Lord had done locked de door."

DONE TOOK MY LORD AWAY.

Done took my Lord a - way, a - way, a - way; Done took my Lord a - way! Can't ye tell me where ter find him?

" If yer wanter go ter heben when yer die,
Stop yer long tongue from tellin' a lie,
I've bin weighed an' weighed agin
An' I thank my Lord I'm free from sin.

REFRAIN :

" God A'mighty spoke an' Nora[1] understood,
He built him an ark out o' gopher wood,
He worked mighty hard on de heart an' bark,
A hundred an' forty years a buildin' de ark.

" God A'mighty spoke ter Nora again
An' said, ' Hurry up, git yo' fam'bly in.
An' take two erlong of ebery t'ing,
From dem as has a hoof ter dem as has a wing.

As I have written in the first of this sketch, it takes the ensemble — the torch-lit grove, the moving, exultant mass of dusky worshippers, the nasal, sonorous voices of these unlettered children of the sun — to give to such songs the full weirdness and wild beauty which they possess. When one has once heard these melodies under these favorable circumstances, it is something never to be forgotten.

[1]Noah

VIII

OLD PLANTATION HYMNS,
HYMNS OF THE SLAVE AND THE FREEDMAN
and
RECENT NEGRO MELODIES

William Eleazer Barton

[William Eleazer Barton was a young Congregational minister who taught school in Tennessee where he probably first came in contact with the songs he would later write about. He was at one time a member of the editorial staff of *The Youth's Companion* and the biographer of his relative Clara Barton. The following three articles appeared in the *New England Magazine* (December 1898, January 1899, and February 1899) and later in 1899 were gathered together for a book, *Old Plantation Hymns*.]

OLD PLANTATION HYMNS.

By William E. Barton, D. D.

ONE of the most genuine surprises ever given to lovers of music occurred in 1871, when a company of students from Fisk University started North, to earn money for that school by singing the plantation hymns of their parents. When Henry Ward Beecher admitted them to Plymouth Church, the papers had not a little to say in a joking way of "Beecher's Negro Minstrels." To the surprise of everybody, the moderate success for which the promoters of the scheme had hoped and the dismal failure which the beginnings of the enterprise prophesied were both forgotten in a most brilliant campaign upon both sides of the ocean, resulting in the building of Jubilee Hall and in the publication of the "Jubilee Songs," by voice and press, wherever the English language is known and even beyond. The story of these negro boys and girls singing their quaint, weird songs before crowned heads reads like a romance. The continued popularity of the airs then first introduced is attested by their use at all manner of occasions, from funerals to yachting parties, and their republication in all manner of books, from collections of Sunday School melodies to books of college songs. Whatever the critic may say about them,—and what he says is usually divided between praise and astonishment,— there is no denying their power. Many of us have seen great congregations swayed by them as a field of grain before the wind. Dvorak calls their tunes our only characteristic American music, and his suite based on their airs is well known. To critics and to common people they are alike enjoyable.

There is a good deal of danger that we shall not discover many of these songs not already familiar. The growing conditions among the negroes are unfavorable to the making of new songs, and the ground has been pretty well hunted over for the old ones. It would be a thing quite worth while to discover a new or old one as sweet as "Swing low, sweet chariot," or as quaint as "Turn back Pharaoh's army," or as pathetic and powerful as "Steal away." If anyone knows any such, he ought to see that they are preserved, both words and music.

It was the writer's privilege to live in the South from 1880 till 1887, and to come into contact with a good many kinds of people. During the earlier years especially he made careful records of most that interested him, and he supplemented these records as the years went by with whatever came in his way. One of the things which never was allowed to escape was an odd song, secular or religious; and wherever possible the quaint air as well as the words was written down at the time. These have waited for eleven years, and it is time that they were printed if they are to appear at all. It is possible that some have been printed already; but even if so, the variations will be of interest. The most of them, however, are probably new to almost all who will see them here, and many, I am confident, have never been printed or even written before.

Conspicuous among the religious songs of the colored people, as of the white people in the Cumberland Mountains, is the large group of "Family Songs," in which the chief or only variation in the successive stanzas is the substitution of "father," "mother," or other relative in order. One of the most unique of these is,

HOWDY, HOWDY!.

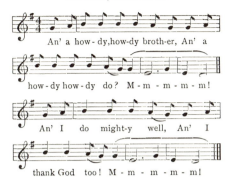

An' a how-dy, how-dy broth-er, An' a

how-dy how-dy do? M-m - m - m - m!

An' I do might-y well, An' I

thank God too! M-m - m - m - m!

This is the entire hymn, except that
it goes on to greet, and be greeted by,
the sisters, mothers, fathers, preachers
and mourners of the company. It is
a song for the opening of service;
and no type can indicate its warmth
and fervor. The "M-m-m-m-m" is a
humming sound with closed lips.
Any one who will close the lips and
hum this sound will discern something
of the perfectly delicious expression of
the joy of meeting.

There are several songs that tell
of going down in the valley to pray.
The valley seems to the colored Christian the proper place for all prayer
save that of ecstatic fervor; and that
fervor voices itself in song rather than
in prayer. Prayer, to the negro, was
so commonly associated with the
thought of trouble that often had no
other outlet, that all the drapery of the
valley seemed to fit its mental association. Sometimes he rose to sing,

"When I git up on de mountain top,
I'll shout an' shout and nebber stop."

Or,

"I'll praise de Lord an' nebber stop!"

but this shout or praise was either
song or hallelujah — it was not commonly prayer. One of these songs,
with a very pretty melody, is given
here.

The words are similar to those
of a song used by the Jubilee singers,
but the melody is different.

DOWN IN THE VALLEY TO PRAY.

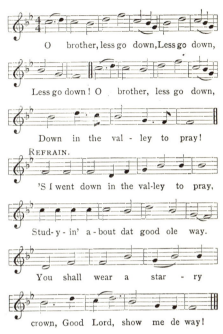

O brother, less go down, Less go down,

Less go down! O brother, less go down,

Down in the val - ley to pray!

REFRAIN.

'S I went down in the val-ley to pray,

Stud-y-in' a-bout dat good ole way.

You shall wear a star - ry

crown, Good Lord, show me de way!

This song does not usually follow
through the family in order, but, being
in the nature of an exhortation, ad-
dresses the "mourners," "sinners,"
"seekers," etc. The "mourners" of
these songs, it should be remembered,
are not necessarily those in affliction,
but those who frequent the "mourners'
bench" and have not yet "got
through." Some of these songs in-
form these mourners that,

"When I was a mourner just like you,
I prayed and prayed till I got through.

Not "till I got through mourning"
or praying, but till that necessary intermediate state, that limbo bordering
upon regeneration, was passed. A period of "mourning" is counted a pre-
requisite for conversion.

The music in this piece is very expressive. The word "down" has always a descending note, and in the
first and third lines covers three notes,
re, do, la; the word "pray" falls as it
were to its knees on the dominant below and is held for four beats.

So many of the negro songs are solemn and in 2:2 or 4:4 time, that when one trips along in 2:4 time with a lively step it is worth noticing. One of these, in which the Christian way is neither a struggle nor a climb, but a joyous progress with confident hope, and almost gleeful measure, is

GOIN' OVER ON DE UDDAH SIDE OF JORDAN.

The *b* flat in the fourth line is meant to suggest a slight variation of tone which cannot be written.

In this, as in many such songs, the melody turns back to the refrain almost before the stanza is completed, so that the held "O!" belongs almost as much to the end of one line as the beginning of the next. The stanzas then take up "my sister," "my mother," and other godly relatives, but "my Lord" is retained in each.

One of the most effective uses of syncopation which I have ever heard is in the song "Tell Bruddah 'Lijah!" or "No harm!" Brother Elijah is probably the prophet, for there is no human character in the Bible too great to be counted a "brother," and some of the allusions to "Brer Jonah" and "Brer Simon Peter" are as unexpected as can well be imagined.

In this hymn the explosive stress upon the word "Sinnah" is startling; and the question, "Ain' you tired of sinnin'?" is wonderfully direct.

TELL BRUDDAH LIJAH.

2—O mourner!
   Ain' you tired ob mournin'?
   Lay down your load ob hell
   An' come along to Jesus!

3—O Christian!
   Ain' you tired ob prayin'?
   I've laid down my load ob hell
   An' come along to Jesus!

4—O preachers!
   Ain' you tired ob shoutin'?
   I've laid down my load of hell
   An' walk de road wid Jesus!

A corrupted version of a Jubilee song is familiar to many people, called "Sooner in de Morning." It should not be "sooner," but "soon," or early. Another song with the same burden, but very different tune, I have often heard in meetings of colored people. There is a marked contrast between the two parts of its melody, the refrain keeping the middle registers, and the verses swinging much lower, beginning an octave below the first part, about middle C. It is a major melody, and moves almost entirely in thirds. The few intermediate tones are quite as likely to be accidentals as to take other notes of the diatonic scale: indeed, the negro rarely sings the seventh note true, to a musical instrument, but generally flats it more or less as in the minor scales. Fondness for these slightly variable tones suggests a reason for the negro's love of a banjo or violin.

SOON IN DE MORNING.

REFRAIN.

I'm goin' up home soon in de morn - ing,
D.C. *O yon - dah stands de two tall an - gels,*

goin' up home soon in de morn - ing,
yon - dah stands de two tall an - gels,

I'm goin' up home soon in de
O yon - dah stands de two tall

FINE.

morn - ing, I'm goin' to live with God.
an - gels, I'm goin' to live with God.

I dun-no what my brother wants to stay here

for! Stay here for! Stay here for! I

dun - no what my broth - er wants to

D.C.

stay here for! I'm goin' to live with God!

2—I dunno what the sinner wants to stay
here for, etc.

3—I dunno what the preacher wants to stay
here for, etc.

4—I dunno what the deacons want to stay
here for, etc.

This song is quite in line with the
view of the world which most of these
hymns present. The world is a wilderness; the Christian has a hard time;
and heaven is his home. The thought
comes out in "Mighty Rocky Road."
It is a melody in 2:4 time, and trips
along over the rocks very lightly,
rising a full octave at a flight at the
thought of being "most done trabbelin'." It is an excellent illustration of
the way in which the twin birth of
these words and notes fitted them to
each other.

MIGHTY ROCKY ROAD.

1. Hit's a mighty rocky road, an' I'm mos' done

trabbelin', Mighty rocky road, an' I'm mos' done

trabbelin', Mighty rocky road, an' I'm mos' done

trab-belin'. I'se bound to ker-ry my soul to

Je-sus, Bound to ker-ry my soul to de Lord.

1—Christian's on de road, an' he's mos'
done trabbelin', etc.

2—Mourner's on de road, an' he's mos'
done trabbelin', etc.

3—Sinner's on de road, an' he's a long time
trabbelin', etc.

4—Dis a rough, rocky road, an' I'm mos'
done trabbelin', etc.

The tune to the last song has a
swing not unlike the war-time melody,

"Great big brick house, an' nobody libin'
in't,
Nobody libin in't, nobody libin' in't,
Great big brick house, an' nobody libin'
in't,
Down in Alabam,"

to which air are sung words whence a
popular college song borrows the
lines,

"Hain't I glad to git out de wilderness,
Leaning on de Lamb."

It was in Alabama, by the way,
that I got the song, "New Born
Again," whose rising and syncopated
"Free grace, free grace, free grace,
Sinner," make the grace more ample
with each repetition. It has a certain
dignity combined with light joyous-
ness which our Gospel Hymns often
strive for in vain. Indeed, there are
several things for us to learn from
these songs.

NEW BORN AGAIN.

Hal - le - lu - jah! Hal - le - lu - jah!
New-born a - gain. Been a long time
talk-in',Bout a start - in' on de way.
Free grace! Free grace! Free grace, sin - ner!

2—Free grace! free grace! free grace, brother!

3—Free grace! free grace! free grace, sister!

4—Free grace! free grace! free grace, mourner!

Another song represents the journey through life in another way. It is not a two-step nor a gay procession, but a solemn yet confident march. It is in stately 4:4 time, and has the suggestion of a quiet but effective drumbeat on its accented notes.

WALK THROUGH THE VALLEY IN PEACE.

REFRAIN.We will walk thro' the val - ley in
1. Brothers,we'll walk thro' the val - ley, etc.
peace,come a - long,We will walk thro' the
val - ley in peace. If Je - sus Himself be our - er then, we will
walk thro' the val - ley in peace.

2—Sisters, we'll walk through the valley, etc.

3—Peter done walked on the water, etc.

4—Daniel done walked through the lion's den, etc.

At a meeting which I used to attend frequently, one of the leading singers was Sister Bemaugh, who often started the tune. One night there came from another settlement a famous singer, a man, who quite usurped Sister Bemaugh's place. There was no denying that she felt it, as he stood up before the congregation whenever a hymn was called for, in a most comfortable frame of mind, his head turned well to the left and the thumb and finger of his right hand holding the tip of his left ear, as he sang song after song. Many of the songs were new to the congregation, and were sung as solos, and he liked them none the less on that account. Several times Sister Bemaugh attempted to start a song; but each time he was ahead of her. At first she joined in the singing; but at length, discouraged and displeased, she gave it up and sat silent. The meeting held late, and Sister Bemaugh, who usually stayed to the very end, prepared to go. She got her lantern, which she had left in one of the front corners, and was somewhat ostentatiously lighting a match, when a hymn was called for, — and the visiting brother could think of none. It was Sister Bemaugh's opportunity. She quickly lighted and turned down the wick, and began to sing, "My good old Auntie's gone along"; and all the congregation fell in with her. I can see her now, as in the dimly lighted tobacco barn where the meeting was held she stood holding her lantern and singing. She was slender and had high cheek bones, but her face was pleasant, and her voice had a certain soul-quality, with a ring of satisfaction. Almost every other note in the song is chromatic, and it is no small task to sing it well; but Sister Bemaugh sang it to perfection, standing and leading, as a woman does not commonly do, — and having sung it to the end, she went along.

If the reader will pick out the notes of this song on the piano, and then sing it, swaying slowly, I think he will like it.

GONE ALONG.

1. My good old aun - tie's gone a -
long, She's gone a - long, She's gone a -
long, My good old aun - tie's gone a -
long, Gone across bold Jor-dan's stream.

REFRAIN.

Thank God, she's got re - li-gion, I do be -
lieve, I do be - lieve, I do believe. Thank
God, she's got re - li - gion, I do be -
lieve, Gone a - cross bold Jor-dan's stream.

2—My good old mother's gone along.

3—My good old father's gone along.

4—My good old brother's gone along.

5—My good old sister's gone along.

No classification of negro hymns is entirely satisfactory; but a very large class is made up of a refrain to which is sung a series of verses in variable order, often having no special relation to the refrain. Many of them are used with scores of different songs, and never twice in the same order. Some present a slight variation in the refrain, but have a uniform response. Of these I have a large number. One very rare one, and one that I count among the best, is "Cold Icy Hand." The burden of the song is the response, "Death goner lay his cold icy hand on me." An indescribable effect is given to the "cold icy hand" by a syncopation. The word "cold" has the accent of the downward beat, and the first syllable of "icy" takes a half note in the middle of the measure. The surprise of the shock which this gives to the nerves, together with the weird tune which prepares one for any uncanny effect, is not unlike the touch of a cold hand. The effect is not less uncanny in the third line of the refrain, in an accidental flat or natural given to the word "cryin'." It is a wail like that of a lost soul.

COLD, ICY HAND.

1. O sin - ner! Sin-ner! you bet-ter pray!
Or your soul be lost-at de jedg-ment day!

Death goner lay his cold, i - cy hand on me!
Death goner lay his cold, i - cy hand on me!

REFRAIN.

Cry - in', O Lord! Cry - in', O my
Lord! Cry-in', O Lord, Death goner lay his
cold, i - cy hand on me.

2—O, sinner, you be careful how you walk on de cross,—
Or your foot may slip an' you' soul be los'.

In all these hymns the notes must adjust themselves to variations in meter. The words of successive stanzas vary in length, and the notes must be varied also. In writing the notes one has to compromise. In singing, they must be adjusted to the different verses, as:

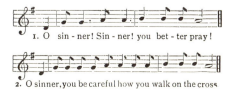

1. O sin - ner! Sin - ner! you bet - ter pray!

2. O sinner, you be careful how you walk on the cross

The foregoing song uses principally stanzas that have reference to death, and contain a warning; but among a great collection of them there is no certain order. Several hymns in common use furnish couplets for this purpose, — most of all, "Jesus my all to heaven is gone." Other hymns are used. I have the music — strikingly like that of one of our college songs — of one hymn which uses half a stanza of "Am I a soldier of the cross?" and it is quite effective used in this way, with the question of the first half unanswered. It is one of the few negro hymns which requires a bass clef. The body of the hymn is sung in unison — the response being sung in bass and all accordant parts.

In the published Jubilee songs, the harmony has been added for piano and quartette; but it is rarely found in negro songs.

SOLDIER OF THE CROSS.

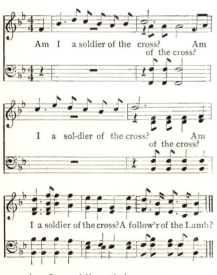

1—Am I a soldier of the cross,
    A follower of the Lamb?

2—Must I be carried to the skies
    On flowery beds of ease?

3—Are there no foes for me to face,
    Must I not stem the flood?

4—Sure I must fight if I would reign,
    Increase my courage, Lord.

In this particular song there is no refrain, the lines being repeated several times to make up a stanza out of half of one. Another hymn, which is sung also by the white people of the Cumberland Mountains, takes the hymn "Did Christ o'er sinners weep," and fits to its stanzas a refrain:

"This world is not my home,
This world is not my home;
This world's a howling wilderness
This world is not my home."

THIS WORLD IS NOT MY HOME.

2—The Son of God in tears
    The wondering angels see.
Be thou astonished, O my soul,
He shed those drops for thee.

The melody above is smooth, flowing and restful, and while sad is not hopeless. It sounds well with the words to which it is wedded.

I have one song which starts in with an introduction which has little to do either in words or music with what follows and which belongs only to the opening stanza, or rather to the first use of the refrain. It is not unlike the recitative which precedes a formal movement, and with change of tempo.

HEAVEN BELLS RINGIN' IN MY SOUL.

No-bod-y knows who I am, . .

who I be till de com-in' day.

REFRAIN. (*Twice as fast.*)

O de heav'n bells ring-in'! De sing-sol-

sing-in'! Heav'n bells a-ringin' in my soul!

Gwine a-way to see my Je-sus,

Gwine a-way to see my Lord.

O de heav'n bells ring-in'! De sing-sol

sing-in'! Heav'n bells a-ring-in' in my soul!

1. { Walked a-round from door to door,
   { What to do I did not know,

Heav'n bells a-ring'-in' in my soul!
Heav'n bells a-ring'-in' in my soul!

2—I'm a-comin' to de Lord, I'm a-comin'
   up too,
   Heaven bells ringin' in my soul;
   I'm comin' to de Lord till heaven I view,
   Heaven bells ringin' in my soul.

3—Heaven is a high an' a lofty place,
   Heaven bells ringin' in my soul;
   But you can't git dar ef you hain't got
   grace,
   Heaven bells ringin' in my soul.

Some of these refrains are litttle
more than reiterated ejaculations, the
monotony of which is somewhat relieved by the variable character of the
couplets which make up the stanzas.

SWEET HEAVEN.

Oh, sweet heav-en! Oh, sweet heav-en!

O sweet heav-en! But how I long to be there.

1. { Some people think that I have no grace, But
   { I'll see my Sav-iour face to face; Lord,

D.C.

how I long to be there.
how I long to be there.

2—I have a right to the tree of life,
   And how I long to be there!
   With them that fought my Jesus' fight,
   And how I long to be there!

3—The grace of God do reign so sweet,
   And how I long to be there!
   It spread abroad, both home and abroad,
   Lord, how I long to be there!

4—The tallest tree in paradise,
   Lord, how I long to be there!
   The Christian calls it the tree of life,
   O, how I long to be there!

5—If you get there before I do,
   O, how I long to be there!
   Look out for me, I'm coming too,
   O, how I long to be there!

In much of our modern preaching
the emphasis has shifted from the life
to come to that which now is; and
sometimes good advice about diet and
hygiene, and of righteousness as tend-
ing to longevity hold the place once
given to immortality. It is not so in
plantation theology. The thought of
heaven is constantly to the fore.

The resurrection is a favorite theme
in these songs, and its figures are well
supplied by Ezekiel's vision. Among
them is one that is very simple in its
movement, starting with plain quarter
notes in 4:4 movement, but growing
irregular in the refrain, and using with
effect a syncopation on, "An' a Lawd,"
and bringing in a strong upward swing
on the long first syllable of "mawn-
in'."

DESE DRY BONES OF MINE.

1. What kind of shoes is dem you wear?
   Dat you may walk up-on de air,

Come to-ged-der in de mawn-in'.
Come to-ged-der in de mawn-in'.

REFRAIN.

An' a Lawd, dese dry bones of mine. .

Shall come to-ged-der in de mawn-in'.

2—If you get dah befo' I do,
  Come togeddah in de mawnin'!
  Look out for me, I'm comin' too,
  Come togeddah in de mawnin'!

The ease with which this rising is to be accomplished in the world to come, has its contrast in a song of rising in the present life. Here Satan appears, and is a familiar figure in negro songs. It is to be noted that while he is a very real and terrible personage, there is always a lively, almost mirthful suggestion in the mention of his name. The melody of this song could not be wedded to a very serious line of thought. The singers appear to feel little troubled over Satan's easy advantage, but cheerfully throw upon him the responsibility for the difficulty of their earthly rising.

The personality of Satan is, therefore, at once a terror and a source of enjoyment to the negro. The place he holds in negro theology is not unlike that which he occupied in the miracle plays of the middle ages.

There seems an inherent tendency to insincerity in negro demonology. Satan is a decided convenience. It is always possible to load upon him what else must be a weight upon the conscience. That Satan holds the sinner responsible for this has its compensation again in the fact that Satan himself is to be dethroned.

HARD TO RISE AGAIN.

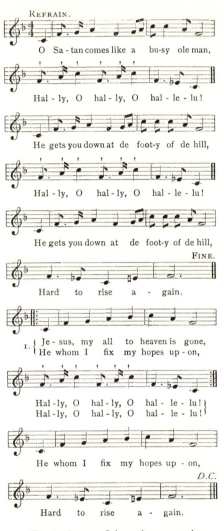

REFRAIN.

O Sa-tan comes like a bu-sy ole man,

Hal-ly, O hal-ly, O hal-le-lu!

He gets you down at de foot-y of de hill,

Hal-ly, O hal-ly, O hal-le-lu!

He gets you down at de foot-y of de hill,

FINE.

Hard to rise a-gain.

1. { Je-sus, my all to heaven is gone,
     He whom I fix my hopes up-on,

Hal-ly, O hal-ly, O hal-le-lu! }
Hal-ly, O hal-ly, O hal-le-lu! }

He whom I fix my hopes up-on,

D.C.

Hard to rise a-gain.

2—Dis is de way I long have sought
  Hard to rise again!
  And mourned because I found it not
  Hard to rise again!

3—De debbil is a liar and a conjurer, too,
  An' ef you don't mind he'll conjure you.

4—Oh, Satan he's a snake in de grass,
  An' ef you don't mind, he'll git you at last.

One song is satisfied to snatch a single line from any convenient hymn, and pair it with one of its own in the refrain, while borrowing couplets right and left for the stanzas.

I WANT TO DIE A-SHOUTING.

2—Am I a soldier of the cross?
   I want to die a-shouting!
 I want to feel my Saviour near,
   When soul and body's parting.
 Must Jesus bear the cross alone?
   I want to die a-shouting!
 No, there's a cross for every one,
   I want to die a-shouting!

3—Oh, Jesus loves the sinner-man,
   I want to die a-shouting!
 I want to feel my Saviour near,
   When soul and body's parting.
 I'm sometimes up and sometimes down,
   I want to die a-shouting!
 But still my soul is Canaan bound,
   I want to die a-shouting!

4—Oh, sinners, turn, why will ye die?
   I want to die a-shouting!
 I want to feel my Saviour near,
   When soul and body's parting.
 Then here's my heart and here's my hand,
   I want to die a-shouting!
 To meet you in the glory land,
   I want to die a-shouting!

While the fitting together of couplets and refrains almost at random leads to some odd and incongruous combinations, upon the whole one is surprised to find with what good taste the mosaic is made, especially when the singing is led by an old-time leader with a wide range of couplets to choose from. Some of these men when confronted by an inquirer with note book and pencil can hardly recall half a dozen of these stanzas; but in the fervor of their worship they not only remember them by the score, but by a sort of instinct rather than taste or judgment fit together words from different sources without a second's reflection or hesitation. It comes to pass sometimes that the words of a certain hymn attach themselves to a given refrain so that one rarely hears them separately. Here is one which I do not remember to have heard except with "Jerusalem, my happy home."

COMFORT IN HEAVEN.

While a majority of the negro melodies are in minor keys, the use of the major is far from being unusual, and is often very striking. A song called "Wake up, children" is of this character. It is impossible to imagine a more appropriate musical setting for the opening words, or a clearer, heartier call to awaken.

WAKE UP, CHILDREN.

O wake up, chil-dren, wake up! O a-
rise! O wake up, chil-dren,
wake up! And I will serve that liv-ing God.

1. { Old Sa-tan tho't he had me fast, And I
{ But thank the Lord, I'm free at last, And I

will serve that liv-ing God.

2—Old Satan wears de hypocrite's shoe,
  And I will serve that living God!
And if you don't mind he'll slip it onto you,
  And I will serve that living God!

The joys of heaven, prominent
among which is its music, afford material for several songs.

I WANT TO GO WHERE JESUS IS.

I want to go where Je-sus is, To
play up-on the gol-den harp,
To play up-on the gol-den harp, . . .
To play up-on the gol-den harp.

1. { Je-sus, my all, to heav'n is gone, To
{ He whom I fix my hopes up-on, To

play up-on the gol-den harp.

A good, ringing, hortatory hymn is
entitled

COME ALONG.

Come a-long, come a-long, I am
sor-ry for to leave you,
On the road to heav-en, come,
friends, will you go? I was but
young when I be-gun, And
now my race is near-ly run.

A cheerful song, with a strong
major melody is "Down by the River."
The Baptists use it at immersion; but
it is not confined to such occasions.

DOWN BY THE RIVER.

Yes, we'll gain this world, Down by the riv-er,
We'll gain this world, Down by the riv-er-side.
1. And if those mourner's would be-lieve,
Down by the riv-er, The gift of life they
would re-ceive, Down by the riv-er-side.

2—When I was a mourner, just like you,
I mourned and mourned till I got through.

Many songs have a line three times repeated, with a fourth but little changed, and thus build a song out of meagre material; but the tunes are usually distinct. A very good one of this sort, and with a good tune, is

THE WINTER SOON BE OVER.

2—Oh, may I tell to sinners round
What a Saviour I have found.

3—Oh, may I tell to sisters all,
Stop your tongue from telling lies.

4—Sing glory, glory, glory to the Lamb,
I have held his bleeding hand.

I used sometimes to preach in a little church built by the colored people, the result of no small sacrifice and hard work. Besides the long Sunday services, held on stated Sundays once a month and whenever they had a preacher, they had innumerable night meetings at "early candle-lighting." For a bell they had a discarded circular saw from the saw mill, fastened to a tree before the door; and when I came in Uncle Joe would say: "Here comes Mistah Bahton now; I'll go out an' knock on de saw." The saw was a very good church bell, and brought the people straggling in from all about. We would spend some time singing while they gathered. The young people wanted book hymns, and had their way in part; but the older people were pleased that I liked the others, and I got many of them in written form. One that was often sung in those meetings was "Pray On." It is a hymn with a fixed refrain and variable stanzas, and is also a family hymn.

PRAY ON.

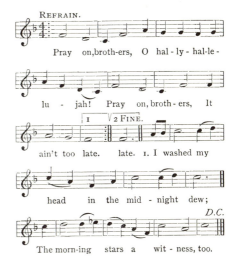

2—If you get there before I do,
Just tell them I am coming too.

3—There grows a tree in Paradise,
The Christian calls it the tree of life.

There was a great revival in the tobacco barn, and the meetings continued late into the night. They were late in beginning, for those who attended were working people, and the "early candle lighting" proved very late for a start. However, those who came first sang, and there was something going on some nights from dusk till nearly daylight; for on the evenings when there was a good benchful of tough old "mourners" who had been there once a year or so for a long time, there was a siege. The faithful called it "marching round Jericho," when, clearing the benches away, they marched round and round the mourners' bench singing and stopping at intervals for prayer or to shout out, "Believe, mourners!" Thomas Hughes, the genial author of "Tom Brown," was making his last visit to this country at the time, and had never been at such a meeting. He made me a brief visit, and I took him there. He was a reverent and interested spectator, seeing the real spirit of worship that underlay some of the odd proceedings, and also having an eye to all that was new to him in the situation.

During this long revival, which lasted a good many weeks, a bright young lady lay dying of consumption in the large house on the hill. As she lay at night near her open window she enjoyed hearing the colored people sing, and there was one hymn that touched her heart with its sweetness and pathos. As she felt her own time "drawing near" and began to listen for the "charming bells," this hymn grew more dear to her; and as the colored people came to know that she cared for it, they grew accustomed to singing it each night, with all its stanzas, for her benefit.

Night after night I heard this song, —an invitation to the sinner, a glad anticipation of heaven, and a salute from the humble but kind hearted worshipers as they closed their meeting in the tobacco barn, to the dying girl in the big house on the hill, who listened nightly for this greeting.

DEM CHARMING BELLS.

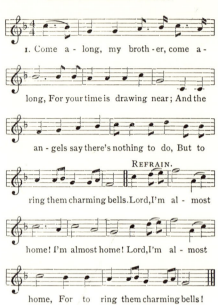

1. Come a - long, my broth - er, come a - long, For your time is drawing near; And the an - gels say there's nothing to do, But to ring them charming bells. Lord, I'm al - most home! I'm almost home! Lord, I'm al - most home, For to ring them charming bells!

2—Come along, my sister, etc.

3—Come along, my preacher, etc.

4—Come along, my deacon, etc.

5—Come along, po' mourner, etc.

6—Come along, O sinner, etc.

7—Come along, Sister Mary, etc.

8—Come along, Sister Martha, etc.

9—Come along, Brother 'Lijah, etc.

10—Come along, true believer, etc.

As cold weather came on, she passed away, and we sent her body to the Northern home whence she had come too late. We had a simple little service in the chapel, and a company of the colored people sang the clear, bell-like notes of the song, which ever since has seemed to me most beautiful, wth its ringing, confident, hopeful and inspiring words,—

"Lord, I'm almost home,
I'm almost home!
Lord, I'm almost home,
For to ring dem charming bells."

The negro hymns seldom make allusion to the Bible as a source of inspiration. They prefer "heart religion" to "book religion." In some places where an ordinary hymn would strengthen assurance by a promise of God in Holy Scripture, the negro appeals to his own revelation from the Lord. The following hymn is an illustration:

WE'RE SOME OF THE PRAYING PEOPLE.

I have another Alabama hymn which, like the above, is made up of a threefold repetition and a concluding line.

The melody of this hymn starts in a way that reminds us of the Gospel Hymn, but when we come to the refrain we find the familiar swing and syncopation of the negro.

WEAR A STARRY CROWN.

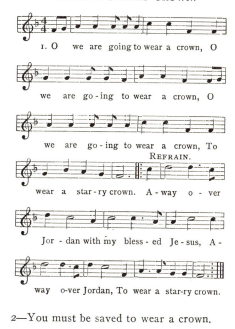

2—You must be saved to wear a crown.

3—You must live right to wear a crown.

4—My mother's gone to wear a crown.

5—My father's gone to wear a crown.

6—The sinner hain't agoin' to wear a crown.

These hymns are fairly representative of a once numerous, but now vanishing class. Some are commonplace enough, both in words and music. But others glow with genuine religious fervor, and afford valuable material for a study of the social and religious life of the negro, besides being an important contribution to American folk lore.

NOTE. Dr. Barton will contribute further articles, with a large number of hitherto unpublished songs, to the next two numbers of the *New England Magazine*. He will be glad to receive and preserve any additional unpublished songs from readers of these articles.—EDITOR.

HYMNS OF THE SLAVE AND THE FREEDMAN.

By William E. Barton, D. D.

I BEGAN my quest for quaint hymns when I was a school teacher, and was neither confined to a single place of worship nor prohibited by the responsibilities of my position from taking notes during service. After I began to preach I had more opportunities; but my field was somewhat restricted, and I was less sensitive to peculiarities which had impressed me in the earlier years of my residence in the South. I partially made my opportunities good, however, by visiting the older people who knew old songs, and writing these down as they sang them. One of my best friends in this regard was Aunt Dinah. It was from her I learned "Death's goner lay his cold icy hand on me;" and I fear that I could never have written it down had I not learned it from some one who would patiently repeat it again and again till I mastered its wonderful syncopations.

It is a peculiarity of the negro music that it can nearly all be swayed to and timed with the patting of the foot. No matter how irregular it appears to be, one who sways backward and forward and pats his foot finds the rhythm perfect. A young lady friend of mine was trying to learn some of the melodies from an old auntie, but found that the time as well as the tune baffled her. At length, when the old woman had turned to her work, the girl got to swaying and humming gently, patting her foot the while. The old woman turned and, patting the girl on the knee, said: "Dat's right, honey! Dat's de berry way! Now you's a-gittin' it, sho nuff! You'll nebbah larn 'em in de wuld till you sings dem in de sperrit!"

Now and then I would go to Aunt Dinah's cabin, and ask her for more songs. She invariably began by declaring that I had long since learned all the songs she knew; but I would plead with her to cudgel her brains for some of the old ones, the ones they sang before the war. After the requisite amount of protesting, she would promise to think and see if she could remember any, but with the declaration that it was hopeless. "I'll go to de do' an' call Sistah Bemaugh," she would say, "an' we'll see ef we can't find some. An' while she's a-comin' ober, you se' down dah, an' I'll finish dis shirt."

I was fortunate to find her ironing, and wise enough not to propose songs if she were at the washtub. It was near a furlong across the hollow to Sister Bemaugh, and there was a sawmill between; but Aunt Dinah and Sister Bemaugh had no trouble about making themselves understood at this distance, and about the time Aunt Dinah had finished the shirt and set her irons down before the open fire, Sister Bemaugh was on hand. Then they both protested that they had sung me every song they knew, —and they invariably found one or two more. One of these songs was "Motherless Child," or "I feel like I'd never been borned." It is one of the most pathetic songs I ever heard.

Not very long ago I attended a concert given by a troupe of jubilee singers, whose leader was a member of the original Fisk company. Toward the end of the programme he announced that a recently arrived singer in his troupe from Mississippi had brought a song that her grandparents sang in slave times, which he counted the saddest and most beautiful of the songs of slavery. It was a mutilated version of Aunt Dinah's song; and it lacked the climax of the hymn as I have it,—the "Gi' down on my knees and pray, PRAY!" The swell on these words is indescribable. Its effect is almost physical. From the utter dejection of the first part it rises with a sustained, clear faith. It expresses more than the sorrows of slavery; it has also the deep religious nature of the slave, and the consolations afforded him in faith and prayer.

Sister Bemaugh did not know this song. Aunt Dinah explained it to her, as she learned it with me, and I wrote down many scraps of their conversation while they thought I was only writing down the hymn; and sometimes they talked for quite a while undisturbed by my presence, as I sat at the ironing-table beating out the tunes which they had sung. Said Aunt Dinah,—I copy from the margin of my score:

"You des' gotter staht dat song in a mourn. Dey hain't no uddah way to git de hang ub it. Fus' time I hear it, I wis' de Lawd I cud lun it. I tried an' tried, an' couldn't. I went home studyin' it, an' all to once it come a-ringin' through me. Den I sung it all night."

The stanzas are double, and the two halves are sung to the same tune.

MOTHERLESS CHILD.

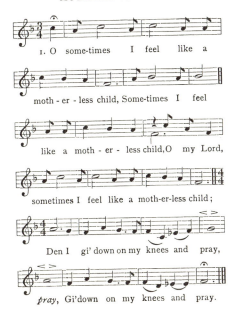

1. O some-times I feel like a moth-er-less child, Some-times I feel like a moth-er-less child, O my Lord, sometimes I feel like a moth-er-less child.

Den I gi' down on my knees and pray, pray, Gi'down on my knees and pray.

1—O, sometimes I feel like a motherless child!
Sometimes I feel like a motherless child!
O my Lord!
Sometimes I feel like a motherless child!
Den I git down on my knees and pray, pray!
Git down on my knees and pray!
O, I wonder where my mother's done gone,
Wonder where my mother's done gone,
I wonder where my mother's done gone.
Den I git down on my knees and pray, pray!
Git down on my knees and pray!

2—O, sometimes I feel like I'd never been borned,
Sometimes I feel like I'd never been borned,
O my Lord!
Sometimes I feel like I'd never been borned,
Den I git down on my knees and pray, pray!
Git down on my knees and pray!
O, I wonder where my baby's done gone,
Wonder where my baby's done gone,
Wonder where my baby's done gone.
Den I git down on my knees and pray, pray!
Git down on my knees and pray!

3—O, sometimes I feel like I'm a long ways from home, etc.
I wonder where my sister's done gone, etc.

4—Sometimes I feel like a home-e-less child, etc.
I wonder where de preacher's done gone, etc.

Sister Bemaugh had not sung so much in church since the visit of the singing brother during the revival, to which I referred in my previous article. Proud as she felt of the fact that they had had to call on her at the end to start a song, she felt sore about the prominence of the strange singing brother that one night, and my effort to learn from her some of the songs which he had sung was futile. They were "no 'count songs," anyway, she thought. While I was writing down another song, I overheard a conversation between her and Aunt Dinah, and wrote down a scrap of it, which

I quote verbatim from the corner of the sheet where I then wrote it.

Quoth Sister Bemaugh to Aunt Dinah: "Does you know why I doesn't sing in church no mo'? Dey hain't used to my voice."

To which Aunt Dinah replied: "Don' you wait for dat. You voice all right. You kin sing des' like a parrot."

Their conversation developed the fact that Aunt Dinah knew one of the most fetching songs which the visitor had sung, and she offered to sing it for me, taking pains to save Sister Bemaugh's feelings. It appeared later that Sister Bemaugh knew it also, though she would not sing it with him. She sang it with Aunt Dinah, however, when it was once started,— and I got it all. One of the quaint things about it is the expression, "Gwineter argue wid de Father and chatter wid de Son." I had often heard the expression, "Gwineter chatter wid de angels," in these songs, but this expression was new to me. "Argue," as here employed, does not mean dispute, but only to converse learnedly; and "chatter" does not imply frivolity, but only familiarity. The underlying theology has always seemed to me interesting.

I'LL BE THERE.

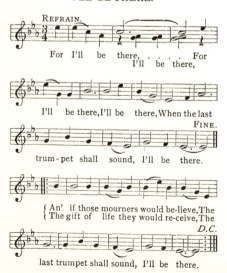

REFRAIN.

For I'll be there, ... For I'll be there,

I'll be there, I'll be there, When the last

FINE.

trum-pet shall sound, I'll be there.

{ An' if those mourners would be-lieve, The
{ The gift of life they would re-ceive, The

D.C.

last trumpet shall sound, I'll be there.

2—I never can forget the day
   When Jesus washed my sins away.

3—Gwine to argue wid de Father and
     chatter wid de Son,
   Gwine talk 'bout de bright world dey
     des' come from.

4—When Jesus shuck de manna tree,
   He shuck it for you, an' he shuck it for
     me.

5—De trumpet shall sound, an' de dead
     shall rise,
   And go to mansions in de skies.

6—Of all de folks I like de bes'
   I love de shouting Methodist.

Both Sister Bemaugh and Aunt Dinah agreed that the church to which they belonged was cold, and sometimes they had to provoke each other to love and good works in view of its depressing influence upon them. It never seemed cold when I was there, but they agreed that by the time meeting would get fairly to going here, their respective home churches would have been "all in a mourn." Aunt Dinah complained (I copy again from the margin of my score):

"Dis chu'ch powerful cold. It des' scrunches me. It's so indifferent from our home chu'ch. Sometimes I goes dah, an I feels de Sperrit, but I hangs my head and squenches it. I knows I'se changed from nature to grace, but when I goes dah, I don' feel like I'se gone to chu'ch. It ain't like it used to be wid me at home. De Sperrit has lifted me right up. I'se shouted dah much as I please, and sometimes I'se des' sot dah an' tickled myself, and den agin I've mighty nigh hugged Sistah Williams to death!"

To this Sister Bemaugh would respond: "When you feels de Sperrit, you mustn't squench him."

Perhaps the next time the complaint and exhortation would be reversed. Anyway, they agreed in their declaration that the church was not what it ought to be, and they sometimes grew almost ecstatic as they hummed and gossiped in the chimney corner while I wrote at the ironing table.

One of Aunt Dinah's hymns was "The heaven bells ringin' and I'm a-goin' home," which was sung to a ringing tune. It requires but little imagination to hear the ringing of bells to its "going, going home." I have heard the same words sung to another tune, but the ring of this one is remarkable.

HEAVEN BELLS RINGIN', AND I'M A-GOIN' HOME.

O de heav'n bells a-ring-in', and I'm a-go-in',go-in'home;De heav'n bells a-ring-in',and I'm a-go-in', go-in'home;De heaven bells a-ring-in',and I'm a-go-in', go-in' home, a-climb-in' up Zi-on's hill.

2—De heaven bells ringin', an' my mother's goin', goin' home, etc.

3—De heaven bells ringin', and my Jesus goin', goin' home, etc.

4—De heaven bells ringin', and de sinner's lost, he's lost a home, etc.

Another of Aunt Dinah's songs was "Mighty Day." The refrain is a four-fold repetition of the question, "O wasn't that a mighty day?"—but this is usually repeated so as to make eight repetitions. The verses follow more or less closely the events of the Apocalypse, and are of variable length.

In their fondness for eschatology, and the joy with which they antici-pate the day of judgment and dwell upon its terrific and sublime features, the hymns are a fair echo and anti-phon of the preaching which they ac-company.

MIGHTY DAY.

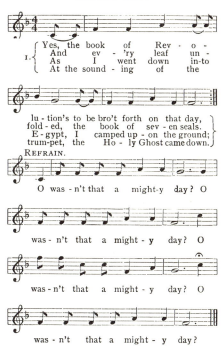

1. { Yes, the book of Rev - o - lu - tion's to be bro't forth on that day,
And ev - 'ry leaf un - fold - ed, the book of sev - en seals.
As I went down in - to E - gypt, I camped up - on the ground;
At the sound - ing of the trum-pet, the Ho - ly Ghost came down. }

REFRAIN.

O was-n't that a might-y day? O was-n't that a might-y day? O was-n't that a might-y day? O was-n't that a might-y day?

2—And when the seals was opened,
  The voice said, "Come and see,"
I went and stood a-looking
  To see the mystery.
The red horse came a-galloping,
  And the black horse he came, too,
And the pale horse he came down the road,
  And stole my father away.

Refrain.

3—And then I seen old Satan,
  And they bound him with a chain,
And they put him in the fi-ar,
  And I seen the smoke arising.
They bound him in the fi-ar,
  Where he wanted to take my soul,
Old Satan gnashed his teeth and howled,
  And missed po' sinner man's soul.

Refrain.

4—Then I see the dead arisin',
  And stand before the Lamb,
And the wicked calls on the mountains
  To hide them from His face.
And then I see the Christian
  A-standin' on the right hand of Jesus,
And a-shoutin' Hallelujah,
  Singin' praises to the Lamb.

5—I bless de Lord I'm goin' to die,
  I'm goin' to judgment by and by.

Another hymn which I heard both at Aunt Dinah's fireside and in meetings was "Anybody Here." Anyone who cares to sing it will recognize in the melody of the second half a strain so decidedly like the Scotch that he might well wed it to one of Burns's poems. The resemblance is apparent, not only in the slurring, hopping effect which almost matches that in "Within a Mile of Edinboro' Town," but also in the threefold repetition of the final tonic note.

ANYBODY HERE?

Is there an-y-bod-y here That loves my Je-sus? An-y-bod-y here that loves my Lord? O, I want to know if you love my Je-sus; I want to know if you love my Lord.

1. The an-gel's wings were tipp'd with gold, That bro't sal-va-tion to my soul.

2—What kind of shoes is them you wear,
That you may walk upon the air?

3—This world 's a wilderness of woe,
Let us all to glory go.

4—I do believe without a doubt
That a Christian has a right to shout.

5—Religion is a blooming rose,
As none but them that feels it knows.

6—You say you're aiming for the skies;
Why don't you stop your telling lies?

7—When every star refuse to shine,
I know King Jesus will be mine.

It was in connection with the song, "Rule Death in His Arms," that I heard Aunt Dinah tell her religious experience to Sister Bemaugh. She was only a little girl, she said, when the war broke out,—"jes' a watertoter." That was as nearly as she could estimate her age, that at the outbreak of hostilities she was large enough to "tote water" to the men in the field. Her uncle, she said, was taken with other slaves to erect fortifications in Virginia before the time when colored troops were allowed to enlist, and while at that work was shot. She saw him while he was dying, and said to him, "You'd better pray;" but he cursed her and said, "I done got past prayin';" and she added, "An' right den he died." She continued the narrative with a good deal of awe, but with no special exhibition of concern for her uncle. Said she: "Dat night I seed him. An' he was in dat ba-a-ad place! An' de debbil des' a-shovin' fire on him wid a pitch-fork! Yeas, ma'am! De debbil has got a pitch-fork! I seed him! An' one club foot! An' my uncle looked up an' seed me. An' I says, 'Aha! You'd orter prayed when I tole you!' An' he says, 'I wish de Lawd I had a-prayed!' Dat's what he said. Sesee, 'You needn't nebbah want to come heah!' An' I says, 'I hain't a-comin' dah, now you des' see!' An' den de ole debbil looked up, an' he says, 'Yes, an' I'm a-comin' to git you bime-by.' An' den I looked, an' I couldn't see what I was a-stannin' on, an' I was right over it. Mus' 'a' been de power of God dat kep' me from fallin' in. An' den I begun to pray. O, but I had a hard time a-gittin' through! I reckon de Lawd mos' made up His mind not to wash away my sins, 'cause I danced so much! But bime-by I learn dis song; and when I learn dat song, de Lawd spoke peace to my soul."

The song is a chant with very irregular lines and a refrain. The figure, "Rule death in his arms," is, I suppose, that of a parent subduing an unruly child. It is almost impossible to write this tune. Even the selection of a key is difficult. It runs an octave below its keynote, and while the range above is only five notes, it is common to sing the "sinner" verse an octave higher, thus covering two octaves and a third. The time, also, varies in the different stanzas, but with the same cadences. The value of this melody is almost wholly in the expression given to it. The notes alone are colorless.

RULE DEATH IN HIS ARMS.

1. When God command-ed Mi-chael in the morn-ing, To stretch at di-vid-ing line, With the sheep up-on his right hand side, And the goats up-on his left.
REFRAIN.
O did-n't Je-sus rule Death in His arms, Yes, rule Death in His arms, On the other side of Jordan, Ah! rule Death in His arms.

2—See the sinnah lyin' on his deathbed,
  An' a Death come a-steppin' in;
You heah the sinnah say to Death,
  "Let me pray God for my sin!"
An' you heah Death say to the sinnah,
  "You been heah long enough to pray
  God for you sin."

3—Yes, you heah Death say to the sinnah-
  man,
  "You been heah long enough to pray
  God for you sin."
God Almighty has sent me heah for
  you,
  An' I can't let you stay."

4—When God commanded Gabriel
  To blow the silver trumpet,
He called the living to judgment,
  And the dead come forth from the
  grave.

5—See the Christian lyin' on his death-
  bed,
  An' a Death come a-steppin' in;
You heah dat Christian say to Death,
  "O Death, you are welcome."

Sister Bemaugh and Aunt Dinah sang this over and over while I was writing it down, first for my benefit and then for their own enjoyment.

I have other songs which I learned from these two good old women, some of them used before and others to follow in this paper. The songs obtained from them were unadulterated by book-religion or any modern tinkering. Every quaver, every slur, every syncopation was there, and I took the greatest pains to write them as they gave them. There was one which they called "De Coffin to Bind Me Down." They made a very long song of it by using the verses again and again, the first line in one verse serving as the third in another, and coupled with a different companion. There were only four lines and the refrain, "De coffin to bind me down;" but out of these they made certainly four times four stanzas.

THE COFFIN TO BIND ME DOWN.

1. { De cof-fin, de cof-fin to bind me
     A fold-ing sheet up-on my
D.C. A sil-ver spade to dig my
                                    FINE.
down, De cof-fin to bind me down.
lips, De cof-fin to bind me down.
grave, De cof-fin to bind me down.
De cof-fin to bind me down, De
                                    D.C.
cof-fin to bind me down.

2—To dust, to dust, to dust we go,
   De coffin to bind me down!
   A golden chain to let me down,
   De coffin to bind me down!

De coffin to bind me down!
De coffin to bind me down!
A folding sheet upon my lips,
De coffin to bind me down!

Besides making a very respectable hymn out of a few lines, these two women could make a reasonably good tune out of three or four notes. I have heard them sing one which I could hardly believe had so small a compass till I came to write it and found that it was all covered by the first three notes of the scale, *do, re, mi.* Such a song is: "I don't want you go on and leave me." It is a pathetic little hymn.

The singer is toddling along with short and broken steps, trying to keep in sight of the Lord, and pleading not to be left behind.

The negroes have many hymns of the "Old Ship of Zion." The talented young southern poet, Irwin Russell, gave an exceedingly funny description of the ark as interpreted in the light of a negro's experience with a river steamer. Such anachronisms sometimes work themselves in perfect good faith into these hymns. But the hymn of this sort which I liked best was one which I learned from Aunt Dinah. The ring and swing of the refrain, "I'm no ways weary," are truly inspiring. I used frequently to hum it on my long mountain rides till there came some measure of relief from fatigue from its buoyant spirit.

I DON'T WANT YOU GO ON AND LEAVE ME.

THE OLD SHIP OF ZION.

2—She has landed many thousands, Hallelujah!

3—King Jesus is her captain, Hallejuh!

4—O, get your ticket ready, Hallelujah!

5—She is coming in the harbor, Hallelujah!

6—She will land you safe in heaven, Hallelujah!

7—She will never rock nor totter, Hallelujah!

Some of the old slave songs survive which had in them the bitterness of a sorrow that never spoke its intensity in plain words, but sought figures from the Bible or veiled its real meaning in inarticulate moans or songs of grief that never uttered the real nature of the sorrow. Yet every minor note was the wail of a broken heart, and every syncopation the snapping of a heartstring. One of these is called "Po' Me."

PO' ME!

2—Hallelujah once, hallelujah twice,
Trouble will bury me down!
De Lawd is on de giving hand,
Trouble will bury me down!

Refrain.

Why, sistering,
Po' me! Po' me!
Trouble will bury me down!
Po' me! Po' me!
Trouble will bury me down!

3—Sometimes I think I'm ready to drop,
Trouble will bury me down!
But, thank de Lawd, I do not stop,
Trouble will bury me down!

Refrain.

But, O my Lawd,
Po' me! Po' me!
Trouble will bury me down!
Po' me! Po' me!
Trouble will bury me down!

One of the most pathetic of all these songs, its minor strains the very acme of sorrow, is "Troubled in Mind." I think that it has been printed, but neither words nor music are as I have heard them.

TROUBLED IN MIND.

2—While I'se walkin' I am troubled,
All day!
I am troubled in mind.

3—O sinnah, I am troubled!
All day!
I am troubled in mind.

4—O my Jesus, I am troubled!
All day!
I am troubled in mind.

The direct references to slavery in the negro songs are surprisingly few. Probably few of the people had come to think of slavery itself as abnormal or of its hardships as justly chargeable to the system; and it is still more probable that the grief which they felt they were constrained to veil behind general lamentation without speaking plainly the sorrows which they regarded as inevitable.

It is noteworthy that these songs, however much they bewail the sorrows of slavery, contain no resentment. The only known exception, if it be an exception, is the joy over the fact that

"When Moses smote the water,
  The waters came together
And drowned old Pharaoh's army. Hallelu!"

The secular songs of freedom, "De Massa Run," "Babylon is Fallen," "Bobolishion's Comin' " and the rest, are tolerably familiar. But there is one hymn which I used often to hear which speaks the freedman's joy in his new manhood. I have heard it sung sometimes in the North by companies of educated jubilee singers, who introduce it with the lines,

"Holy Bible! Holy Bible!
Holy Bible, Book Divine, Book Divine!"

But I never heard these words sung as a verse of this or any native plantation hymn in the South. Their references to the Bible are few, and such as are given in the songs of this series, namely, allusions to well-known narrative portions of Scripture. The "Holy Bible" stanza was probably the addition of some "reading preacher." It is quite as appropriate, however, as those which are sung to the song in the South; for the freedman, preferring death to slavery, and singing his solemn joy in a strong and stirring strain, comforts himself in the thought of the possibility of death, with the details of the first-class funeral, in which he is to play the chief rôle. Such a funeral as is described in this hymn is, next to heaven, the desire of the average colored man even in a state of grace. But apart from all this, which may provoke a smile, there is something that thrills one in the words:

"Before I'd be a slave,
I'd be buried in my grave,
And go home to my Lord and be saved!"

BEFORE I'D BE A SLAVE.

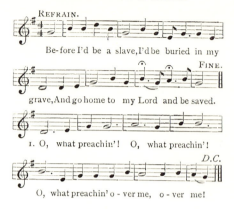

2—O, what mourning, etc.

3—O, what singing, etc.

4—O, what shouting, etc.

5—O, weeping Mary, etc.

6—Doubting Thomas, etc.

7—O, what sighing, etc.

As I write the words of this hymn I seem to hear old Uncle Joe Williams sing them. Slavery had not been unkind to him. He always hired his time from his master and made money enough to pay for his labor, and had a good start toward buying his wife and children when freedom came. But this is the hymn he loved to sing, sitting before his door in the twilight.

For the most part the war did little for negro song. The melodies which are most characteristic gain little from association with outside influences. But here and there we may trace in words or music a theme which the war suggested and which is worth noting. Choicest among these specimens is "Sinner, You'd Better Get Ready." In several ways it seems a departure from ordinary negro music, but it is quite characteristic. It is in triple time; it is major; and the melody of the refrain, which is its more important part, is entirely in thirds, unless we take account of the three notes before the last one, which as now sung make a slight variation, but which are easily changed to conform to the rule. As written, the lower notes are as sung; the upper harmony is as it would be played. With this slight change it can be played on a keyless bugle.

SINNER, YOU BETTER GET READY.

2—I looked at my hands, my hands was new;
I looked at my feet, my feet was, too.

3—My name's written in de book of life,
If you look in de book you'll find it there.

4—De good old chariot passing by,
She jarred the earth and shook the sky.

Another song that uses almost wholly the open notes is "Little David, Play on Your Harp." It is less like a bugle song than "Sinner, You Better Get Ready," but it is striking in its use of major thirds and fifths, the more so as, following the negro predilection for minor beginnings, this decidedly major tune starts on *la*. Its opening notes are, *la sol do mi do, la sol do, do do mi, do mi sol.*

LITTLE DAVID, PLAY ON YOUR HARP.

4—Peter walked upon the sea,
And Jesus told him, "Come to me."

5—Elijah slew the prophets of Baal;
The rain came down and did not fail.

6—If you belong to Gideon's band,
Then here's my heart and here's my hand.

7—They cast Brer Jonah overboard,
And a big whale swallowed Brer Jonah whole.

If the foregoing suggest a bugle, not less so do some others suggest the tap of the drum. There is no better example than one lately given me by Rev. George W. Moore, field missionary of the American Missionary Association, and husband of one of the original jubilee singers, whose voice still is often heard at annual meetings of that association. Anyone who will for a moment disregard the tones, and tap the notes or sing them in monotone with a rat-tat-a-tat, will see that the time of the song "I'm Goin' to Sing" is such as might well have been derived from the beat of an army drum.

I'M GOIN' TO SING.

O I'm goin' to sing, Goin' to

sing, Goin' to sing, Goin' to

sing all a - long my way.

O I'm goin' to sing, Goin' to

sing, Goin' to sing, Goin' to

FINE.

sing all a - long my way.

1. We want no cow-ards in our band, Who
2. Are there no foes for me to face, Must

will their col-ors fly; We call for val - iant
I not stem the flood? Is this vile world a

D.C.

heart - ed men Who're not a - fraid to die.
friend to grace, To help me on to God?

Some of these war songs are exceedingly simple in structure, often having only a single line that can be called a permanent part of the hymn. This is often repeated, sometimes shortened, and again lengthened by a hortatory ejaculation or a direct address; but the rest of the hymn is built up as occasion demands,—and in some cases the one line, or germ cell of the song, is found to vary greatly in different versions. Sometimes a single couplet attaches itself to the refrain in such a way as to be commonly recognized as the first stanza, but for the rest the song hunts about for couplets from "Jesus, My All," or other hymns with lines of the same length. Some of these, however, are rather effective.

STAY IN THE FIELD.

REFRAIN.

O stay in the field, chil-der-en-ah

Stay in the field, chil-der-en-ah,

FINE.

Stay in the field, Un-til the war is end-ed.

1. {I've got my breastplate, sword, and shield,
And I'll go march-ing thro' the field,

D.C.

Till the war is end - ed.

2—Satan thought he had me fast,
Till the war is ended;
But thank the Lord I'm free at last,
Till the war is ended.

No other couplet of this as I learned it has any military suggestion. The other verses used are such as are given in the songs with constant refrains and variable stanzas.

There are several simple songs that fit a military pledge of fealty to familiar words, with a simple but effective tune, as:

SOLDIER FOR JESUS.

REFRAIN.

1. I'm a sol - dier for Je - sus, En-

list - ed for the war, And I'll fight un -

FINE.

til I die. 1. Am . . I a

sol - dier of the cross, And

D.C.

shall I fear to own His cause.

2—This is the way I long have sought
  And mourned because I found it not.

3—I've got my breastplate, sword and shield,
  And I will die upon the field.

There are suggestions of enlistment in songs about joining the band. The allusions are generally indefinite, but such as might well come from a general suggestion of military figures adapted for use in worship.

GWINE TER JINE DE BAND.

3—Swing low, chariot, pillar in de East,
  All God's chillen gwine ter hab a little feast—ah!

4—Swing low, chariot, pillar in de West,
  All God's chillen gwine ter hab a little rest—ah!

—Swing low, chariot, pillar in the South,
  All God's chillen gwine ter hab a little shout—ah!

Each stanza of the above hymn ends with a euphonic Ah! which connects it with and merges into the refrain. A like syllable is used at the end of the second line of the refrain.

Now and then the word "Union," pronounced in three syllables, is added to the "band," and may indicate yet more plainly the army origin of some of these songs. One of these is:

STAND ON A SEA OF GLASS.

2—When Jesus shook the manna tree,—
  Stand on a sea of glass,
  He shook it for you and shook it for me,—
  Stand on a sea of glass,

3—Talles' tree in Paradise,—
  Stand on a sea of glass,
  Christian calls it de tree of life,—
  Stand on a sea of glass,

The negro pronunciation of "This Union" was said to be turned to good account by certain merchants living in the border states during the war, among whom a popular placard bore a picture of a contraband throwing up his hat and shouting, "Dis Union Forever!" The words were so spaced as to leave the phrase beautifully ambiguous, and it was explained as "This Union forever," or "Disunion forever," according to the exigencies of the occasion.

Another version, with a different tune, is found in a grouping of the "Union band" with that theme of perpetual interest and ecstatic contemplation, the big camp meeting in the promised land. There are many songs that dwell on the last of these, and some that combine the two.

BIG CAMP MEETING IN THE PROMISED LAND.

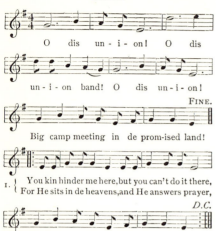

O dis un-i-on! O dis

un-i-on band! O dis un-i-on!

FINE.

Big camp meeting in de prom-ised land!

1. { You kin hinder me here, but you can't do it there,
For He sits in de heavens, and He answers prayer,

D.C.

Big camp meeting in de promised land!

2—I hain't got time for to stop an' talk,
De road is rough and it's hard to walk.

I have one song that seems to be made up from an army march tune and the two hymns, "All Hail the Power" and "Am I a Soldier of the Cross?"

CROWND HIM LORD OF ALL.

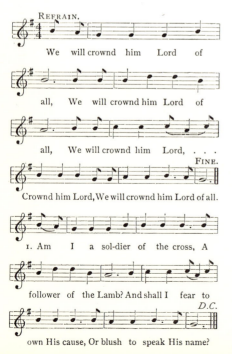

REFRAIN.

We will crownd him Lord of

all, We will crownd him Lord of

all, We will crownd him Lord, . . .

FINE.

Crownd him Lord, We will crownd him Lord of all.

1. Am I a sol-dier of the cross, A

follower of the Lamb? And shall I fear to

D.C.

own His cause, Or blush to speak His name?

One feature of army life impressed the negro deeply. It was the calling of the roll and the lining up of the men to answer to their names. It has its echoes in several hymns, some of which have been published; but the most striking one which I have ever heard I give below:

WHEN THAT GENERAL ROLL IS CALLED.

REFRAIN.

I'll be there in the morning, I'll be

there in the morn-ing, I'll be

there in the morn-ing, When that

gen-er-al roll is called, I'll be there, When that

gen-er-al roll is called, I'll be there.

1. Gwine to see my father, I'll be there; Gwine to

see my fa-ther, I'll be there; Gwine to there.

2—Goin' to see my mother, etc.

3—Goin' to see my sister, etc.

4—Goin' to see my brother, etc.

5—Goin' to see my Jesus, etc.

These are quite enough to illustrate the effect of the war upon the songs of the negro, and are the principal hymns of this kind which have come to my notice.

These retain, for the most part, the genuine negro characteristics, but illustrate the imitative bent of the negro mind, and manifest more or less distinctly outside influences.

There is an element of religious selfishness in some of these songs and a rejoicing in the relative exclusiveness of religion as the singers understand it. We have noticed it already in such couplets as:

"Wait till I get in the middle of the air,
There won't be nary sinner there."

It constitutes the burden of some songs. I do not know that it is more pronounced in these than in some more pretentious hymns. I hear quite often in evangelistic meetings a song of heaven in which, as I first heard it, the words were:

"I shall know Him, I shall know Him,
    And alone by His side I shall stand,
I shall know Him, I shall know Him,
    By the print of the nails in His hand."

Such songs are as open to criticism on the ground either of an unspiritual materialism or of a religious self-seeking as are any of the negro hymns. Recently, however, I have heard this one sung, "And *redeemed* by His side I shall stand," which eliminates one objectionable feature.

The hymn which I give as illustrating this characteristic is "I'm Going to Walk with Jesus by Myself." The tune is much the same as that of "Who Will Drive the Chariot When She Comes?" And this reminds me that many of these tunes that seem monotonously alike when written, have a much wider variety when sung to different words and with the *ad libitum* of the negro singer. In this the melodies are much like those of Scotland. Who ever would have known by ear alone that the tune of "I'm wearin' awa, John," is the very same as that of "Scots wha hae wi' Wallace bled"? And for that matter, who, knowing the pathetic sweetness of the one and the martial solemnity of the other, would have suspected that both these airs are simply the silly old ditty of "Hey, tuttie, tattie"? Even so these negro melodies are not to be too lightly scorned because of their monotony, which is often more apparent than real.

I'M GOIN' TO WALK WITH JESUS
BY MYSELF.

1. I am goin' to walk with Je-sus by my-
2. I'm goin' to talk with Je-sus by my-
3. I'm goin' to see King Je-sus by my-
4. I'm goin' to live with Je-sus by my-

self, by my-self, I am goin' to walk with
self, by my-self, I am goin' to talk with
self, by my-self, I am goin' to see King
self, by my-self, I am goin' to live with

Je - sus by my-self, by my-self, I'm
Je - sus by my-self, by my-self, I'm
Je - sus by my-self, by my-self, I'm
Je - sus by my-self, by my-self, I'm

goin' to walk with Je - sus, I'm
goin' to talk with Je - sus, I'm
goin' to see King Je - sus, I'm
goin' to live with Je - sus, I'm

goin' to walk with Je - sus, I'm
goin' to talk with Je - sus, I'm
goin' to see King Je - sus, I'm
goin' to live with Je - sus, I'm

goin' to walk with Je - sus by my-self.
goin' to talk with Je - sus by my-self.
goin' to see King Je - sus by my-self.
goin' to live with Je - sus by my-self.

A good many of the hymns of the colored people deal with ecstatic experiences; but most of them are sufficiently modest in their claims of regenerate character and of fruits meet for repentance. Now and then, however, there is a song whose singer professes to have received sanctification. It has been my privilege to know a number of people, white and black, who were thought by others to be sanctified in the sense in which that term is commonly (and incorrectly) used; but these people always denied it. On the other hand, I have known

a number of people who thought themselves to be sanctified, and in no case
could any one else be made to believe
it. However, here is the hymn, which
is rather a rare one of its sort.

It may be noted that while conversion implies a long struggle to "get
through," sanctification, as here interpreted, is not related to antecedent experience. It occurs simply while
"walking along."

DONE BEEN SANCTIFIED.

1—One day I'se walkin' along,
    The Lord done sanctified me.
One day I'se walkin' along,
    He sanctified my soul.
Mourner, behold de Lamb of God,
    The Lord done sanctified me.
He sanctified me, he'll sanctify you,
    He sanctified my soul.

2—I went to the valley to pray,
    The Lord done sanctified me;
I climbed to the mountain top,
    He sanctified my soul.
Sinner, behold de Lamb, etc.

3—Before I learned to pray,
    The Lord done sanctified me;
I'd trouble all the day,
    He sanctified my soul.
Brother, behold the Lamb of God, etc.

4—I'se lost and now I'm found,
    The Lord done sanctified me;
My soul is heaven bound,
    He sanctified my soul.
Preachers, behold the Lamb of God,
    etc.

A good old·hymn is "Don't you
want to go?" I count it one of the
gems of negro song.

DON'T YOU WANT TO GO?

Jordan and the sea furnish abundant figures for these songs; and the river applies equally well to baptism or to death. One of these songs is, "You can't cross here." It is a dialogue, and a warning to the sinner who will one day attempt to cross where he will not be able.

This brings us around again to the theme of the resurrection, which always suggests a song. This time it may as well be, "Dese bones gwine ter rise again." Sometimes family names are interjected before the third "I know," and varied.

YOU CAN'T CROSS HERE.

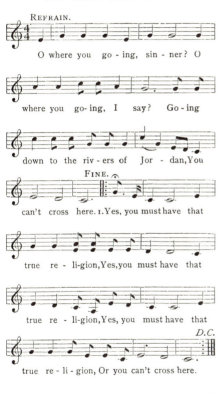

2—Lord, I'm so glad my soul's converted,
   Lord, I'm so glad my soul's converted,
   Lord, I'm so glad my soul's converted,
   You can't cross here.

3—I'm so glad my soul's converted,
   I'm so glad I've got religion;
   Yes, I'm going down to Jurdin,
   You can't cross here.

4—I'm so glad that Jesus loves me,
   I'm so glad I'm going to heaven,
   I'm so glad my soul's converted,
   You can't cross here.

THESE BONES GWINETER RISE AGAIN.

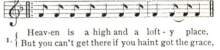

2—Little did I think dat he was so nigh;
   Dese bones gwineter rise again;
Spoke, and he made me laugh and cry;
   Dese bones gwineter rise again.

3—When Gabriel makes his trumpet sound,
De saints shall rise and bust de ground,

4—You kin hender me here, but you can't do it dah,
For he sits in de heavens and he answers prah,

With this good old hymn, I bring this paper to a close. It is a fitting one for a finale. It is irregular in its composition, but with a flowing metre and with phrases of equal length as measured, though wedded to lines of two, four, seven, ten and more syllables. It has the characteristic introductory refrain and the monotonous croon for the couplet and response. It has also the clear faith, the fondness for the supernatural and the joyous conception of the Christian life common to these songs.

Note. Dr. Barton's first paper was published in the New England Magazine for December, 1898. A third and final paper will appear in the February number. So large a collection of these songs has not, we believe, appeared outside the Fisk and Hampton collections, and the total is nearly equal to either of those books.—Editor.

RECENT NEGRO MELODIES.

By William E. Barton, D. D.

IN two previous articles I have given fifty-four old plantation hymns, including both those of unquestioned antiquity and those which show the influence of the war and the effects of newly found freedom. In the present paper I propose to consider some which show more recent influences.

I cannot pretend, however, that the classification which I have made is strictly chronological. Material is lacking for a hard and fast division of these songs into historical groups. A song which I have recently learned, and which the man who sang it for me assured me was composed by a man well known to him, has all the characteristics of the older melodies. I have selected, in part, the songs that had common or contrasting features in melody or doctrine, and I shall include in this article some songs that were simply left over from the preceding ones. And the so-called "railroad songs" which make up a part of this article, though in their present form modern, represent a very old type of hymn structure, and had their beginnings far back in the days of slavery. No one man made them, nor are they ever written or ever complete. But I have endeavored to follow the general principle of grouping these songs according to their probable age.

Beside the "railroad songs" proper, there are some that are about the railroad. One of these will illustrate how modern influences in the South have affected the content of negro hymns.

To the negro on the levee the steamboat is the greatest thing afloat. But to the negro of the interior the place of the steamer in religious typology is assigned to the locomotive. There are several songs about the Gospel Train, some of which are familiar. The railroad seems so supernatural that it is hard to convince some faithful old souls that heaven is not at one or the other terminus. There is a good old song with this suggestion. It is in triple time, and pronounces "evening" in three sharp syllables.

GIT ON THE EVENING TRAIN.

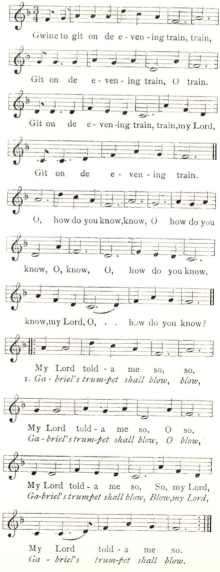

Gwine to git on de e - ven - ing train, train,

Git on de e - ven - ing train, O train.

Git on de e - ven-ing train, train, my Lord,

Git on de e - ven - ing train.

O, how do you know, know, O how do you

know, O, know, O, how do you know,

know, my Lord, O, . . how do you know?

My Lord told - a me so, so,
1. Ga - briel's trum-pet shall blow, blow,

My Lord told - a me so, O so,
Ga - briel's trum-pet shall blow, O blow,

My Lord told - a me so, So, my Lord,
Ga-briel's trumpet shall blow, Blow, my Lord,

My Lord told - a me so.
Ga - briel's trum-pet shall blow.

2—Old Death stayin' in de grave, grave, etc.

3—Swing low, chariot, swing low, low, etc.

4—Prayer, prayer is de way, way, etc.

5—Let God's people git 'board, 'board, etc.

6—Gwine to heaven on de mor-en-ing train, train, etc.

7—My Lord send a me here, here,
My Lord send a me here, to pray.

8—Do thyself a no harm, harm.

Railroad songs are so named from the fact that they are sung by large bodies of men in the construction of railroads and other public works. Not many of them originated on the railroad, but their use in the army building fortifications, and in these more modern kinds of labor, has probably served to elongate them. The wise contractor employing colored men at work of this character lets them sing. The songs require little expenditure of breath, and are long drawn, monotonous chants. They usually have a Scripture theme, and often tell at length a long Scripture story with the negro's own improvements and interpretations thrown in. The refrain comes at considerable and irregular intervals, just often enough to quicken the lagging interest of any who may have dropped out. Only the leader attempts to sing the words, though perhaps a few nearest him catch a strain here and there; but the tune, which often runs along for a dozen verses between *la* and *do*, is hummed by others far and near, and gives the time to which the spades sink into the clay or the picks descend.

To hear these songs, not all of which are religious, at their best, one needs to hear them in a rock tunnel. The men are hurried in after an explosion to drill with speed for another double row of blasts. They work two and two, one holding and turning the drill, the other striking it with a sledge. The sledges descend in unison as the long low chant gives the time. I wonder if the reader can

imagine the effect of it all, the powder smoke filling the place, the darkness made barely visible by the little lights on the hats of the men, the echoing sounds of men and mules toward the outlet loading and carting away the rock thrown out by the last blast, and the men at the heading droning their low chant to the *chink! chink!* of the steel. A single musical phrase or a succession of a half dozen notes caught on a visit to such a place sticks in one's mind forever. Even as I write I seem to be in a tunnel of this description and to hear the sharp metallic stroke and the syncopated chant.

One occasionally hears these long songs in an evening meeting. They are interminable, and the only way to end them is to stop. One of them, a part of which has been published, and the whole of which no one man knows, is "Walk Jerusalem just like John." Different versions of it have been printed, but none like the one I have.

This song throws in almost at random couplets like:

Walk around from do' to do',
What to do I did not know;

Walk Jerusalem on Zion's hill,
Walk about on heaven and earth;

Satan thought he had me fast,
Thank the Lord I'm free at last.

I bless the Lord I'm going to die,
I'm going to judgment by and by.

Oh, John he heard the trumpet blow,
Hills and mountains fall below.

It has no proper end. It goes on at the will of the leader, and, unlike the ordinary hymn, which may be ended either with a stanza or the refrain and usually is meant to end with the latter, this is meant never to end so far as the structure of the song is concerned. It may end with "When

I come to die," or "Jes' like John"; but in either case it gives the air of incompleteness, like the old Scotch and Irish songs which ended so often on *re* and were ready to begin again. Some of these songs have a proper end, and may stop with the refrain any time; but the refrain is of variable occurrence, and may come every two lines, or run on for an epitomized biography of some Bible character.

WALK JERUSALEM JES' LIKE JOHN.

Walk Je - ru - sa - lem, jes' like John.

When I come to die, I want to be

read - y, . . When I come to die.

1. Walk Je - ru - sa - lem, 'jes like John,

Walk Jer - ru - sa - lem up and down,

(Omit or repeat at will.)

Walk Je - ru - sa - lem, walk Je - ru sa - lem.

Walk Je - ru - sa - lem 'jes like John,

Walk Je - ru - sa - lem round and round.

While the narrative portions of this song and others like it are used as a solo, which is a great saving of breath, there is a humming accompaniment, with many an "Amen" and "Yes," and frequently a chuckle or "holy laugh," especially at any suggestion of giving the devil what is conceived to be his due, or of any sharp turn of Providence for the worsting of sinners. One of these songs, which I have heard both on the railroad and

in an evening meeting, is "The New Burying Ground."

NEW BURYING GROUND.

1. O, my Lord, Good and kind,
   To - morrow's the day, First go - in' by,
   O - pen the grave, Let him down,

Take the lit - tle babe, Leave its
Take the lit - tle babe, To the
There he's go - in t'lay Till the

moth - er be - hind.
new bur - ry - in' ground.
Judg - ment day.

Judgment day! God's a call - in'! Stars a - fall - in'!

Char - iot's com - in' down To the

new bur - yin' ground! O, Je - sus,

come this a - way! Let not your char - iot

wheels de - lay! Want you to live

hum - ble-l-humble-l-Humble your - selves! The

bells done rung, Bells done ring, Angels done sing.

O don't it look like a judg - ment day?

Gwine to glo - ry an' - a - hon - or! Praise

Jesus! Gwine to glory an'-a-honor! Praise the Lamb!

2—All along down by de watery shore,
De waters run steady, level as a die;
Hearse come down next day gone by;
Take de lill babe to new burying
    ground.
Yes, I went down to the valley to pray,
Met ole Satan on de way.
Look out, Satan, out my way!
Took my sword an' cut him down;
Satan shot one ball at me;
Missed my soul and got my sin.

Refrain.

3—O, no, brethering, dat ain't all,—
Golden girdle round my waist,
Starry crown upon my head,
Palm of victory in my hand.

Refrain.

4—I went to meeting on a certain day,
Went fo' to hear what de preacher say.
Bout de time dat I got in,
Spoke one word condemned my sin.
Went back home an' counted de cost,
Heard what a treasure I had lost.

Refrain.

5—Yes, mysteree! Come and see!
Heard a great voice shoutin' in de new
    buryin' ground.
B for book and be forgiven,
Wrote by wise men sent from heaven.
If you want to go to heaven when you
    dies,
Stop you long tongue from telling lies.
Stars a-fallin'! God's a-callin'!
Don't dat look like judgment day?

Refrain.

6—I went down by the tottery sho',
Found a ship all ready to go.
Cap'n he come, troubled in mind,
"Wake up! wake up, you sleep, sleepy
    man!"
O, cap'n, if it's me,
Pray you cast me overboard!
Cast Brer Jonah overboard;
Whale did swaller Brer Jonah whole.
Three long nights, three long days,
Jonah lied in de body of de whale.
Las' words I hear Brer Jonah say,
He had no place to lie his head.
God commanded fish to land,
Cast Brer Jonah on dry sand.
Gourd vine growed all over his head.
Inchworm come long and cut it down.

Refrain.

7—Hit 'em wid de hammer cryin', "Sin-
    ner, repent!"
Wrought sorrow in de Jedge-e-ment.
Green trees burn, and why not dry?
Sinner man die, and why not I?
Sea ob glass all full of fire,
I'm gwine to jine God's heavenly choir.

H for Hannah, happy was she,
Lill boy Samuel on her knee.
B for book an' God forgiven,
Young child Jesus came from heaven.

Refrain.

8—Sing ole hymn at new buryin' ground,
Dar gwine lay his body down.
He gave me pree, and sot me free
An' bought my soul from libertee.
Death come along at break of day,
Take de lill baby on his way.
Give me a horn and tell me to blow,
Come along, don't you want to go?
Bell done ring, angels done sing,
God A'mighty bought my heart and
    tongue.
Went down hill, fell on my knees,
Help me, Jesus, if you please.

Refrain.

Another of these is "How Long
Watch-a-Man?" The melody of this
is worthy of special attention. It is
sweet, full, dignified and descriptive.
The variations of "Watch-a-man" are
very telling, and the repeated and re-
tarded final tonic notes, suggestive of
the passing of time as seen by the
"Watch-a-man" are fine. It deserves
to be fitted with a strong, full harmony and to be widely known. I consider it a gem. It is partly in 3:4 and
partly in 4:4 time, and the fitting of
these into a smooth, flowing melody
in perfect taste is noteworthy. The
words are not so good.

HOW LONG, WATCHMAN?

O how long, watch-a-man? How long,

watch-a-man, How long, watch-a-man?
FINE.

How long, watch-a-man? How long?

1. { How long did it rain? Can any one tell? }
   { For for-ty days and nights it fell. }
D.C.

How long, watch-a-man? How long?

2—Oh, dey called ole Noah foolish man,
   Built his ark upon dry sand.
   Foolish Jews come a-ridin' by,
   Hawk and spit on Noah's timber.
   My sister done broke de ice an' gone
   Sitting in heaven wid 'er raiment on.

Refrain.

3—Watah come up to de cellah door,
   Marched an' slipped on de upper floor,
   Den I went up to de winder an' peep
     out;
   I see ole Noah passin' by,
   Try an' help me out er my miseree.
   I know ole Noah felt and seen,
   I b'lieve God A'mighty locked de door.
   Come along my muddah to de watah
     side,
   Come along an' be baptized.

Refrain.

4—My dungeon open, my chains flew wide,
   Glory to God, I've found him at last.
   Brer Jonah lied in de bowels ub de
     whale,
   Brer Jonah prayed in de bowels ub de
     whale.
   De ark got stuck on de mountain-top,
   God commanded de rain to stop.
   De rainbow show, de sun he shine,
   Glory to God, my sins are forgiven.

Refrain.

5—How long was Noah buildin' of de ark?
   Mo'n a hundred years he kept to work.

6—How long was Jonah in the bowels of
   the whale?
   For three whole days and nights he
     sailed.

7—How long will the righteous in heaven
   be?
   For ever and ever their Lord they see.

A good many people, no one of whom knew it all, contributed first and last to give the foregoing hymn the degree of completeness which is here shown.

The negro is reluctant to bring a service to a close. When, late at night, the end finally comes, there is often a quotation concerning the heavenly assembly:

"Where congregations ne'er break up,
   And Sabbaths have no end."

The thought enters several of their own songs, among them one of the interminable ones such as we are now considering. It runs on in narrative form with long or short stanzas, but calls for active and repeated responses in the refrain, "I believe!" The refrain changes, also, from time to time, to suit the tenor of the stanzas, but the end is always the same, "And Sabbath has no end."

SABBATH HAS NO END.

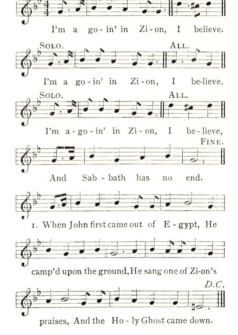

When John first came out of Egypt, He camp'd upon the ground, He sang one of Zion's praises, And the Holy Ghost came down.

2—He done blessed him and cheered him
   And told him not to weep,
   For the power was in Christ Jesus
   To raise him from his sleep.

Refrain.

Mighty meeting in Zion,
     I believe,
Mighty meeting in Zion,
     I believe,
Mighty meeting in Zion,
     I believe,
   And Sabbath has no end.

3—When Jesus came to the world,
   He came to do no harm,
   But they placed on him a thorny crown,
   And the blood came streaming down.

Refrain.

Wasn't that a shame?
I believe,
Wasn't that a shame?
I believe,
Wasn't that a shame?
I believe,
And Sabbath has no end.

4—Not all the blood of beasts
On Jewish altars slain
Could give a guilty conscience peace,
Or wash away the stain.
Behold he wore the mortgage,
He was Almighty God;
At once they might have 'stroyed him,
But he saved them by his word.

Refrain.

I know, 'twas Jesus,
I believe.
I know, 'twas Jesus,
I believe,
I know, 'twas Jesus.
I believe,
And Sabbath has no end.

5—Want you to look at you dying Saviour,
Want you to look at you dying Lord;
Stand near the cross and view him,
Behold the Lamb of God.
They rebuked him and they scorned
him,
And told him to come down,
Before the cross of suffering,
They changed him for his crown.
Jesus came in many mysterious ways,
His wonders to perform,
He placed his footsteps in the seas,
And rode upon the storm.

Refrain.

I'm going to heaven,
I believe.
I'm going to heaven,
I believe.
I'm going to heaven,
I believe,
And Sabbath has no end.

6—They took my blessed Jesus,
And led him to the whiteoak island,
They hewed him out a yoke,
And they yoked it on to him.
His ankle bones they done give way,
His knees they smote the ground,
And every star shall disappear,
King Jesus shall be mine.

Refrain.

I'm going to Zion,
I believe,
I'm going to Zion,
I believe,
I'm going to Zion,
I believe,
And Sabbath has no end.

7—I met old Judas at the spring.
The history how he talked,—
"For thirty pieces of silver,
I show you where my Jesus walk."

Refrain.

Walked the road to heaven,
I believe,
Walked the road to heaven,
I believe,
Walked the road to heaven,
I believe,
And Sabbath has no end.

8—Mary saw her father coming,
Done run and met him too,
She told him 'bout her brother,
Who was dead and passed away.

Refrain.

Then come forth Lazarus,
I believe,
Then come forth Lazarus,
I believe,
Then come forth Lazarus,
I believe,
And Sabbath has no end.

9—Well, they taken my blessed Jesus,
They led him to the low ground of
sorrow,
They hewed him out a Roman cross,
They placed it on his shoulder.
They speared him long in his side!
They speared him long in his side!
(Wasn't that a shame!)
There came out water and blood!
There came out water and blood!
(O my Lord!)
The blood was for redemption,
The water for baptism.

Refrain.

So we'll rock trouble over,
I believe,
So we'll rock trouble over,
I believe,
So we'll rock trouble over,
I believe.
And Sabbath has no end.

This last hymn I have heard in different places, but the part relating to
the crucifixion I have not heard ex-

cept at religious services. The last of these hymns which I shall give is one that I heard but once. I do not know that it is used as a song to work with, but suspect that the "ham-mer-ring!" which is the constant response, may be used sometimes to time the descent of the pick or sledge. As I heard it, however, it was sung at an evening meeting, a single voice telling the story, repeating twice each line, while the congregation sang a heavy bass "Ham-mer-ring!"

THE CHRISTIANS' HYMN OF THE CRUCIFIXION.

2—Mary wept (Ham-mer-ring)
  And Martha mourned. (Ham-mer-ring)
If thou'd been here, (Ham-mer-ring)
My brother hadn't died. (Ham-mer-ring)
They buried him, (Ham-mer-ring)
And on the third day (Ham-mer-ring)
He ascended high, (Ham-mer-ring)
To his Father's house. (Ham-mer-ring)
Jesus came, (Ham-mer-ring)
His friend he rise, (Ham-mer-ring)
And found a home (Ham-mer-ring)
Above the skies. (Ham-mer-ring)
O, Lazarus, (Ham-mer-ring)
I know Lazarus! (Ham-mer-ring)
Come forth, Lazarus! (Ham-mer-ring)
Want you to loose him (Ham-mer-ring)
And let him go. (Ham-mer-ring.)

A good many of these railroad songs, I am satisfied, originated in those grewsome vigils wherein a dozen or more people "sit up" with the dead. The night is largely spent in singing, and the set songs run out long before morning. The family sleep, or are supposed to sleep, often in the same room, and if not there then in a room within easy hearing distance, and the singing is thought to comfort them, as well as to help in keeping the watchers awake and to apply the occasion to the profit of those present. The song about "The New Burying Ground" is evidently of this kind. Its references to the little babe that had been taken, the mother left behind, and to the next day as that of the burial, plainly show its original meaning; but it is sung now on other and very different occasions.

These songs are long, low, monotonous croons, wherein the recitative is half sung, half spoken, and the voices other than that of the leader merely hum with occasional ejaculations and an intermittent refrain. The songs are modified by their subsequent uses, but originating, as they do, without a distinct purpose to make a song, they are most irregular in everything but rhythm, which is always such that they can be swayed to and patted with the foot. They afford a good illustration of the way in which the more elaborate songs originate.

There are some of the more recent plantation hymns which have added an element of culture without diminishing religious fervor. One of the best of these is "Were You There When They Crucified My Lord?" It dwells on the details of the crucifixion, and the separate stanzas add only a single line each to the song. It is a tender and beautiful hymn, the climax of its effect depending largely on the hold and slur on the exclamation "Oh!" with which the third line begins, and the repetition and expression of the word *"tremble! tremble! tremble!"*

WERE YOU THERE?

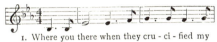

1. Where you there when they cru - ci - fied my
2. Were you there when they nail'd him to the
3. Were you there when they pierced him in the
4. Were you there when the sun re-fused to

Lord? (Were you there?) Were you
cross? (Were you there?) Were you
side? (Were you there?) Were you
shine? (Were you there?) Were you

ad lib.

there when they cru-ci-fied my Lord? O
there when they nail'd him to the cross? O
there when they pierced him in the side? O
there when the sun refused to shine? O

some-times it caus - es me to
some-times it caus - es me to
some-times it caus - es me to
some-times it caus - es me to

rit. *p* *pp p*

trem - ble! trem-ble! trem - ble! Were you
trem - ble! trem-ble! trem - ble! Were you
trem - ble! trem-ble! trem - ble! Were you
trem - ble! trem-ble! trem - ble! Were you

there when they cru - ci - fied my Lord?
there when they nail'd him to the cross?
there when they pierced him in the side?
there when the sun re - fused to shine?

PETER ON THE SEA.

1. Pe - ter! (Pe - ter,) Pe - ter, (Pe - ter,)
2. Ga - briel! (Ga-briel,) Ga-briel, (Ga-briel,)
3. Who did (who did) Jo - nah? (who did?)
4. Whale did (whale did) Jo - nah! (whale did!)
5. Dan - iel (Dan - iel) li - on's (Dan - iel!)

Pe - ter on the sea, sea, sea, sea!
Ga-briel, blow your trump, trump, trump, trump!
Who did swal - low Jo - nah, Jo - nah?
Whale did swal - low Jo - nah, Jo - nah!
Dan - iel in the li - on's, li - on's!

Pe - ter, (Pe - ter,) Pe - ter, (Pe - ter,)
Ga - briel, (Ga - briel,) Ga - briel, (Ga -briel,)
Who did (who did) Jo - nah? (who did?)
Whale did (whale did) Jo - nah! (whale did!)
Dan - iel (Dan - iel) li - on's (Dan - iel!)

Pe - ter on the sea, sea, sea, sea!
Ga-briel, blow your trump, trump, trump, trump!
Who did swal - low Jo - nah, Jo - nah?
Whale did swal - low Jo - nah, Jo - nah!
Dan - iel in the li - on's, li - on's!

Pe - ter, (Pe - ter,) Pe - ter, (Pet - er,)
Ga - briel, (Ga - briel,) Ga - briel, (Gabri-el,)
Who did (who did) Jo - nah? (who did?)
Whale did (whale did) Jo - nah! (whale did!)
Dan - iel (Dan - iel) li - on's, (Dan - iel!)

Pe - ter on the sea, sea, sea, sea!
Ga-briel, blow your trump, trump, trump, trump!
ho did swal - low Jo - nah, Jo - nah?
hale did swal - low Jo - nah, Jo - nah!
Dan - iel in the li - on's, li - on's!

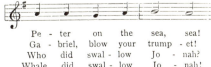

Pe - ter on the sea, sea!
Ga - briel, blow your trump - et!
Who did swal - low Jo - nah?
Whale did swal - low Jo - nah!
Dan - iel in the li - on's!

Pe - ter on the sea, sea, sea!
Ga - briel, blow your trump - et, blow!
Who did swal - low Jo - nah? Who?
Whale did swal - low Jo - nah! Whale!
Dan - iel in the li - on's den!

The foregoing modern song keeps much of the spirit of the older ones. It is in striking contrast with the preceding song. It is a lively staccato, is full of responses, is not in the least shy of the fourth and seventh notes, and is thoroughly up to date except perhaps in its theology. No higher criticism has yet eliminated from negro theology a vestige of the miraculous. Peter on the sea, Gabriel with his trumpet, Jonah and the whale and Daniel in the lions' den are all here in a swift-moving panorama, and with a lively good humor that is nothing less than mirth-provoking.

One of the most interesting places in which I have ever attended worship is a well built and fairly well appointed meeting house erected by the colored people, well out in the country, and adorned with crude frescoes that show a desire to beautify the sanctuary of the Lord. I have been there in summer when the temperature of the day did not exceed that of the meeting, and I have been there in winter when the minister announced that he was "cold, brethren; cold two ways, cold in de body and cold speritually"; and yet I have never been wholly disappointed in seeing something worth while. The records of the business meeting of Saturday are read on Sunday morning with a good many exclusions from the church "for immoral conduct," as the charge has invariably read when I have been there; and not infrequently there are people to be received into membership with ecstatic experiences proved by a repetition of them on the spot. The preaching begins very moderately, but as one after another comes to the front, the tide rises until the preacher in charge, who is said to have been the longest settled pastor in Kentucky, rises and begins; and then there is a demonstration. The company has long been swaying back and forth in the rhythm of the preacher's chant, and now and then there has come a shout of assent to the oft repeated text. Each time the preacher's almost incoherent talk

becomes articulate in a shout, "I have trod de wine-press," there are cries of "Yes!" "Praise de Lawd!" and "Glory!" from the Amen corner, where sit the "praying brethren," and the Hallelujah corner, where sit the "agonizing sistering." In the earlier demonstrations the men rather lead, but from the time when Aunt Melinda cries out "Nebbah mind de wite folks! My soul's happy! Hallelujah!" and leaps into the air, the men are left behind. Women go off into trances, roll under benches, or go spinning down the aisle with eyes closed and with arms outstretched. Each shout of the preacher is the signal for some one else to start; and, strange to say, though there are two posts in the aisle, and the women go spinning down like tops, I never saw one strike a post. I have seen the pastor on a day when the house would not contain the multitude cause the seats to be turned and take his own position in the door with a third of the audience inside and the rest without, and have heard him provoke the most ecstatic response to a reference to his wife such as this, "O, I love dat yaller woman out dar in dat buggy, but I love my Jesus bettah!" I have seen the minister in grave danger of being dragged out of the pulpit by some of the shouters who in their ecstasy laid hold upon him. I have seen an old man stand in the aisle and jump eighty-nine times after I began to count, and without moving a muscle of his thin, parchment-like face, and without disturbing the meeting.

There is more or less variation in the service at this church, but there is one invariable feature, the collection; and the more white people there are present, the more important is this feature. Two deacons sit at a table in front of the pulpit; a song is sung, and the contributors walk up the aisle and deposit their contributions amid exhortations and plaudits thrown in at the end of the line. Each coin is scrutinized, and there is no opportunity to pass a mutilated coin at par, as some people do in dealing with the Lord, or make a button do duty for legal tender. One day some one started a new fashioned hymn, and the people came up slowly. The preacher interrupted the hymn midway saying, "Breddern, dah hain't no money in dat tune. Sing one of de good ole tunes." In response to this suggestion they sang "Jes' gwine ober in de heabenlye lan'." It has a high air, covering only a diminished fifth, and running mostly on the tonic note, but the monotony is broken and a decided character is given to the melody in the refrain, "De heabenlye lan'," when from the last syllable of "heabenlye" to "lan'" the voice rises from E flat tonic to D flat, which it holds with a strong accent on a half note filling the last half of the measure.

JES' GWINE OBER IN DE HEABENLYE
LAN'.

2—Sinnah jine de church an' he run pretty
      well,
Jes' gwine ober in de heabenlye lan'!
An' afore six weeks he's on his road to hell,
Jes' gwine ober in de heabenlye lan'!
   De heabenlye lan'!
   De heabenlye lan'!
Jes' gwine ober in de heabenlye lan'!

3—Hebben is a high an' a lofty place,
   Jes' gwine ober in de heabenlye lan'!
But yer can't git dah ef you hain't got de
      grace,
Jes' gwine ober in de heabenlye lan'!
   De heabenlye lan'!
   De heabenlye lan'!
Jes' gwine ober in de heabenlye lan'!

4—Satan he's like a snake in de grass,
   Jes' gwine ober in de heabenlye lan'!

An' ef you don' mind he'll git you at las',
Jes' gwine ober in de heabenlye lan'!
   De heabenlye lan'!
   De heabenlye lan'!
Jes' gwine ober in de heabenlye lan'!

5—Way ober yander in de harves' fiel',
   Jes' gwine ober in de heabenlye lan'!
De angels are rollin' at de chariot wheel,
Jes' gwine ober in de heabenlye lan'!
   De heabenlye lan'!
   De heabenlye lan'!
Jes' gwine ober in de heabenlye lan'!

What conception the worshipers have of an angel is patent, for two of them are wrought into the frescoes of the room. The feet of one turn abruptly to the right, and the feet of the other to the left. One of them is cross eyed; both are white. There was every indication that this song brought a good collection.

A good many of the negro songs are written in the pentatonic scale. The same is true of a majority of Scotch songs and the songs of Oriental nations. When Luther W. Mason went to Japan to teach our system of music in the government schools, he sought out melodies common among us that are written in the scale of five notes. The first which he taught and which they received with great pleasure was one that we received from the Orient, I think from India, "There is a happy land." Few of the thousands of thousands who have sung this air all round the world have thought how a part of its hold upon so many million of hearts is its omission of the two notes 4 and 7 from the diatonic scale. Several of the best of the Scotch songs are of this character, as "Auld Lang Syne," and, with the exception of one or two notes which I believe are modern, "Annie Laurie." It is a little strange that just when the breaking up of Primrose and West's minstrel troupe might seem to indicate, and probably does indicate, a decline of interest in the burnt cork show that has been so popular for generations, and still is popular in England, there should be a great increase of so called "coon songs," some of whose airs are very pleasing, arranged for the piano. To any one who desires to write a fair imitation of a characteristic negro melody, one simple rule is good to start with: compose it on the black keys of the piano. It takes more than this rule, however, to make a good negro song, and the best of them are ill adapted to a piano. The violin or banjo fits them best, for they have no frets to distribute the error in tone. A sharp and B flat are not mathematically the same, but they must be represented by one tone on the piano. The negro is able to make this fine discrimination when he uses accidentals, and this makes it impossible to represent the tones exactly upon the staff; but the five notes of the simpler scale suffice for most of the hymns. "In Dat Great Day" is an example of a song whose tune is major and which ranges over an octave and a half with no suggestion of a lack of sufficient tone variety. There is great contrast between the startling warning, almost breathless, "Whah you runnin', sinnah?" and the clear, exultant "O Is-a-rel" The entire piece is of great power. It is a negro *Dies Iræ.* The use of the major is all the more remarkable because the eschatological theme and the sombre succession of incidents described would naturally suggest the minor.

This song illustrates a way in which the negro varies his melodies. In theory the song is sung in unison, and there is no harmony proper. But in practice the more independent singers introduce grace notes and slurs, and the higher and lower voices range above and below in fifths and thirds in the more descriptive portions, especially in the latter verses. In this song the melody of "O Isarel! O Isarel!" is given in the first line where those words are used, and in the notes which run nearest the tonic; but as the song proceeds this simple theme is worked out quite elaborately and with much greater variety than the notes here given indicate, but in a manner which they illustrate.

IN THAT GREAT DAY.

2—Don' you see de dead arisin'? etc.

3—Don' you heah de trumpet soundin'?

4—Don' you see dem tombs a-bustin'?

5—Yes, we'll see our chillen risin'.

6—Don' you see de chariot comin'?

7—Don' you see de sinnah tremblin'?

8—Don' you heah de saints a-shoutin'?

This quaint *Dies Iræ* may well be paired with an equally quaint "Hallelujah Churus." It is a Baptist hymn, "Been down into the Sea." Its exultant hallelujahs suggest, as one hears them, some passages in Handel's great masterpiece. I cannot expect any one to agree with this statement who merely picks out the notes on the piano; but one who hears the piece sung by a great congregation will not think the statement wholly extravagant.

BEEN DOWN INTO THE SEA.

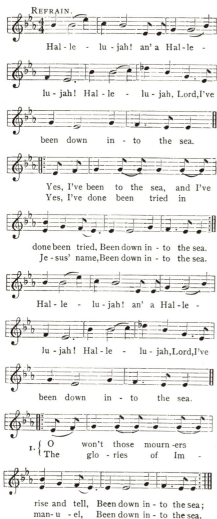

Hal - le - lu - jah! an' a Hal - le -
lu - jah! Hal - le - lu - jah, Lord, I've
been down in - to the sea.

Yes, I've been to the sea, and I've
Yes, I've done been tried in

done been tried, Been down in - to the sea.
Je - sus' name, Been down in - to the sea.

Hal - le - lu - jah! an' a Hal - le -
lu - jah! Hal - le - lu - jah, Lord, I've
been down in - to the sea.

1. { O won't those mourn -ers
     The glo - ries of Im -

rise and tell, Been down in - to the sea;
man - u - el, Been down in - to the sea.

2—Hallelujah! an' a hallelujah!
Hallelujah, Lord! I've been down into the
   sea!
Why don' dem mourners rise an' tell—
   Been down into the sea—
The glories of Immanuel?
   Been down into the sea!

3—Hallelujah! an' a hallelujah!
Hallelujah, Lord! I've been down into the
   sea!
I do believe without a doubt—
   Been down into the sea—
That a Christian has a right to shout,
   Been down into the sea!

4—Hallelujah! an' a hallelujah!
Hallelujah, Lord! I've been down into the
   sea!
Yes, I've been to the sea and I've been bab-
   tized,
Been down into the sea;
I've been babtized in Jesus' name,
   Been down into the sea!
Hallelujah! an' a hallelujah!
Hallelujah, Lord! I've been down into the
   sea!

Now and then there is a piece that
not only uses the diatonic scale, but
makes the most of it. One effective
song, "When the Chariot Comes,"
uses the seven toned scale, and empha-
sizes the fact by the prominence of its
major thirds. For instance, the
first time the word "comes" is used,
it is cut into five syllables with emphatic rough breathings, and fitted to
a *do-sol-mi-sol-do*.

WHEN THE CHARIOT COMES.

1. O who will drive the cha - riot when she
cu - hu - hu - hu - hums? O who will drive the
cha - riot when she comes? O who will drive the
cha - riot? O who will drive the cha - riot?
O who will drive the chariot when she comes?

2—King Jesus, he'll be driver, when she
   cu-hu-hu-hu-hums, etc.

3—She'll be loaded with bright angels, etc.

4—She will neither rock nor totter, etc.

5—She will run so level and steady, etc.

6—She will take us to the portills, etc.

Among the eschatological songs, I do not remember any that have affected me as did the song, "Who's Dat Yandah?" At the end of each inquiry, "Who's dat yandah?" is a rest of two beats in the middle of the measure; and the effect is more startling than the syncopation of a note. It is an emphasized silence of eager and fearful expectancy. It is a pure minor, and runs almost wholly in thirds. This song is so painfully realistic in its tone picturing as to cause an involuntary turning of the head in expectation of some majestic Presence. It starts with a refrain, which is repeated after every stanza and again at the end, as is usually the case where the song opens with the refrain.

2—Sinnah, sinnah, you'd bettah pray,
    Looks like-a my Lord comin' in de sky!
Or you' soul be los' at de jedgment day,
    Looks like-a my Lord comin' in de sky!

3—Wait till I gits in de middle of de air,
    Won't be nary sinnah dere.

4—De debbil is a liar and a conjurer, too,
    An' ef you don' mind he'll conjure you.

5—I nebbah can fo'git de day,
    When Jesus washed my sins away.

6—Washed my haid in de midnight dew,
    De mawning star's a witness, too.

7—Sinnahs jines de church, and dey sing and dey shout,
    An' afore six months des all turned out.

8—When I was a mourner jes' like you,
    My knees got 'quainted wid de hillside, too.

WHO'S DAT YANDAH?

In this and the two preceding articles I have given nearly seventy of these songs. It has been a sincere pleasure to prepare them for preservation in this form. Growing out of the heart experience of the negro, the older ones are absolutely natural and unaffected, and exhibit no attempt to express the religious life in conventional terms. Even their crudest oddities are of interest as data for study in religious and social development, and this is by no means the limit of their value.

I have not counted it a part of my duty to write harmonies for these songs, but have endeavored to preserve the melodies as accurately as possible.

These songs are such excellent exponents of "heart religion" that they are certain to disappear before the swift coming "book religion," save as they are carefully recorded and preserved. I exhort all teachers, pastors and others who are able to secure these songs to do so, with the music wherever possible, and to see that they are suitably preserved in print.

IX

NEGRO "SPIRITUALS"

Marion Alexander Haskell

[There is a pleasant new note in this article written just before the end of the nineteenth century. The usual white nostalgia for "the good-old-days" is still faintly present, but here, too, is recognition that if old folkways are to be preserved it must not be at the expense of the "folk's" rights to a fuller life, or by any attempt to perpetuate the conditions from which his folkways emerged. Yet, for the better part of the next fifty years there would be folklorists who mourned such progress. The article appeared in *The Century Magazine*, XXXVI (August, 1899), pp. 577-581.]

BY THE FIREPLACE.

NEGRO "SPIRITUALS."

BY MARION ALEXANDER HASKELL.

THE education of the negro in the South is gradually abolishing a species of folk-song as interesting as it is unique—the old negro "spirituals," the most truly characteristic music that the race has as yet produced.

Spirituals are the religious songs composed by the negroes themselves, never written or printed, but passing from one generation to another with such additions and variations as circumstances may suggest.

It is a curious fact that the music which the negro originates differs essentially in spirit from that which most pleases his fancy as coming from other sources. In borrowing he chooses gay, stirring strains, but his own native songs are nearly always minor and sad in character. Even the dance-tunes, to the rhythm of which bare little black feet while away many an idle hour, are generally a sort of rhythmic monotone with minor cadences. Most of the songs of the jubilee singers, while of the nature readily adopted by the negro, are foreign to his creative genius; but in the spirituals its stamp is unmistakable.

As the negro becomes educated he relinquishes these half-barbaric, but often beautiful, old words and melodies, and their place is taken by the denominational hymns and the Moody and Sankey songs, which are becoming more and more popular wherever schools have sprung up. But among those who are as yet innocent of any educational aspirations, especially among the coast negroes, upon whom the yoke of civilization rests but lightly, spirituals still hold undisputed sway, and hymns are regarded as the sacred property of city churches and those who have attained greatness through knowledge of reading, writing, and "figgahs."

The musical talent of the uneducated negro finds almost its only expression in religious song, and for this there is a simple explanation. A race strongly imbued with religious sentiment, one rarely finds among them an adult who has not gone through that emotional experience known as conversion, after which it is considered vanity and sinfulness to indulge in song other than that of a sacred character. The new-found child of the church knows but little of that which he must forego, for his mother before him sang only spirituals, and to these he naturally turns as to old friends whom his own religious experiences have clothed in new dignity and light.

These spirituals have never been systematically collected, and they bid fair to become, a few years hence, only things of the past. To those who have heard them from childhood they are too familiar to seem interesting or valuable, and the stranger who seeks to collect them will meet with many difficulties.

The negro feels that the white man's religion is very different from his own, and is sensitive about submitting to an uncomprehending critic a sacred thing, which he fears may be ridiculed, or at best regarded as strange and peculiar.

Then, again, the imitative tendency of the race leads them to adopt the white man's methods as fast as they can be learned, and the would-be student of spirituals is likely to find the obliging colored brethren serving him with hymns picked up from a white person and rendered with pride in various degrees of perversion.

One can sometimes steal, unobserved by the many, into a camp-meeting and hear the spirituals sung there, but a white presence is very apt to disturb the workings of the "Sperrit," which must come upon the assemblage in full force to make the meeting a real success.

The best way, after all, is to be cradled by an old mauma, who sits at evening in a squeaky rocking-chair by an open fireplace, and sings the baby to sleep, while the flicker of the firelight, the peaceable tone of the old rocker, and the long, mysterious shadows on the wall seem but parts of the old melodies that nightly mark the stations to dreamland.

The low-country or coast child will reap a richer harvest than the child whose mauma comes from the up-country. The songs of the coast are more plaintive, more poetic and imaginative, carrying in their minor cadences a sense of loneliness and a pathos that seem born of the sound of the waters. They have in them something of the dignity of the solitary palm and the moss-draped oaks which have stood as silent witnesses of their birth, as they were first sung amid the creative excitement of a camp-meeting, or about the graves of those who have entered into that rest for which the singers cry.

The up-country spirituals are not lacking in imagination, but they often present abstract ideas, whereas the low-country spirituals are invariably pictures. Both species deal at times with biblical subjects, but the coast negro sings them as personal experiences, and frequently alters them to suit his own conceptions, while his up-country brother sings them as he interprets them in the Scriptures. Thus, in the up-country one hears:

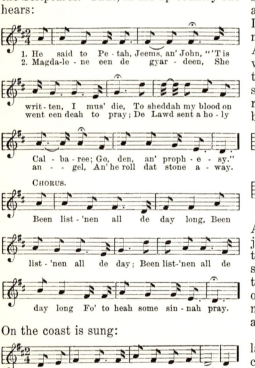

1. He said to Pe-tah, Jeems, an' John, "'T is
2. Magda-le-ne een de gyar-deen, She

writ-ten, I mus' die, To sheddah my blood on
went een deah to pray; De Lawd sent a ho-ly

Cal-ba-ree; Go, den, an' proph-e-sy."
an-gel, An' he roll dat stone a-way.

CHORUS.

Been list-'nen all de day long, Been

list-'nen all de day; Been list-'nen all de

day long Fo' to heah some sin-nah pray.

On the coast is sung:

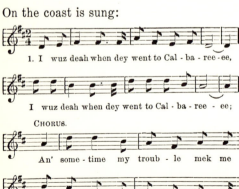

1. I wuz deah when dey went to Cal-ba-ree-ee,

I wuz deah when dey went to Cal-ba-ree-ee;

CHORUS.

An' some-time my troub-le mek me

trim-ble, trim-ble, trim-ble; Lawd, I

did'n' know my tri-als wuz so hard.

2 I wuz deah when dey crucified my Lawd,
 I wuz deah when dey crucified my Lawd.—CHO.
3 I wuz deah when he wo'ed de purple robe, etc.
4 I wuz deah when dey crown him wid de t'orn, etc.
5 I wuz deah when dey nail him to de cross, etc.
6 I wuz deah when de pilots took him down, etc.

With the pilots coming and going among them, carrying ships down to the ocean, one readily sees how they came to suppose the scriptural Pilate to be one of this company.

Spirituals are often composed on the spur of the moment by a preacher or a member whose voice can insure the attention of the assemblage. At a meeting held in Columbia, South Carolina, in 1897, the preacher chose as the subject of his sermon "Paul and Silas Imprisoned," and for an hour or more commanded the strictest attention of his hearers. At the end of this time interest began to flag visibly, and apparently the spirit of exhortation had fled from the minister. After a hard struggle to rouse the audience by another reading of the prison scene, he suddenly burst forth in a loud shout:

Y' all heah! Do dy-se'f no harm! Y'all heah!

etc.

Do dy-se'f no harm! Oh-h-h! Y'all heah!

At each repetition additional voices would join in, until the whole house had caught the words and rhythm; their bodies began to sway, and the excitement became so great that the meeting was brought to a close out of regard for some of the more emotional members, who were working themselves into a frenzy.

Another spiritual which has become popular among the country negroes of this locality was first sung by a convert while giving his experience in camp-meeting, and runs as follows:

1. Got a let-tah dis maw-nin', Um-m-m-m;

2. Could not read dat let-tah, Um-m-m.

3 Took it to my deacon, um-m-m.
4 Deacon could not read it, um-m-m.
5 Took it to my pastor, um-m-m.
6 Pastor could not read it, um-m-m.
7 Took it to my Jesus, um-m-m.
8 Jesus read dat lettah, um-m-m.

9 Lettah read about my soul, um-m-m.
10 Gospel train a-comin', um-m-m.
11 Lettah read about jedgment, um-m-m.
12 Sinnah, bettah git ready, um-m-m.
13 Gospel train a-comin', um-m-m.
14 Sinnah, bettah git on boa'd, um-m-m.[1]

This spiritual is a special favorite because it has no end, and serves as a perfect medium for the expression of any reflection which may occur to the singer. The day after it was first heard in camp-meeting one old cook, at least, was thinking aloud to its melody and rhythm from morn till eve. At one moment she would piously repeat an order just given, "Come an' mix dem cakeses, um-m-m." At the next, with her mind attuned to holy thoughts, she would continue, "Deah I 'll meet my Lawd, um-m-m."

Another spiritual which is very effective at revivals, being especially well suited to "shouting" (the term applied to the rhythmic bodily movements which the worshipers go through when deeply moved or excited), is the following:

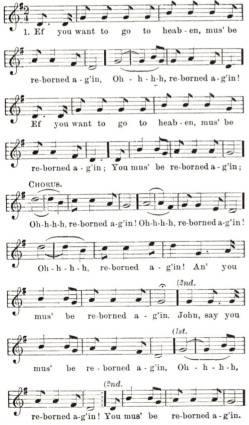

_{1. Ef you want to go to heab-en, mus' be re-borned a-g'in, Oh-h-h-h, re-borned a-g'in! Ef you want to go to heab-en, mus' be re-borned a-g'in; You mus' be re-borned a-g'in;}

CHORUS.

Oh-h-h-h, re-borned a-g'in! Oh-h-h-h, re-borned a-g'in! Oh-h-h-h, re-borned a-g'in! An' you mus' be re-borned a-g'in. John, say you mus' be re-borned a-g'in, Oh-h-h-h, re-borned a-g'in! You mus' be re-borned a-g'in.

[1] The "um-m-m" is sung with closed lips.

The length of this spiritual is almost infinite, for any biblical character may be put in place of John, and the song continued until the list is exhausted.

As a child I can remember being shown a little cabin which stood in a tangle of wild honeysuckle, woodbine, and yellow jasmine, with hollyhocks, four-o'clocks, larkspurs, and other old-fashioned flowers running to waste in the neglected garden, and listening with awe to the story of Maum Rizpah, who once lived there. Whence she came no one could tell, and all that remained of her was her song, well known to the colored people on the plantation, and believed to have been composed by her. She had appeared soon after the war and had taken quiet possession of this unused cabin, whence no one sought to drive her, and where, as the superstitious negroes thought, she worked her charms. She was half Indian, and the proud dignity of her bearing, in addition to her other peculiarities, led to the belief that she was a witch. As such she was secretly visited by the colored people in times of sickness or misfortune, and their offerings served as her subsistence. Her one visible occupation was singing—always the same pathetic strain, which came to be familiar on the plantation, though no presumptuous voice dared echo it until after her death, when it was generally sung. During the day she would sit in her cabin crooning it softly to herself, rocking to and fro, with sometimes a little bundle in her arms; but at night, and especially when the moon shone over the fields around her little hut, she would stand in the doorway, and the song would float out on the still night air with a sweetness and pathos that stamped itself indelibly upon the memory of her hearers. She had been dead for years when I was taken to see her cabin, and the little wooden cross had fallen into decay over the grave by the edge of the wood, but the tears stood in my old mauma's eyes as she told me all she knew of the singer's history, and how, over the open grave on a moonlight night, the whole plantation sang:

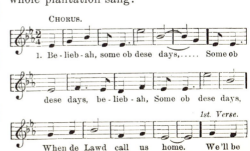

CHORUS.

_{1. Be-lieb-ah, some ob dese days,..... Some ob dese days, be-lieb-ah, Some ob dese days,}

_{1st. Verse.}

_{When de Lawd call us home. We'll be}

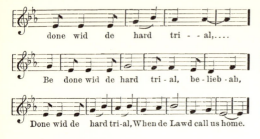

done wid de hard tri - - al,....

Be done wid de hard tri - al, be - lieb - ah,

Done wid de hard tri-al, When de Lawd call us home.

2 An' we 'll walk de golden street,
   An' we 'll walk de golden street, beliebah.
   Walk de golden street,
   When de Lawd call us home.—CHO.

3 An' we 'll try on de long white robe, etc.
4 An' we 'll try on de slippah-shoe, etc.
5 An' we 'll weah de golden crown, etc.
6 An' we 'll weah a golden belt, etc.

It was my good fortune to be down in an out-of-the-way little settlement in Beaufort County, South Carolina, during a protracted revival among the negroes of that region, and there I learned four spirituals which rank foremost in my affections.

The meetings were held in a little log church furnished with a few wooden benches, a table on a platform as a pulpit, and lighted by two long pine torches stuck in the cracks of the wall. Sometimes, in their devotions, the members forgot the torches, which burned so close to the wall as to ignite the mud-bedaubed logs; but this had occurred often enough to make the deacons expert in extinguishing the blaze, which no longer created any excitement. Soon after dark the congregation began to collect, the women often carrying in their arms babies, which they laid in a row, on shawls and blankets near the door, to sleep undisturbed throughout the service. By nine o'clock the preacher had arrived, and from then until midnight the woods reëchoed with the sound of prayer and praise.

The service began generally with this spiritual:

1. Dey is a tree in Par - a - dise, Po'
2. I tell my chillen, as a mat - tah o' fac', You

sin - nah call um tree ob life.
once git to heaben you wun' come back.

CHORUS.

Je - sus, Mahs - tah, Dy'n' on de cross.

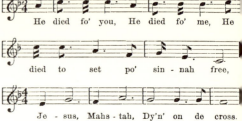

He died fo' you, He died fo' me, He

died to set po' sin - nah free,

Je - sus, Mahs - tah, Dy'n' on de cross.

3 Ef you want to see ole Satan run,
   Jes fiah off dat gospel gun.
   Jesus, Mahstah, etc.

After prayer and exhortation a voice would raise the sweet old melody of "De Mo'nin' Dove," and the first verse would wail through the dark woods slowly, softly, and sadly. Then, with a quickening of tempo and a ring of triumph as the eagle in his flight crossed their spiritual vision, they sang: "Sometime I feel like a yeagle een de yeah." Again with the pathos which so largely makes the beauty of the negro voice, "Sometime I feel like a muddahless chile," etc.

1. Some-time I feel like a mo'n - in' dove,

Some-time I feel like a mo'n - in' dove,

Some-time I feel like a mo'n - in' dove,

Feel like a mo'n-in' dove. Feel like a mo'nin' dove.

2 Sometime I feel like a yeagle een de yeah, etc.
3 Sometime I feel like a muddahless chile, etc.
4 Sometime I wish dat I nebbah been bawned, etc.

Another exhortation was followed by the fine old shouting spiritual:

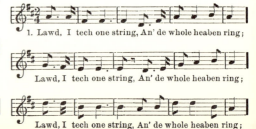

1. Lawd, I tech one string, An' de whole heaben ring;

Lawd, I tech one string, An' de whole heaben ring;

Lawd, I tech one string, An' de whole heaben ring;

Lawd, I don' want to stay heah no lon-gah!

2 Lawd, dig my grabe wid a silvah spade, etc.
Lawd, I don' wan' to stay heah no longah.

3 Lawd, lowah me down wid a golden chain, etc.

4 Dey 's a milk-white robe een de heab'n for me, etc.

5 Dey 's a slippah-shoe een de heab'n for me, etc.

Before the close of the service they always sang the pathetic, dirge-like "Why will Ye Die?" Often, as they sang, the dark faces would be bathed in tears, sobs mingling with the wail of the melody, and many and heart-felt were the petitions for mercy offered up after the hymn.

1. When you see de stahs a - fall-in', Een dat

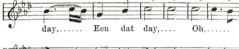

day,...... Een dat day,.... Oh,......

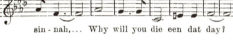

sin - nah,... Why will you die een dat day?

2 When you heah de trump a-callin'
Een dat day, een dat day,
Oh, sinnah, why will ye die, een dat day?

3 When you see de moon a-bleedin', etc.

4 When you see de yearth a-rentin', etc.

5 When you see de rocks a-rendin', etc.

6 When you see my Faddah's chillen, etc.

Equilibrium was, however, always restored by the following, the most remarkable of the collection. Each one sang it with exultation, a feeling of exemption, and a righteous joy in the probable gruesome fate of his neigh-bor, and then departed to his home with a complacency delightful to behold.

1. Whut dat sin - nah - man gwine do.... een dat

day?.......... Whut dat sin - nah - man gwine

do.... een dat day?...... Whut dat

sin-nah-man gwine do een dat day?............

When de right-eous go march-in' home!

2 Whut dat hickhatic [1] gwine do een dat day
When de righteous go marchin' home?

3 Whut dat backbite gwine do een dat day, etc.

4 Whut dat backslide gwine do een dat day, etc.

5 Whut dat t'ief gwine to do een dat day, etc.

6 Whut dat liah gwine do een dat day, etc.

An answering voice in the background would cry between the verses:

Sin - nah, mo'n!..

And each one, contemplating the fate of his neighbor, was satisfied.

A graduate of Hampden-Sidney told me recently, as an example of the splendid work of this institute, that these old spirituals are now rarely heard on the lips of the Virginia negro. It is inevitable that they give way before the advance of education. While rejoicing in the progress of the race, one cannot but feel that these quaint old spirit-uals, with their peculiar melodies, having served their time with effectiveness, deserve a better fate than to sink into oblivion as unvalued and unrecorded examples of a by-gone civilization.

[1] Heretic.

X

THE SOCIAL IMPLICATIONS
OF THE NEGRO SPIRITUAL

John Lovell, Jr.

[In 1939 the present editor read and never forgot John Lovell, Jr.'s ground-breaking study "The Social Implications of the Negro Spiritual" for the *Journal of Negro Education* (October 1939, pp. 634-643). Dr. Lovell originally intended to add four additional studies, but was never able to continue the work. Very little written since, except for an article and a few communications by Russell Ames in *Science and Society* (Summer, 1950, and Spring, 1951) has added much to Lovell's original thesis. We have used Dr. Lovell's study as our final paper so that it can serve as a catalyst for all the assorted materials that precede it, and as a clear-eyed look by a black scholar at the white comments of an earlier day.]

The Social Implications of the Negro Spiritual*

JOHN LOVELL, JR.

EARLY CRITICISM OF SPIRITUALS

May 30, 1867 is an important date in the history of Negro culture. On that date, in the New York *Nation*, there appeared a notice of the first attempt to collect and understand Negro

---

* Literature on the Spiritual and on the related topics I discuss here is voluminous and ubiquitous. The bibliography I suggest here is far from complete, but is fully representative.

I—*Basic Collections and Studies of Negro Spirituals*

Allen, William Francis, Ware, Charles Pickard, and Garrison, Lucy McKim, *Slave Songs of the United States*. New York: Peter Smith, 1929 (c. 1867).

Barton, William E., *Old Plantation Hymns*, n.d.

Brown, Sterling, *The Negro Poetry and Drama*. Washington: Associates in Negro Folk Education, 1937. Bronze Booklet No. 7.

Dann, Hollis Ellsworth, *Fifty-Eight Spirituals for Choral Use*. Boston: C. C. Birchard and Co., n.d.

DuBois, W. E. Burghardt, "The Sorrow Songs" in *Souls of Black Folk*, pp. 250-264. Chicago: A. C. McClurg and Co., 1903.

Fenner, Thomas P., *Fifty Cabin and Plantation Songs* in *Hampton and Its Students*, ed. by Armstrong, M. F. and Ludlow, Helen W. New York: G. P. Putnam's Sons, 1874.

Harris, Joel Chandler, *Uncle Remus, His Songs and His Sayings*. New York: D. Appleton Co., 1892.

Higginson, Thomas Wentworth, "Negro Spirituals" in *Atlantic Monthly*, XIX (June 1867), 685-694.

Krehbiel, Henry Edward, *Afro-American Folksongs*. New York: G. Schirmer, n.d. (c. 1914).

Johnson, James Weldon and Johnson, J. Rosamund, *The Book of American Negro Spirituals*. New York: Viking Press, 1937 (c. 1925).

Johnson, James Weldon and Johnson, J. Rosamund, *The Second Book of Negro Spirituals*. New York: Viking Press, 1926.

Locke, Alain Leroy, *The Negro and His Music*. Washington: Associates in Negro Folk Education, 1936.

Odum, Howard W. and Johnson, Guy B., *The Negro and His Songs*. Chapel Hill: University of North Carolina Press, 1925.

Scarborough, Dorothy, *On the Trial of Negro Folk-Songs*. Cambridge: Harvard University Press, 1925.

White, Clarence Cameron, *Forty Negro Spirituals*. Philadelphia: Theodore Presser, 1927.

II—*Pictures and Explanations of Spiritual Backgrounds*

Aptheker, Herbert, *Negro Slave Revolts in the United States, 1526-1860*. New York: International Publishers, n.d. (c. 1939). Reprinted from *Science and Society*, I (1937): 512-538; II (1938): 386-392.

Douglass, Frederick, *My Bondage and My Freedom*. New York and Auburn: Miller, Orton and Mulligan, 1855.

Hare, Maud Cuney, *Negro Musicians and Their Music*. Washington: Associated Publishers, n.d. (c. 1936).

Higginson, Thomas Wentworth, *Army Life in a Black Regiment*. Boston: Houghton Mifflin and Co., 1900 (c. 1870).

Jackson, George Pullen, *White Spirituals in the Southern Uplands*. Chapel Hill: University of North Carolina Press, 1933.

Macon, J. A., *Uncle Gable Tucker; or, Reflection, Song, and Sentiment in the Quarters*. Philadelphia: J. B. Lippincott, 1883.

Metfessel, Milton, *Phonophotography in Folk Music*. Chapel Hill: University of North Carolina Press, 1928.

Mitchell, Margaret, *Gone With the Wind*. New York: Macmillan Co., 1936.

Nation, IV: No. 100, Thursday, May 30, 1867: "Literary Notes."

Robinson, Avis P., *Social Conditions of Slavery as Taken from Slave Narratives*. (Unpublished Master's Thesis, Howard University, 1938.)

Siebert, William H., *The Underground Railroad from Slavery to Freedom*. New York: Macmillan Co., 1898.

Still, William, *The Underground Railroad*. Philadelphia: Porter and Coates, 1872.

Talley, Thomas W., *Negro Folk Rhymes: Wise and Otherwise*. New York: Macmillan, 1922.

Texas Folk-Lore Society Publications, Nos. 1 to 7 (7 v.), 1916-1928.

Weatherford, W. D., *The Negro from Africa to America*. New York: George H. Doran, n.d. (c. 1924).

spirituals. One of the prospective compilers announced the forthcoming volume, and added almost shamefacedly: "No one up to this time has explored for preservation the wild, beautiful, and pathetic melodies of the Southern slaves."[1] Since then, a thousand pens have dipped themselves in the sunlight, and they have scribbled at least a million lines, in praise, in defense, in explanation, in interpretation, in eulogy of the Negro spiritual. They have mined out its religion, its psychology, its philosophy. But the vast wealth of the spiritual in terms of the social mind of a very powerful cultural unit has just been scratched. In that respect, we have pierced only slightly deeper than we had on May 30, 1867.

James Weldon Johnson,[2] R. C. Harrison,[3] and Alain Locke[4] have sketched the periods of the creation and appreciation of the spiritual. They tell us that the spirituals were probably started on their way about 100 years before slavery died; that the heyday of the spiritual was about 1830 to 1865; that from 1865 to 1880 aroused American were collecting them, like fine orchids or trampled old masters; that from 1880 to 1910, men like Harris, Page, and Smith were using them for local color; that since 1910, Negroes, notably DuBois and Johnson, have rolled them through their subjective consciousnesses, with admirable results. White critics, like Krehbiel, Dorothy Scarborough and Guy Johnson, have gone through them with a fine-tooth comb. The farthest advance any of these writers have made into the social meaning of the spiritual is found in Krehbiel, and DuBois. Krehbiel wrote:[5]

Is it not the merest quibble to say that these songs are not American? They were created in America under American influences and by people who are Americans in the same sense that any other element of our population is American—every element except the aboriginal.

Concerning the spiritual DuBois wrote some of America's finest prose.[6] He hinted at the African genius for transmuting trouble into song. His only social comment on the American spiritual, however, concerns "Nobody Knows the Trouble I've Seen," and that comment is incidental to a gorgeous picture:[7]

Weeden, Howard, *Songs of the Old South.* (Verses and Drawings.) New York: Doubleday, Page and Co., 1900.

Woodson, Carter G., *The Negro in Our History.* Washington: Associated Publishers, n.d. (c. 1931).

III—*General Background Books and Articles*

Austin, Mary, *The American Rhythm.* Boston: Houghton, Mifflin and Co., 1930.

Barnes, Nellie, *American Indian Verse.* Lawrence: University of Kansas Humanistic Studies, Vol. II, No. 4, 1921.

Child, Francis James, *English and Scottish Popular Ballads.* 5 v. Boston: Houghton Mifflin and Co., n.d. (c. 1888).

Hoffmeister, Karel, *Antonin Dvorak,* translated by Rosa Newmarch. London: John Lane, n.d. (c. 1928).

Kennedy, R. Emmett, *Black Cameos.* New York: Albert and Charles Boni, 1924.

Linton, W. J., *Poetry of America.* London: George Bell and Sons, 1878.

Lovell, John, Jr., "Negro-True" (review of Richard Wright. *Uncle Tom's Children*) in JOURNAL OF NEGRO EDUCATION, VIII (Jan. 1939): 71-73.

Pound, Louise, *American Ballads and Songs.* New York: Charles Scribner's Sons, n.d. (c. 1922).

[1] *Nation,* May 30, 1867, p. 428.
[2] *The Book of American Negro Spirituals,* 1937 ed., pp. 10-23.
[3] *Texas and Southwestern Lore* No. 6, 1927. pp. 144-153.
[4] *The Negro and His Music,* pp. 10-21.
[5] *Afro-American Folksongs,* p. 26.
[6] "The Sorrow Songs" in *The Souls of Black Folk,* 1903 ed.
[7] *Ibid.,* p. 255.

When struck with a sudden poverty, the United States refused to fulfill its promises of land to the freedmen, a brigadier-general went down to the Sea Islands to carry the news. An old woman on the outskirts of the throng began singing this song; all the mass joined her, swaying. And the soldier wept.

No literature can fail to look stunted when deprived of its social strength. Take away the fire of Elizabethan England and the grand tragedies of Shakespeare are just twice-told tales. Milton's "Lycidas" was just another elegy before Tillyard came along in the 1920's and showed that it was the cry of a young man against a system that threw stumbling-blocks before him on his road to fame. The high priests of the spiritual have worn themselves out with appeals to the gods of art and religion, and the people have not heard them, for they live in a social world. The result is that today white people look askance at explanations for the spiritual, and Negroes are ashamed to discuss it.

Sterling Brown,[8] two short years ago, prepared the first direct case for the social implications of the Negro spiritual. He brought Frederick Douglass and Harriet Tubman to the stand to testify that these "religious" songs had social meanings: for example, deliverance for the Israelites meant freedom for the slaves; Canaan meant Canada. With good evidence and keen insight, he says:[9]

Against the tradition of the plantation as a state of blessed happiness the spirituals speak out with power and tragic beauty. Too many rash critics have stated that the spirituals showed the slave turning his back on this world for the joys of the next. The truth is that he took a good look at this world and told what he saw.

But the pursuit of this point lay outside the scope of Brown's book. And so we still have 800 to 1,000 original songs, comprising an epic tradition in the class of the *Iliad,* the Songs of Roland, or the Lays of the Nibelungs, with no clear analysis of the soil from which they sprung or of the process of their growth. In other epic traditions, patient scholars have found the seeds of racial and national culture. They look there first. And yet for how many years have the dabblers in American "Negroitis" ignored or treated with disgraceful cavalierness the heart of the Negro spirituals!

SOIL OUT OF WHICH SPIRITUAL GREW

What is this soil, capable of such rich products? Descriptions of it are fully available. There is, first of all, the African environment—not the romantic Africa of the movies but the Africa which puts blood and sand into the bodies of its natives. Woodson[10] tells us of the social and political genius of the African tribes, from whom American slaves were recruited. He describes their metal workers, architects, their experts in industrial arts. None of the vicious tactics of slave-mongers, white or black; none of the patronizers or traducers of things African can obscure the cultural accomplishments of these people who, under new conditions, expressed themselves in the Negro spiritual. They left their imprint on America before the white man came, as seen in such terms as canoe, buckra, and tobacco.[11] In

---

[8] *Negro Poetry and Drama,* ch. II.
[9] *Ibid.,* p. 18.

[10] *The Negro in Our History,* 1931 ed., pp. 37-52.
[11] *Ibid.,* p. 58.

music, says Locke,[12] there is an African gulf-stream flowing completely around Southern America, the coast islands, Hayti, the Bahamas, the Eastern provinces of Cuba, Vera Cruz, Yucatan, Guiana; and influencing such well-known dances as the tango of the Argentine, the carioca of Trinidad, and the beguine of Guadeloupe. Weatherford[13] speaks highly of the Africans' trading and military ability, their agricultural science, and of the revelations of their social life through religious activities.

The horrors of the slave trade—in Africa, on the middle passage, and in America—could not take away the social consciousness of these people. Nor was their moral fibre loosened thereby. They realized that if they reached America, each of them had 15 to 20 partners who had been blotted out in the process of transferrence. They saw the American plantation system steadily and whole. Their memories stored up the pictures of masters, overseers, auctioneers and buyers, patrollers, and other brutalizers of men. Read the slave narratives for their social implications, as Mrs. Robinson has done,[14] and you will see this remarkable mind at work.

Naturally, men as sensitive as these slaves were going to react definitely, and sometimes turbulently, to all these things. Sometimes they howled with alarm at brutalities;[15] but often they fought back, and learned the advantages of resistance.[16] Their physical reaction, seen in hundreds of recorded slave revolts and thousands of unrecorded ones,[17] is important enough. It destroys the almost universal belief that the African Negro is docile because he "accepted" slavery. Almost universally he did not accept slavery, and laws compelling every able-bodied white man to patrol duty around the plantations—or a sum for a substitute—and the consternation and fear in every nook and cranny of the slavocracy are devastating proof.

But the physical revolts are not so important as the mental revolts. Uprising slaves were shot or hanged and that was the end of them physically; but the mind of the slave seethed ceaselessly, and was a powerful factor in the abolition movement. *Gone With the Wind* resounds with "Go' Down, Moses" and "Jes a few more days ter tote de wee-ry load"[18] as well as with evidence of the pitiless progress of the group intelligence in: "that black grapevine telegraph system[19] which defies white understanding." Linda Brent, Douglass, Lewis and Milton Clarke, Josiah Henson, Elizabeth Keckley, Solomon Northrup, and a dozen others[20] tell what slaves were thinking, and how their thinking stimulated a great secret movement. Siebert[21] and Still[22] clinch the belief that the majority of slaves were collecting information, plotting and planning, seeking outlets, ammunition,

---

[12] *Op. cit.*, p. 138.
[13] *The Negro from Africa to America*, pp. 33-36, 43.
[14] "Social Conditions of Slavery as Taken from Slave Narratives"—unpublished Master's thesis, Howard University, 1938.
[15] Frederick Douglass, *My Bondage and My Freedom*, p. 123.

[16] *Ibid.*, p. 95.
[17] Herbert Aptheker, *Negro Slave Revolts in the United States, 1526-1860.*
[18] Pp. 306, 308, 349, etc.
[19] *Ibid.*, p. 813.
[20] Robinson, *op. cit., passim.*
[21] *The Underground Railroad from Slavery to Freedom*, 1898.
[22] *The Underground Railroad*, 1872.

supplies. A host of American writers, like Mark Twain, are further evidence. If the Negro spiritual came from the heart of the slave, it should be covered with such sentiments. It is. The demonstration of that fact in every particular is necessary.

THE SPIRITUAL AS CRITICISM OF EVERYDAY LIFE

The spiritual, then, is the key to the slave's description and criticism of his environment. It is the key to his revolutionary sentiments and to his desire to fly to free territory. With it, we can smash the old romantic molds, which are still turning out readymade Negroes.[23] But let us not put the emphasis on the negative side. Most important of all, the Negro spiritual is a positive thing, a folk group's answer to life.

Many students of the spiritual are misled by the religious and folk elements into believing that the social contribution is *nil*. We have already quoted Weatherford to the effect that the African Negro mixed his social life and his religion so thoroughly that neither can be said to dominate perpetually. That is true of the American Negro, and of nearly all peoples. The English and Scottish popular ballads are solid folk stuff: hardly a one is without mystical tone, or reference to some religious practice in everyday life, and several are exclusively Christian stories, *e.g.*, "St. Stephen and Herod," "Judas," "Dives and Lazarus." Their social implications are multitudinous.[24] American folk stuff is

no different.[25] Casey Jones serenely mentions his "trip to the holy land,"[26] and many American ballads, non-Negro, begin like "Charles Guiteau": "Come all you tender Christians."[27] In her introduction, Miss Pound refers generously to the social revelations in these all-American songs, and dedicates her collection to, among others, "those who care for traditional pieces as social documents which reflect the life and tradition of those who preserve them."[28] Religion enhances the power and desire of the folk to reveal their deepest social selves. This is true no more of Negroes than of anybody else.

WHAT IS WRONG WITH EXTANT INTERPRETATIONS

This brings us to what is wrong with the extant interpretations of the spiritual, excluding Sterling Brown's. The answer is: two forms of sentimentalism, one from the gone-with-the-wind South, the other from the we-fought-for-freedom North. The first is rather obvious in Natalie Taylor Carlisle:[29]

As many Southerners have observed, the old time darky's trusting religious faith, his loyalty to his daily tasks, his love for "ole marse" and "ole mist'ess," and his richly flavored sayings make a very attractive memory.

It is less obvious, but no less present, in Howard Odum and Guy Johnson.[30] The second is plain in Higginson,[31]

---

[23] See the present writer's review of Richard Wright's *Uncle Tom's Children* in JOURNAL OF NEGRO EDUCATION, VIII (Jan. 1939): 71-73.

[24] Francis J. Child, *English and Scottish Popular Ballads*, 1888 ed.

[25] Louise Pound, *American Ballads and Songs*, 1922 ed.

[26] *Ibid.*, p. 133.

[27] *Ibid.*, p. 146.

[28] *Ibid.*, p. vii.

[29] *Texas and Southwestern Folklore* No. 5, 1926, p. 137.

[30] *The Negro and His Songs*: chapters on "Presenting the Singer and His Song," "The Religious Songs of the Negro," and "Examples of Religious Songs."

[31] "Negro Spirituals" in *Atlantic Monthly*, XIX (June 1867): 685-694.

Allen and his associates,[32] and Kreh-biel,[33] who wrote: "Slavery was the sorrow of the Southern blacks; religion was their comfort and refuge." It is less plain in James Weldon Johnson, DuBois, Locke, and Maud Cuney Hare,[34] who wrote: "These were hynms that glowed with religious fervor and constant belief in ultimate victory through the gateway of death." In these last, it is impassioned and beautiful, but sentimentalism still, and therefore thin as literary interpretation.

Escape and Religion

These interpretations harp on two connected theories: that the spiritual was exclusively a method of escape from a troublesome world to a land of dreams, before or after death; and that its chief motivation is pure religion. In opposition to the escape theory, let me submit the realistic interpretations of the whole system that are found in the slave narratives. These slaves knew that their masters suffered as much as they, economically and mentally, and said so. They did not perenially commiserate their lot, and they rarely wished themselves anyone else. They were not the kind of people to think unconcretely; and the idea that they put all their eggs into the basket of a heaven after death, as the result of abstract thinking, is absurd to any reader of firsthand materials in the social history of the slave. This is not to say that they were not intrigued by the possibilities of various escapes. They were interested in religion, underground railroads, swamps,

abolition, colonization—anything that might provide a way out of the dark. But there was no exclusive surrender in songs and dreams.

George P. Jackson[35] has shown that some spirituals are perhaps derived from white camp meetings. Let us accept that. The white camp meeting was a frontier institution. The frontiersman's religion was one of his weapons. He enjoyed it ecstatically. But he did not separate it from the rest of his world. Mr. Jackson demonstrates that in the camp meeting hymn the companionships of the rough journey to camp became the common pilgrimage to Cannan; the meetings and partings on the ground became the reunion of believers in Heaven; and the military suggestions of encampment suggested the militant host of the Lord. The sweetnesses of life were the delights of Heaven; the pains of life, the pains of hell.[36] The camp meeting hymn parallels the spiritual in every respect, except that it is inferior poetry. The whites left the camp meeting and went out to conquer the wilderness. The Negroes left spiritual singing and plotted to upset the system of slavery. In each case, the song was just a stimulation for the march.

Concerning the theory of pure religion, there is practically no evidence that the slave swallowed the American philosophies of religion, and much to the contrary. Professor Brown finds satirical parodies growing up side by side with the spirituals, like this:[37]

I don't want to ride in no golden chariot,
I don't want to wear no golden crown,

---

[32] *Slave Songs of the United States.*
[33] *Op cit.,* p. 29.
[34] *Negro Musicians and Their Music,* p.

[35] *White Spirituals in the Southern Uplands.*
[36] *Ibid.,* p. 216.
[37] Brown, *op. cit.,* 21.

I want to stay down here and be
Just as I am without one plea.

Nat Turner was a preacher and knew
his Bible well; but his religion was
not pure in the best sense, for it led
him to bloody massacres, coldly
planned. Douglass thinks Master
Thomas's religion cheap and worthless when it did not improve his attitude toward his slaves,[38] and his
thinking was representative on this
subject. How could the slave accept
seriously a religion which he saw making brutes of those who were handing
it to him?

Most slaves, as most people, were
mildly religious; a few, as always a
few, were fanatical; but in the spiritual, religion is chiefly an arsenal of
pointed darts, a storehouse of images,
a means of making shrewd observa-
tions. Everybody talks about the keen-
ness of imagery in the African, whether
at home or in America.[39] Higginson
shows[40] that an African word, Myo—
from *mawa*, to die—is often substituted for Jordan. Natalie Carlisle,
Harrison, Bales[41] present sharply-
chiseled songs about woodchoppers,
"long-tongue liars," and death scenes
with doctor, mother, father, sister, actively participating. The slave had a
genius for phrase-making and dramatic situations; the Biblical lore was
a gold mine for him; he needed it to
make a social point; that just about
tells the story.

This is not to distort or belittle the
slave's religion. That religion struck
far more deeply than the gorgeous dis-
play of externals with little effect upon
everyday living, which the American
white man had set up. The presentday
African is cynical of American religion and its missionaries in the same
sense. The slave's religion is in his
spiritual, yes, but not in the externals.
It is in the principles he lives by, hid
deep beneath the soil, and meaning
something. It is a hard, thickly-rooted
plant, not a flower of the empyrean.
The things called religious in his
spiritual are his artistic fancy at work.
Witness his "Singin' wid a Sword in
Ma Han'," for its marvellous flights
and subtle double-meanings, or his introduction of modern arrangements,
like a train, instead of boats and chari-
ots. Remember that America got her
first railroad only in 1828. Witness
also his revision of camp meeting
hymns:[42]

CAMP MEETING
(same as old Methodist Hymn)
And then away to Jesus
On wings of love I'll fly

NEGRO SPIRITUAL
Dey'll take wings and fly away,
For to hear de trumpet soun'
In dat mornin'

THE TRUE SOCIAL INTERPRETATION

Approaching the heart of the spiritual, we must recognize three fixed
stars. First, there is the Negro's ob-
session for freedom, abundantly
proved by every firsthand document
connected with the slave himself.
Douglass says of the spirituals:[43]

. . . they were tones, loud, long and deep,
breathing the prayer and complaint of souls

[38] *Op. cit.*, 193-200.
[39] Notable examples can be found in Krehbiel, *op. cit.*, p. 45; Hare, *op. cit.*, p. 64;
Book of American Negro Spirituals, 15-16;
23-24; etc.
[40] *Life in a Black Regiment*, pp. 274-275.
[41] *Texas and Southwestern Lore*, No. 5,
1926, pp. 88, 140, 143, 150-151.

[42] Jackson, *op. cit.*, p. 302.
[43] *Op. cit.*, p. 99.

boiling over with the bitterest anguish. Every tone was a testimony against slavery, and a prayer to God for deliverance from chains.

Second was the slave's desire for justice in the judgment upon his betrayers which some might call revenge. And third was his tactic of battle, the strategy by which he expected to gain an eminent future. These three are the *leit motif* of nearly every spiritual.

Higginson says the slaves were jailed in Georgetown, S.C. in 1862 for singing "We'll Soon Be Free." This song opens "We'll soon be free When de Lord will call us home" and continues with such phrases as: "My brudder, how long fore we done suffering here" . . . "It won't be long Fore de Lord will call us home" . . . "We'll walk de miry doad Where pleasure never dies" . . . "We'll walk de golden street Where pleasure never dies" . . . "We'll soon be free When Jesus sets me free" . . . "We'll fight for liberty When de Lord will call us home." Higginson was told by a little drummer-boy: "Dey tink *de Lord* mean for say *de Yankees*."[44] Aptheker,[45] on this same point, reports that the slaves were certain as far back as 1856 that the Republican party would free them. They smiled when whipped and said that Fremont and his men heard the blows they received.

Beginning with a song and a background like this, and others in the same category—such as "Many Thousands Go," a farewell to "peck o' corn," "pint o' salt," "hundred lash," "mistress' call;" and the spirituals on "the ole nigger-driver" or "the pater-roler

get you"—it is easy, by the code found here, to work out into the open field of spirituals. Of course, the chariot in "Swing Low" is some arm of freedom reaching out to draw him in; and the number of times it succeeded shows that it was no hopeless hope. Of course "My Lord delibered Daniel . . . why can't he deliber me" means just what it says. And the falling rocks and mountains hit the slave's enemies. You would never get the communities all over the South which tasted slave revolts, especially in 1831, 1856, and 1860,[46] to believe that these rocks and mountains were ethereal or that they couldn't fall at any time. You would never get post-Sherman Georgia to believe that there was no fire in hell for sinners. The slave song was an awesome prophecy, rooted in the knowledge of what was going on and of human nature, and not in mystical lore. Its deadly edge threatened; and struck.

THE SPIRITUAL'S FINEST TOUCH

These, however, are not the finest touches of the spiritual. The really significant poetry is found in the plans for the future. Take a simple spiritual like "I Got Shoes." "When I get to heav'm" means when I get free. It is a Walt Whitman "I," meaning any slave, present or future. If I personally don't, my children or grandchildren, or my friend on the other end of the plantation will. What a glorious sigh these people breathed when one of their group slipped through to freedom! What a tragic intensity they felt when one was shot down trying to escape! So, the group-mind speaks in the

[44] *Atlantic Monthly,* XIX (June 1867): 692.
[45] *Op. cit.,* p. 58.

[46] Aptheker, *op. cit.,* p. 72.

group way, all for one, one for all. "When I get to heav'm, gonna put on my shoes" . . . that means he has talents, abilities, programs manufactured, ready to wear. On Douglass's plantation, the slaves bossed, directed, charted everything—horse-shoeing, cart-mending, plow-repairing, coopering, grinding, weaving, "all completely done by slaves."[47] But he has much finer shoes than that which he has no chance to wear. He does not means he will outgrow work, but simply that he will make his work count for something, which slavery prevents. When he gets a chance, he says, he is going to "shout all ober God's heav'm"— make every section of his community feel his power. He knows he can do it.

Here this slave was, tearing down a wreck and building a new, solid world, and all along we thought he was romanticizing. We gave him credit for dainty little fantasies of song. He was writing some of the stoutest poetry ever created. His subjects are social living, democracy, revolution, morals, Nature, Death, Love, the subjects of all great poets.[48] Which do you prefer, gentle reader: the sentimental spiritual, or the thumping, two-fisted, uproarious, not-to-be-denied: "O no man can hinder me! O no man, no man, no man can hinder me!"

And so, we cannot accept the pretty little platitudes to be found in such excellently written books as Odum and Johnson's *The Negro and His Songs*. Satan is not a traditional Negro goblin; he is the people who beat and cheat the slave. King Jesus is not just the abstract Christ; he is whoever helps the oppressed and disfranchised, or gives him a right to his life. Babylon and Winter are slavery as it stands— note "Oh de winter, de winter, de winter'll soon be ober, children;" Hell is often being sold South, for which the sensitive Negro had the greatest horror. Jordan is the push to freedom. The "great 'sociation," the "welcome table," the "big baptizin'," the "union," "viewin' the land" were concrete things which fit into the scheme at one time or another.

A few spirituals were swinging, narrative verse. "Dust and Ashes" is a very imaginative story of the crucifixion, and "In dat Great Gittin'-up Mornin'" reveals a fine fancy at work on a few facts taken from Revelations. Either of these, in some versions, may run beyond a hundred stanzas. Good narrative verse is a composite of wit and awareness of striking experiences. That composite is much in evidence here.

SUMMARY: THE SPIRITUAL IS ESSENTIALLY SOCIAL

Let us try to sum up. The Negro slave was the largest homogenous group in a melting-pot America. He analyzed and synthesized his life in his songs and sayings.[49] In hundreds of songs called spirituals, he produced an epic cycle; and, as in every such instance, he concealed there his deepest thoughts and ideas, his hard-finished plans and hopes and dreams. The exploration of these songs for their social truths presents a tremendous problem. It must be done, for, as in

---

[47] *Op. cit.*, p. 69.
[48] The present writer has projected four articles to follow this one, as follows: "Democracy in the Spiritual," "The Fighting Spiritual," "The Slave Looks at Progress," and "The Heav'm of the Negro Spiritual."

[49] See Thomas W. Talley, *Negro Folk Rhymes: Wise and Otherwise*, 1922.

the kernel of the *Iliad* lies the genius of the Greeks, so in the kernel of the spiritual lies the genius of the American Negro. When it is done—when the Negro and his white helper have learned about the large soul of the Negro here imprisoned, respect for the Negro will rise, and his gifts will not be held in contempt. Men will know that he was fully civilized, though a slave. Men will appreciate the glowing words of Douglass:[50]

For much of the happiness—or absence of misery—with which I passed this year with Mr. Freeland, I am indebted to the genial temper and ardent friendship of my brother slaves. They were, every one of them, manly, generous and brave, yes; I say they were brave, and I will add, fine looking. It is seldom the lot of mortals to have truer and better friends than were the slaves on this farm. It is not uncommon to charge slaves with great treachery toward each other, and to believe them incapable of confiding in each other; but I must say, that I never loved, esteemed, or confided in men, more

---

[50] *Op. cit.*, pp. 268-269.

than I did in these. They were as true as steel, and no band of brothers could have been more loving.

Douglass tells how they resisted oppression and tyranny, how they worked together and never moved without mutual consultation. He provides another basis for our contention that the spiritual was a language well understood in all its burning import by the slave initiate, but harmless and graceful to an unthinking outsider.

Douglass captured the all-round greatness of the slave, reflected in the spiritual. Antonin Dvorak, Roland Hayes, Marian Anderson, Paul Robeson have captured it in their handling of spirituals. When some more of us do, American Negroes and Americans generally will want to seek democracy by moving out on the track laid by these slaves, who sang:

You got a right,
I got a right,
We all got a right to the tree of life.

AN EPILOGUE [1]

J. Rosamond Johnson

Many collectors and theorists claim that the spirituals in many instances have digressed from those originally heard before the Civil War, and are not genuine. That is true in respect to antiphonal and polyphonic treatment, also the use of so-called sophisticated harmonies. But what if these changes have occurred? Environment can change a stone. The slave songs of America have rolled along through various moods of rhythmic and melodic conditions, and yet the idioms and characteristics of the Negro remain steadfast, regardless of progress by way of rag-time, syncopation, jazz, and blues. . . .

The latest Negro innovation in dance form is the "stomp." Analyzing it, you will find it definitely based on an incessant rhythm of the African drumbeat. At this very moment, as I write, a jazz-band of colored musicians is rehearsing at the Lafayette Theatre Hall, which is just across the street from where I live. At first I was annoyed, but the unceasing beat aroused my interest to such an extent that I jotted down bits of the rhythm and incoherent melody, thinking perhaps I could use them in this volume. Then I sent over to ask the leader what on earth was the name of the piece they were playing. My messenger brought back this answer: "Tell Mr. Johnson it ain't got no name *yet*—we's just makin' it up—that's all." I have called attention to this incident to confirm the fact that the same method as was sometimes used in the making of the spirituals is also used today by Negro groups in originating new types of modern dance tunes. . . .

W. C. Handy, with his famous composition the "St. Louis Blues," has combined the elements of the spirituals and the tangana beat of the African drum with the wailing chant of the primitive Negro lover

---

1. From *Rolling Along in Song* edited by J. Rosamond Johnson. Copyright 1937 by The Viking Press, Inc., copyright © renewed, 1965 by Mrs. Nora E. Johnson. Reprinted by permission of The Viking Press, Inc.

and its jazz and rag-time idioms, and has given a new impetus to our modern composers. Duke Ellington has also given a new note, especially in dance form. William Grant Still, a young American composer of the modern school, has contributed commendable work. . . .

The rendition of "Rhapsody in Blue" is always a signal for applause; it is a composition that thrills its listeners. The writer is among many others who consider that it is the greatest one-hundred-percent exposition of Negro American idioms and characteristics, and that it is a firm stepping-stone in the right direction for the development of a modern American school of music. It is gratifying to be able to quote Mr. Gershwin's dedication:

> For Mr. Handy — whose early blues songs are the forefathers of this work.
>
> George Gershwin,
> August 30, 1926.

SELECTED BIBLIOGRAPHY

Allen, William Francis, Ware, Charles Pickard, and Garrison, Lucy McKim. *Slave Songs of the United States*. New York: A. Simpson, 1867. Republished, Oak (paper), 1967.

Ames, Russell. *The Story of the American Folk Song*. New York: Grosset & Dunlop, 1955.

——. "Protest and Irony in Negro Folksong," *Science & Society* (Summer, 1950).

——. "Implications of Negro Folk Song," *Science & Society* (Spring, 1951).

American History and Encyclopedia of Music. Vol. 4. New York-Toledo-Chicago: Irving Squire, 1908.

Armstrong, Mary Frances, and Ludlow, Helen W. *Hampton and Its Students, by two of its teachers . . . with fifty cabin and plantation songs*. Arranged by Thomas P. Fenner. New York: G. P. Putnam's Sons, 1874.

Ballanta-Taylor, Nicholas. *Saint Helena Island Spirituals*. New York: G. Schirmer, 1925.

Barton, William E. *Old Plantation Hymns*. Boston: Lamson, Waffler Co., 1899.

——. "Old Plantation Hymns," *New England Magazine* (December, 1898).

——. "Hymns of the Slave and the Freedman," *Ibid.* (January, 1899).

——. "Recent Negro Melodies," *Ibid.* (February, 1899).

Bremer, Fredrika. *Homes of the New World*. 2 Vols. New York: Harper & Bros., 1853.

Brown, John Mason. "Songs of the Slave," *Lippincott's Magazine* (December, 1868).

Burlin, Natalie Curtis. *Songs and Tales from the Dark Continent*. New York: G. Schirmer, 1920.

——. *Hampton Series of Negro Folksongs*. 4 Vols. New York: G. Schirmer, 1918-1919.

Cable, George Washington. "The Dance in Place Congo," *The Century Magazine* (February, 1886).

——. "Creole Slave Songs," *Ibid.* (April, 1886).

Chase, Gilbert. *America's Music*. New York: McGraw Hill, 1955.

Coleridge-Taylor, Samuel. *Twenty-Four Negro Melodies*. Transcribed for the piano with a Preface by Booker T. Washington. Boston: Oliver Ditson, 1905.

Courlander, Harold. *Negro Folk Music, U.S.A.* New York: Columbia University Press, 1963.

Cuney-Hare, Maude. *Negro Musicians and Their Music*. Washington, D. C.: Associated Publishers, 1936.

Dett, Robert Nathaniel. *Religious Folk-Songs of the Negro as sung at Hampton Institute*. Hampton, Va.: Hampton Institute Press, 1927.

DuBois, William Edward Burghardt. *Souls of the Black Folk*. Chicago: McClurg, 1903.

Fisher, Miles M. *Negro Slave Songs in the United States*. Ithaca, N.Y.: Cornell University Press, 1953. Paper ed., Citadel.

Georgia Writers Project: Works Progress Administration, Savannah Unit. *Drums and Shadows; Survival Studies Among the Georgia Coastal Negroes*. Athens, Ga.: University of Georgia Press, 1940.

Grissom, Mary Allen (compiler). *The Negro Sings a New Heaven*. Chapel Hill: University of North Carolina Press, 1930.

Haskell, Marion Alexander. "Negro Spirituals," *The Century Magazine* (August, 1899).

Hayes, Roland. *My Songs*. Boston: Little, Brown, 1948.

Herzog, George. *Research in Primitive and Folk Music in the United States*. Bulletin No. 24. Washington, D.C.: American Council of Learned Societies, 1936.

Higginson, Col. Thomas Wentworth. "Negro Spirituals," *Atlantic Monthly* (June, 1867).

Jackson, George Pullen. *Spiritual Folk-Songs of Early America*. New York: J. J. Augustin, 1937.

——. *White and Negro Spirituals, their life-span and kinship, tracing 200 years of untrammeled song-making and singing among our country folk* . . . New York: J. J. Augustin, 1944.

Johnson, Guy B. *Folk Culture on St. Helena Island, South Carolina*. Chapel Hill: University of North Carolina Press, 1930.

Johnson, J. Rosamond (ed.). *Rolling Along in Song; a Chronological Survey of American Negro Music*. New York: Viking Press, 1937.

Johnson, James Weldon (ed.). *The Books of American Negro Spirituals*, 2 Vols. in 1. New York: Viking Press, 1940.

——(ed.). *The Book of American Negro Spirituals*. New York: Viking Press, 1925.

Jones, Le Roi. *Blues People: Negro Music in White America*. New York: Morrow, 1963. Paper ed., Apollo.

Kemble, Frances Anne. *Journal of a Residence on a Georgian Plantation, in 1838-1839*. New York: Harper & Bros., 1863.

Krehbiel, Henry Edward. *Afro-American Folksongs*. New York: G. Schirmer, 1914. Republished, New York: Frederick Ungar, 1962.

Landeck, Beatrice. *Echoes of Africa in Folk Songs of the Americas*. New York: McKay, 1961.

Locke, Alain. *The Negro and His Music*. Washington, D. C.: Associates in Negro Folk Education, 1936.

Lomax, John and Allen. *Negro Folk Songs as Sung by Leadbelly*. New York: Macmillan, 1936.

McIlhenny, Edward Avery. *Befo' de War Spirituals*. Boston: Christopher Publishing Co., 1933.

Marsh, J. B. T. *The Story of the Jubilee Singers with their Songs*. Boston: Houghton, Mifflin, 1880.

Nelson, Rose K., and Cole, Dorothy L. *The Negro's Contribution to Music in America.* New York: The Bureau for Intercultural Education, 1941.

Odum, Howard W., and Johnson, Guy B. *The Negro and his Songs: A Study of Typical Negro Songs in the South.* Chapel Hill: University of North Carolina Press, 1925.

——. *Negro Workaday Songs.* Chapel Hill: University of North Carolina Press, 1926.

Parish, Lydia. *Slave Songs of the Georgia Sea Islands.* New York: Creative Age Press, 1942.

Peterson, C. G. [sister of Luis Moreau Gottschalk]. *Creole Songs from New Orleans.* New Orleans: L. Grunewald Co., 1902.

Pike, Gustavus D. *The Jubilee Singers and their campaign for twenty thousand dollars.* Boston: Lee, Shepard & Dillingham, 1873.

Scarborough, Dorothy. *On the Trail of Negro Folk Songs.* Cambridge, Mass.: Harvard University Press, 1925. Republished, Hatboro, Pa.: Folklore Associates, 1963.

Pipes, William H. *Say Amen, Brother!* New York: William Frederick Press, 1951.

Stowe, Harriet Beecher. *Men of Our Times.* Hartford: Hartford Publishing Co., 1868. Chapter on Frederick Douglass and Slave Songs.

Spaulding, H. G. "Under the Palmetto," *Continental Monthly* (August, 1863). Section on Shouts and Shout Songs.

Talley, Thomas W. *Negro Folk Rhymes.* New York: Macmillan, 1922.

Thurman, Howard. *Deep River; Reflections on the Religious Insight of Certain of the Negro Spirituals.* New York: Harper, 1955.

Tiersot, Julien. *La Musique Chez les Peuples Indigènes de l'Amérique du Nord* (Notes d'Ethnographie Musicale, Ser. 2) Paris: Librairie Fischbacher, 1910.

Trotter, J. M. *Music and Some Highly Musical People.* Boston: Lee & Shepard, 1878.

Washington, Booker. T. *Up From Slavery.* New York: Doubleday, Page & Co., 1901.

White, Newman Ivey. *American Negro Folk-Songs.* Cambridge, Mass: Harvard University Press. Republished, Hatboro, Pa.: Folklore Associates, 1965.

Wood, Henry Cleveland. "Negro Camp-Meeting Melodies," *New England Magazine* (March, 1892).

Work, John Wesley and Frederick J. *Folk Songs of the American Negro.* Nashville: Work Brothers, 1901.

——. *New Jubilee Songs.* Nashville: Work Brothers, 1901.

Work, John Wesley. *The Folk Songs of the American Negro.* Nashville: Fisk University Press, 1915. Republished, Howell, Soskin, 1940.

SONG INDEX